*From* **The Best of Bridge**

# The Rest
# *of* The Best
## and more

Written by The Best of Bridge Publishing Ltd.

Robert
**ROSE**

# The Rest of The Best and More
## Recipes from The Best of Bridge Cookbooks

Disclaimer
The recipes in this book have been carefully tested by our kitchen and our tasters. To the best of our knowledge, they are safe and nutritious for ordinary use and users. For those people with food or other allergies, or who have special food requirements or health issues, please read the suggested contents of each recipe carefully and determine whether or not they may create a problem for you. All recipes are used at the risk of the consumer.

We cannot be responsible for any hazards, loss or damage that may occur as a result of any recipe use.

For those with special needs, allergies, requirements or health problems, in the event of any doubt, please contact your medical adviser prior to the use of any recipe.

Library and Archives Canada Cataloguing in Publication

The rest of the best and more : from the Best of Bridge cookbooks / written by the Best of Bridge Publishing Ltd.

Includes index.
ISBN 978-0-7788-0400-0

1. Cooking.  2. Cookbooks.  I. Best of Bridge Publishing Ltd

TX715.6.R475 2012        641.5        C2011-907193-2

Cover design by: KARO, Calgary, Alberta
Production by: PageWave Graphics Inc.

Photography by: Lisa Preston
Bilodeau Preston Photography
Calgary, Alberta

Published by Robert Rose Inc.
120 Eglinton Avenue East, Suite 800, Toronto, Ontario, Canada  M4P 1E2
Tel: (416) 322-6552  Fax: (416) 322-6936
www.robertrose.ca

Printed in China

01  02  03  04  05  06  07  08  09  PPLS  20  19  18  17  16  15  14  13  12

## DEDICATION

TO ALL OF THE FRIENDS AND MARKETING MANAGERS
WE'VE NEVER MET:

HOW MANY TIMES HAVE WE HEARD, "THE BEST OF BRIDGE
COOKBOOKS ARE THE ONLY COOKBOOKS I USE." "YOUR
BOOKS ARE MY BIBLE." YOU SEND SUCH GOOD LETTERS –
AND RECIPES. YOU REPORT ON THE PROLIFERATION
OF BEST OF BRIDGE COOKBOOKS IN YOUR CORNER
OF THE WORLD – AND WE KNOW IT WAS YOU AND YOUR
ENTHUSIASM. YOU ARE ALL OUR MARKETING MANAGERS –
AND FRIENDS THAT WE HAVEN'T MET – YET!

PLEASE – KEEP TAPPING US ON THE SHOULDER, WRITING
LETTERS AND SHARING YOUR NEWS. YOUR FRIENDSHIP
IS ONE OF THE BEST PARTS OF THIS 30-YEAR ENDEAVOR.
HERE'S TO ANOTHER BESTSELLER – YOU'VE DONE IT AGAIN!

KAREN BRIMACOMBE      HELEN MILES

MARY HALPEN      VAL ROBINSON

LINDA JACOBSON      JOAN WILSON

# FOREWARNING

BACK IN 1998 WHEN WE PUBLISHED "THE BEST OF THE BEST AND MORE", WE WERE ABSOLUTELY AMAZED AND DELIGHTED WITH THE RESPONSE. NOT ONLY DID NEW COOKS APPRECIATE THIS INTRODUCTION TO THE SIX-BOOK BEST OF BRIDGE SERIES, BUT OUR LOYAL FANS OF MANY YEARS EMBRACED THE CONVENIENCE OF ONE BOOK OF FAVORITES - AND MORE GREAT RECIPES TO BOOT.

THEN CAME THE MAIL: "WHERE IS 'YUMMY CHICKEN' AND WHAT ABOUT 'SEAFOOD LASAGNE'? WHY DID YOU LEAVE OUT 'CAJUN BREAD PUDDING' AND WHAT HAPPENED TO 'FRENCH LEMON PIE'?"

IT'S 2004. AFTER SIX YEARS AND ANOTHER BOOK, "A YEAR OF THE BEST" (2001), WE'VE HAD AN EPIPHANY. "LET'S DO ANOTHER BOOK WITH ALL THE REST OF OUR FAVORITES, INCLUDE MORE OF THE EXCITING NEW RECIPES WE'VE GATHERED AND CALL IT "THE REST OF THE BEST AND MORE - VOLUME 2" - ALL THE GREAT BEST OF BRIDGE RECIPES IN JUST TWO BOOKS - IT'S ALL YOU'LL EVER NEED!"

SO - WE'VE TASTED, TESTED, REVISED SOME OF THE "OLDIES" AND LEARNED A LOT ABOUT NEW FOODS AND FLAVORS.

WE HOPE YOU'LL HAVE AS MUCH FUN IN YOUR KITCHEN AS WE'VE HAD IN OURS. THE "LADIES OF THE BRIDGE" STILL PROMISE YOU "SIMPLE RECIPES WITH GOURMET RESULTS". YOU ARE GOING TO LOVE THIS BOOK!

# Table of Contents

FRONT COVER RECIPE

BAKED POTATO AND LEEK SOUP
WITH CHEDDAR AND BACON (PAGE 120)

## MUFFINS AND BREADS

Berry Best Muffins
A Pail Full of Muffins
Cranberry Muffins
Welsh Cakes
Lemon Loaf
How Cheesy Do You Want It?
Pita Crisps
Parmesan Crisps

## LUNCH AND BRUNCH

Breakfast Fruit Kabobs
Midnight French Toast
Night-Before Eggs Benedict
Puffy Hot Pepper Jack Cheese Omelet
Chili Cheddar Frittata
Crab or Chicken Crêpes
Spinach & Camembert Strudel
Cotswold Cheese Flan
Quiche Lorraine
Vegetarian Fiesta Casserole
Vegetarian Texas Tacos
Chilies Rellenos with Sage Cheese
Rene's Sandwich Loaf
Roast Beef Sandwiches with Brie
and Caramelized Onions

# BERRY BEST MUFFINS

RAID THE BERRY PATCH! FROZEN BERRIES WORK TOO.

## TOPPING

| | | |
|---|---|---|
| ½ CUP | GOLDEN BROWN SUGAR, FIRMLY PACKED | 125 ML |
| ⅓ CUP | FLOUR | 75 ML |
| 1½ TSP. | GRATED LEMON ZEST | 7 ML |
| ½ CUP | PECANS OR WALNUTS, TOASTED & CHOPPED | 125 ML |
| 2 TBSP. | BUTTER, SOFTENED | 30 ML |

## MUFFINS

| | | |
|---|---|---|
| 1½ CUPS | FLOUR | 375 ML |
| ¾ CUP | SUGAR | 175 ML |
| 2 TSP. | BAKING POWDER | 10 ML |
| 1½ TSP. | GRATED LEMON ZEST | 7 ML |
| 1 TSP. | CINNAMON | 5 ML |
| ¼ TSP. | SALT | 1 ML |
| ½ CUP | MILK | 125 ML |
| ½ CUP | BUTTER, MELTED & COOLED | 125 ML |
| 1 | LARGE EGG, BEATEN | 1 |
| 1½ CUPS | BERRIES (A MIXTURE OF BLACKBERRIES, BLUEBERRIES & RASPBERRIES) | 375 ML |

PREHEAT OVEN TO 350°F (180°C).

TOPPING: IN A MEDIUM BOWL, MIX TOGETHER BROWN SUGAR, FLOUR AND LEMON ZEST. STIR IN NUTS AND BUTTER. MIXTURE SHOULD BE CRUMBLY.

# BERRY BEST MUFFINS

CONTINUED FROM PAGE 8.

MUFFINS: IN A LARGE BOWL, COMBINE FLOUR, SUGAR, BAKING POWDER, LEMON ZEST, CINNAMON AND SALT. MAKE A WELL IN THE CENTER AND ADD MILK, BUTTER AND EGG. MIX UNTIL SMOOTH. CAREFULLY FOLD IN BERRIES. PLACE PAPER LINERS IN MUFFIN CUPS AND FILL EACH F FULL. TOP EACH MUFFIN WITH 1 TBSP. (15 ML) OF TOPPING MIXTURE. BAKE ON MIDDLE RACK FOR 20-25 MINUTES, UNTIL A TOOTHPICK INSERTED IN THE MIDDLE COMES OUT CLEAN. PLACE ON A RACK AND COOL 5 MINUTES. REMOVE MUFFINS FROM TINS AND SERVE WARM. MAKES 12 MEDIUM MUFFINS. (PICTURED OPPOSITE PAGE 36.)

CONSCIOUSNESS: THAT ANNOYING
TIME BETWEEN NAPS.

# A PAIL FULL OF MUFFINS

A CLASSIC! THE BATTER KEEPS IN THE REFRIGERATOR FOR UP TO 6 WEEKS.

| | | |
|---|---|---:|
| 2 CUPS | BOILING WATER | 500 ML |
| 2 CUPS | 100% BRAN | 500 ML |
| 3 CUPS | SUGAR | 750 ML |
| I CUP | BUTTER | 250 ML |
| 4 | EGGS | 4 |
| I QT. | BUTTERMILK (PLAIN YOGURT IS A GOOD SUBSTITUTE) | I L |
| 5 CUPS | FLOUR | 1.25 L |
| 3 TBSP. | BAKING SODA | 45 ML |
| I TBSP. | SALT | 15 ML |
| 4 CUPS | BRAN FLAKES | I L |
| | CHOPPED DATES, RAISINS OR BLUEBERRIES (OPTIONAL) | |

POUR BOILING WATER OVER BRAN AND LET STAND. CREAM SUGAR AND BUTTER. ADD EGGS TO SUGAR MIXTURE AND BEAT WELL. ADD BUTTERMILK AND BRAN MIXTURE. SIFT FLOUR, SODA, SALT AND ADD TO BRAN FLAKES. FOLD DRY INGREDIENTS INTO LIQUID MIXTURE SLOWLY UNTIL MIXED. STORE IN AIRTIGHT CONTAINER IN REFRIGERATOR, AT LEAST 24 HOURS. BEFORE BAKING, ADD DATES, RAISINS OR BLUEBERRIES. BAKE AS FEW OR AS MANY MUFFINS AS YOU WANT. SPOON INTO GREASED MUFFIN TINS. BAKE ON MIDDLE RACK AT 400°F (200°C) FOR 15-20 MINUTES. MAKES 6 DOZEN MUFFINS.

# CRANBERRY MUFFINS

KEEP ORANGES IN THE FRIDGE AND CRANBERRIES IN THE FREEZER - YOU'RE ALWAYS PREPARED.

| | | |
|---|---|---|
| 2 CUPS | CRANBERRIES, FRESH OR FROZEN, COARSELY CHOPPED | 500 ML |
| 1/3 CUP | SUGAR | 75 ML |
| 1 TBSP. | GRATED ORANGE ZEST | 15 ML |
| 1/2 CUP | ORANGE JUICE | 125 ML |
| 2 CUPS | FLOUR | 500 ML |
| 1 TSP. | BAKING POWDER | 5 ML |
| 1/2 TSP. | BAKING SODA | 2 ML |
| 1/2 TSP. | SALT | 2 ML |
| 1/2 CUP | BUTTER | 125 ML |
| 1 CUP | SUGAR | 250 ML |
| 1 | EGG | 1 |

PREHEAT OVEN TO 375°F (190°C). LIGHTLY GREASE MUFFIN TINS. COMBINE CRANBERRIES, 1/3 CUP (75 ML) SUGAR, ORANGE ZEST AND ORANGE JUICE. SET ASIDE. MIX DRY INGREDIENTS TOGETHER. SET ASIDE. CREAM BUTTER, 1 CUP (250 ML) SUGAR AND EGG IN LARGE BOWL. ADD CRANBERRY MIXTURE AND DRY INGREDIENTS. MIX UNTIL JUST BLENDED AND SPOON INTO MUFFIN TINS. BAKE ON MIDDLE RACK FOR 20 MINUTES. MAKES 18 MEDIUM MUFFINS.

# WELSH CAKES

THIS MAKES ABOUT 20 LITTLE CAKES FOR BRUNCH, BRIDGE OR AFTERNOON TEA!

| | | |
|---|---|---|
| 1½ CUPS | FLOUR | 375 ML |
| ½ TSP. | SALT | 2 ML |
| ½ TSP. | BAKING POWDER | 2 ML |
| ½ CUP | SUGAR | 125 ML |
| 1 TSP. | NUTMEG | 5 ML |
| ½ CUP | BUTTER | 125 ML |
| 1 | EGG | 1 |
| 2 TBSP. | ORANGE JUICE (OR LESS) | 30 ML |
| ½ CUP | CURRANTS | 125 ML |
| 2 TBSP. | BUTTER (MORE IF NEEDED) | 30 ML |

SIFT DRY INGREDIENTS TOGETHER. CUT IN BUTTER UNTIL CRUMBLY. ADD EGG AND MIX. ADD ENOUGH ORANGE JUICE TO BIND DOUGH TOGETHER. ADD CURRANTS AND MIX WELL. ROLL ON A FLOURED SURFACE TO ½" (1.3 CM) THICKNESS AND CUT CAKES WITH A 2" (5 CM) CUTTER. MELT BUTTER IN A FRYING PAN AND COOK CAKES OVER MEDIUM HEAT UNTIL LIGHTLY BROWNED, ABOUT 3-4 MINUTES EACH SIDE.

IF THE BROOM FITS, FLY IT.

# LEMON LOAF

SUPERB FLAVOR. FREEZES WELL.

| | | |
|---|---|---|
| 1/2 CUP | BUTTER | 125 ML |
| I CUP | SUGAR | 250 ML |
| 2 | EGGS, BEATEN | 2 |
| 1/2 CUP | MILK | 125 ML |
| 1 1/2 CUPS | FLOUR | 375 ML |
| I TSP. | BAKING POWDER | 5 ML |
| I TSP. | SALT | 5 ML |
| | GRATED ZEST OF I LEMON | |
| 1/2 CUP | CHOPPED WALNUTS (OPTIONAL) | 125 ML |

## DRIZZLE

| | | |
|---|---|---|
| 3 TBSP. | LEMON JUICE | 45 ML |
| 1/4 CUP | SUGAR | 60 ML |

PREHEAT OVEN TO 350°F (180°C). IN A LARGE BOWL, CREAM BUTTER AND SUGAR. ADD BEATEN EGGS AND MILK. ADD DRY INGREDIENTS, LEMON ZEST AND WALNUTS. MIX WELL. PLACE IN A 2 X 5 X 9" (5 X 13 X 23 CM) GREASED LOAF PAN AND BAKE FOR I HOUR. REMOVE FROM OVEN AND COOL ON A RACK FOR 5 MINUTES. PRICK CAKE WITH FORK AND POUR DRIZZLE OVER LOAF. LET STAND AT LEAST I HOUR BEFORE REMOVING FROM PAN.

# HOW CHEESY DO YOU WANT IT!

## HOW EASY DO YOU WANT IT??

| | | |
|---|---|---|
| I | LOAF FROZEN BREAD DOUGH, THAWED UNTIL SLICEABLE (APPROXIMATELY I HOUR) | I |
| 1/4 CUP | BUTTER | 60 ML |
| I-2 CUPS | GRATED CHEDDAR CHEESE (PARMESAN WORKS TOO) | 250-500 ML |

CUT LOAF INTO 10-12 PIECES. DIP BOTH SIDES IN BUTTER, THEN CHEESE. ARRANGE IN BUNDT PAN. LET RISE 2-3 HOURS. BAKE 20 MINUTES AT 375°F (190°C). IF MAKING THE NIGHT BEFORE, COVER BUNDT PAN WITH DAMP TEA TOWEL AND BAKE WHEN READY. TO SERVE - PULL APART AND PUT IN A BREAD BASKET.

# PITA CRISPS

## YOU JUST WHIPPED THESE UP? - CLEVER!

| | | |
|---|---|---|
| I | PKG. MINI PITAS, SPLIT | I |
| 1/4 CUP | MELTED BUTTER | 60 ML |
| 1/4 CUP | LIQUID HONEY | 60 ML |
| 1/4 CUP | SESAME SEEDS | 60 ML |

BRUSH PITA HALVES WITH BUTTER AND HONEY. SPRINKLE WITH SESAME SEEDS. BROIL UNTIL CRISP AND GOLDEN. WATCH CAREFULLY! SERVE WITH ASIAN CHICKEN SALAD ON PAGE 104.

## PARMESAN CRISPS

GREAT TO SERVE WITH SOUP OR SALAD!

| 3/4 CUP | COARSELY SHREDDED FRESH | 175 ML |
| | PARMESAN CHEESE | |
| 1 TSP. | FLOUR | 5 ML |

PREHEAT OVEN TO 350°F (180°C). LINE A COOKIE SHEET WITH PARCHMENT PAPER OR COAT WITH VEGETABLE OIL. IN A SMALL BOWL, STIR CHEESE AND FLOUR TOGETHER. SPOON 1 ROUNDED TEASPOON (7 ML) CHEESE MIXTURE ONTO BAKING SHEET. GENTLY SPREAD MIXTURE TO FORM SMALL CIRCLES, ABOUT 2" (5 CM) IN DIAMETER. FILL SHEET WITH 4 OR 5 CIRCLES, LEAVING AT LEAST 2" (5 CM) BETWEEN EACH ONE. BAKE IN CENTER OF OVEN UNTIL GOLDEN, ABOUT 5-7 MINUTES. COOL CRISPS COMPLETELY ON BAKING SHEET BEFORE REMOVING. REPEAT UNTIL ALL CHEESE MIXTURE IS USED. CRISPS CAN BE MADE UP TO 1 DAY BEFORE SERVING. STORE AT ROOM TEMPERATURE IN AN AIRTIGHT CONTAINER. MAKES 10-12 CRISPS.

MARITAL STATUS: NOT GOOD

WIFE'S NAME: PLAINTIFF.

# BREAKFAST FRUIT KABOBS

AN ATTRACTIVE ADDITION TO ANY BRUNCH MENU.

|  |  |  |
|---|---|---|
|  | WATERMELON |  |
|  | CANTALOUPE |  |
|  | HONEYDEW |  |
|  | PINEAPPLE |  |
|  | STRAWBERRIES |  |
|  | SEEDLESS GRAPES |  |
|  | KIWI FRUIT |  |
| 6-8 | WOODEN SKEWERS | 6-8 |

## HONEY-LIME DRIZZLE

| 1/2 CUP | PLAIN YOGURT | 125 ML |
|---|---|---|
| 1 TSP. | HONEY | 5 ML |
| 1/4 TSP. | FRESHLY GRATED NUTMEG | 1 ML |
| 2 TSP. | LIME JUICE | 10 ML |
| 1 | LIME, THINLY SLICED | 1 |

PREPARE FRUIT IN BALLS OR CHUNKS AND THREAD ON
SKEWERS. ARRANGE ON A PLATTER. COMBINE YOGURT,
HONEY, NUTMEG AND LIME JUICE. DRIZZLE OVER KABOBS.
GARNISH WITH LIME SLICES.

NEVER BUY A CAR YOU CAN'T PUSH.

# MIDNIGHT FRENCH TOAST

## WHAT A WAY TO END THE DAY - AND START THE NEXT!!

| | | |
|---|---|---|
| I | DOZEN EGGS | I |
| 1/2 CUP | CREAM | 125 ML |
| 1/2 TSP. | VANILLA | 2 ML |
| | GRATED ZEST OF I ORANGE | |
| 2 TBSP. | ORANGE LIQUEUR OR | 30 ML |
| | ORANGE JUICE | |
| I | LOAF FRENCH BREAD, SLICED I" (3 CM) | I |
| | THICK | |

MIX EGGS, CREAM, VANILLA, ORANGE ZEST AND LIQUEUR IN 9 X 13" (23 X 33 CM) PAN. PLACE SLICED BREAD IN PAN, MAKING SURE SLICES ARE WELL COATED. COVER WITH LID OR PLASTIC WRAP. PLACE IN FRIDGE OVERNIGHT.

NEXT MORNING, PLACE BREAD SLICES ON WELL GREASED COOKIE SHEET. BAKE AT 375°F (190°C) FOR 20-25 MINUTES. SERVE WITH FRUIT OR MAPLE SYRUP. SERVES 6.

WRINKLED WAS NOT ONE OF THE THINGS I WANTED TO BE WHEN I GREW UP.

# NIGHT-BEFORE EGGS BENEDICT

PROMISE - THIS WORKS!! THE HOLLANDAISE CAN ALSO BE MADE THE DAY AHEAD.

| 8 | LARGE EGGS | 8 |
| 2 | SLICES BREAD | 2 |
| 8 | SLICES BACK BACON, FRIED | 8 |
| 4 | ENGLISH MUFFINS, SLICED IN HALF | 4 |

IN A LARGE FRYING PAN, BRING WATER TO A BOIL. REDUCE HEAT TO SIMMER. BREAK 1 EGG AT A TIME INTO A SMALL BOWL, AND THEN SLIDE INTO WATER. REPEAT WITH REMAINING EGGS. COOK UNTIL THE WHITE IS OPAQUE AND JUST SET, ABOUT $2\frac{1}{2}$-3 MINUTES. SPOON EGGS INTO A NON-METALLIC DISH FILLED WITH ICE WATER. COVER AND REFRIGERATE UP TO 24 HOURS. WHEN READY TO SERVE, CAREFULLY REMOVE EGGS FROM WATER AND TRIM EDGES WITH A KNIFE. SLIDE EGGS INTO A PAN OF SIMMERING WATER; WARM 1-2 MINUTES. USING A SLOTTED SPOON, PLACE EGGS ON A SLICE OF BREAD TO DRAIN. (NO - YOU DON'T EAT THE BREAD!)

WHILE EGGS ARE WARMING, TOAST MUFFIN HALVES UNDER THE BROILER. PLACE A SLICE OF BACON ON EACH MUFFIN HALF. PLACE EGGS ON TOP AND SPOON ON HOLLANDAISE SAUCE (PAGE 19).

# NIGHT-BEFORE EGGS BENEDICT

CONTINUED FROM PAGE 18.

## NEVER-FAIL BLENDER HOLLANDAISE

| | | |
|---|---|---:|
| I CUP | BUTTER | 250 ML |
| 4 | EGG YOLKS | 4 |
| 1/4 TSP. | SALT | I ML |
| 1/4 TSP. | SUGAR | I ML |
| 1/4 TSP. | TABASCO SAUCE | I ML |
| 1/4 TSP. | DRY MUSTARD | I ML |
| 2 TBSP. | FRESH LEMON JUICE | 30 ML |

HEAT BUTTER TO A FULL BOIL, BEING CAREFUL NOT TO BROWN. COMBINE ALL OTHER INGREDIENTS IN BLENDER. WITH BLENDER TURNED ON HIGH, SLOWLY POUR BUTTER INTO YOLK MIXTURE IN A THIN STREAM UNTIL ALL IS ADDED. MAY BE REFRIGERATED FOR SEVERAL DAYS. WHEN REHEATING, HEAT OVER HOT (NOT BOILING) WATER IN TOP OF DOUBLE BOILER. MAKES ABOUT 1 1/4 CUPS (300 ML) OF SAUCE. SERVES 4.

ETHERNET: A DEVICE USED TO CATCH THE ETHERBUNNY.

# PUFFY HOT PEPPER JACK CHEESE OMELET

**PUFFY AS A SOUFFLÉ - "AS GOOD AS IT GETS" JACK!**

| | | |
|---|---|---|
| 4 | LARGE EGGS, SEPARATED | 4 |
| | SALT & PEPPER TO TASTE | |
| PINCH | GROUND NUTMEG | PINCH |
| 1/3 CUP | SOUR CREAM | 75 ML |
| 1 TBSP. | BUTTER | 15 ML |
| 1/2-3/4 CUP | SHREDDED HOT PEPPER JACK CHEESE | 125-175 ML |

PREHEAT OVEN TO 350°F (180°C). IN A MEDIUM BOWL, BEAT EGG WHITES WITH SALT AT HIGH SPEED UNTIL STIFF, MOIST PEAKS FORM; SET ASIDE. IN ANOTHER BOWL, BEAT EGG YOLKS WITH PEPPER AND NUTMEG UNTIL VERY THICK AND LEMON COLORED. WHISK IN SOUR CREAM. POUR YOLK MIXTURE OVER BEATEN WHITES AND GENTLY FOLD TOGETHER. MELT BUTTER IN A 10" (25 CM) OVENPROOF FRYING PAN OVER MEDIUM HEAT. TILT TO COVER BOTTOM OF PAN. POUR IN EGG MIXTURE. COOK WITHOUT STIRRING UNTIL OMELET IS PUFFY AND LIGHTLY BROWNED ON BOTTOM (2-3 MINUTES). LIFT EDGE CAREFULLY TO CHECK COLOR. TRANSFER PAN TO OVEN; BAKE UNTIL OMELET TOP IS PALE GOLDEN BROWN (6-8 MINUTES) AND KNIFE INSERTED IN CENTER COMES OUT CLEAN. SPRINKLE EVENLY WITH CHEESE; THEN, USE A SPATULA TO LOOSEN EDGE. CAREFULLY TIP OMELET OUT OF PAN,

# PUFFY HOT PEPPER JACK CHEESE OMELET

CONTINUED FROM PAGE 20.

ALLOWING TOP EDGE TO FOLD OVER. SLIDE OMELET ONTO A WARM PLATTER AND SERVE IMMEDIATELY. SERVES 2. (PICTURED OPPOSITE PAGE 37.)

VARIATION: ADD SAUTÉED MUSHROOMS AND BELL PEPPERS BEFORE FOLDING OMELET IN HALF.

# CHILI CHEDDAR FRITTATA

THE AROMA WILL GET EVERYONE OUT OF BED!

| | | |
|---|---|---|
| ½ LB. | SHARP WHITE CHEDDAR, SHREDDED | 250 G |
| 4 OZ. | CAN MILD CHILIES OR JALAPEÑOS, DRAINED, RESERVE LIQUID | 115 G |
| ⅓ CUP | OIL-PACKED, SUNDRIED TOMATOES, CHOPPED | 75 ML |
| | LOTS OF FRESH BASIL | |
| 9 | EGGS, WELL BEATEN | 9 |

SPRAY A 9" (23 CM) GLASS BAKING DISH. SPRINKLE IN CHEESE, CHILIES, SUNDRIED TOMATOES AND BASIL. BEAT EGGS WITH RESERVED CHILI LIQUID AND POUR OVER ALL. BAKE AT 350°F (180°C) FOR 30 MINUTES. SERVES 6. THIS DOUBLES WELL.

# CRAB OR CHICKEN CRÊPES

CRÊPES MAY BE MADE AHEAD OF TIME AND STORED FROZEN BETWEEN LAYERS OF WAXED PAPER.

## CREPE BATTER

| | | |
|---|---|---:|
| I CUP | COLD WATER | 250 ML |
| I CUP | COLD MILK | 250 ML |
| 4 | EGGS | 4 |
| ½ TSP. | SALT | 2 ML |
| 2 CUPS | FLOUR | 500 ML |
| | | |
| 2 TBSP. | BUTTER | 30 ML |

WHIRL CREPE INGREDIENTS IN BLENDER FOR 2 MINUTES. REFRIGERATE 2 HOURS. USING 6" (15 CM) CREPE PAN OR SMALL NONSTICK FRYING PAN, MELT A LITTLE BUTTER AND POUR ABOUT ¼ CUP (60 ML) BATTER INTO PAN, TIPPING UNTIL BATTER COVERS THE BOTTOM. COOK AND TURN UNTIL CREPE IS GOLDEN ON BOTH SIDES. TRANSFER TO PLATE. REPEAT METHOD UNTIL ALL BATTER IS USED.

## FILLING

| | | |
|---|---|---:|
| ¼ CUP | CHOPPED GREEN ONION | 60 ML |
| I TBSP. | BUTTER | 15 ML |
| ½ CUP | SHERRY | 125 ML |
| 3 CUPS | CRAB OR COOKED DICED CHICKEN | 750 ML |
| | SALT & FRESHLY GROUND PEPPER TO TASTE | |

# CRAB OR CHICKEN CRÊPES

CONTINUED FROM PAGE 22.

## SWISS CHEESE SAUCE

| | | |
|---|---|---:|
| ¼ CUP | BUTTER | 60 ML |
| ⅓ CUP | FLOUR | 75 ML |
| 2 CUPS | MILK, HEATED | 500 ML |
| | SALT & FRESHLY GROUND PEPPER | |
| | TO TASTE | |
| 2 | EGG YOLKS | 2 |
| ½ CUP | WHIPPING CREAM | 125 ML |
| ¾ CUP | GRATED SWISS CHEESE | 175 ML |

TO MAKE FILLING: SAUTÉ ONION IN BUTTER; ADD SHERRY AND MIX IN CRAB, SALT AND PEPPER. SET ASIDE.

TO MAKE SAUCE: IN A SAUCEPAN, MELT BUTTER AND ADD FLOUR. BLEND. GRADUALLY ADD MILK, SALT AND PEPPER, STIRRING CONSTANTLY. BOIL FOR 1 MINUTE THEN REMOVE FROM HEAT. BEAT YOLKS AND CREAM TOGETHER. ADD EGG MIXTURE TO SAUCEPAN, STIRRING CONSTANTLY. FOLD IN CHEESE (SAUCE SHOULD BE THICK). SET ⅓ OF THE SAUCE ASIDE. POUR REMAINING SAUCE INTO THE FILLING. FILL AND ROLL CRÊPES AND PLACE IN A SHALLOW 9 X 13" (23 X 33 CM) BAKING DISH. DRIZZLE WITH RESERVED SAUCE. HEAT IN WARM OVEN UNTIL SERVING TIME.

NOTE: THIN SAUCE WITH CREAM IF NECESSARY.

# SPINACH AND CAMEMBERT STRUDEL

THIS IS A HIT AT BRUNCH OR LUNCH - THE FLAVORS ARE OUTSTANDING. CAN BE PREPARED AND FROZEN AHEAD OF TIME.

| | | |
|---|---|---|
| 10 OZ. | BAG FRESH SPINACH, COOKED & CHOPPED | 284 ML |
| 2 TSP. | BUTTER | 10 ML |
| 1/2 | SMALL ONION, THINLY SLICED | 1/2 |
| 1/2 CUP | RICOTTA CHEESE | 125 ML |
| 3 OZ. | CAMEMBERT CHEESE, RIND DISCARDED, CUT INTO SMALL PIECES | 85 G |
| 1/4 CUP | GRATED PARMESAN CHEESE | 60 ML |
| 3 TBSP. | PINE NUTS, TOASTED | 45 ML |
| 1/4 TSP. | SALT | 1 ML |
| PINCH | FRESHLY GROUND PEPPER | PINCH |
| PINCH | NUTMEG. | PINCH |
| 6 | SHEETS PHYLLO | 6 |
| 1/3 CUP | MELTED BUTTER | 75 ML |

COOK SPINACH IN A LITTLE WATER; DRAIN; SQUEEZE OUT ALL LIQUID AND CHOP. IN SMALL FRYING PAN HEAT BUTTER AND SAUTÉ ONION UNTIL SOFT. IN A BOWL, COMBINE SPINACH, ONION, RICOTTA, CAMEMBERT, PARMESAN, PINE NUTS, SALT, PEPPER AND NUTMEG.

PREHEAT OVEN TO 375°F (190°C).

LAY 1 SHEET OF PHYLLO ON COUNTER, LONGEST SIDE FACING YOU. BRUSH WITH MELTED BUTTER. REPEAT UNTIL YOU HAVE 6 SHEETS ON TOP OF

# SPINACH AND CAMEMBERT STRUDEL

CONTINUED FROM PAGE 24.

ONE ANOTHER. SPOON ON SPINACH MIXTURE 3" (8 CM) WIDE AND 2" (5 CM) FROM THE BOTTOM. LEAVE ABOUT 1" (2.5 CM) AT EACH SHORT END. FOLD PHYLLO OVER MIXTURE AND CONTINUE TO ROLL. BRUSH BUTTER ON EDGE TO SEAL. PLACE PARCHMENT PAPER ON A COOKIE SHEET. BRUSH REMAINING BUTTER OVER TOP AND SIDES OF STRUDEL AND LIFT ONTO COOKIE SHEET. USING A SHARP KNIFE, SCORE DIAGONALLY (NOT TOO DEEP), ABOUT 2" (5 CM) APART. BAKE 35-40 MINUTES. IF FREEZING, WRAP TIGHTLY IN PLASTIC WRAP. TO BAKE FROZEN, ADD 10 MORE MINUTES TO BAKING TIME. LET STAND FOR 10-15 MINUTES. WHEN READY TO SERVE, SLICE AT SCORED INTERVALS. SERVES 6.

AMAZING!! YOU HANG SOMETHING IN YOUR CLOSET FOR AWHILE AND IT SHRINKS TWO SIZES.

# COTSWOLD CHEESE FLAN

THIS RECIPE IS FROM THE COTSWOLD REGION OF ENGLAND WHERE THEY MAKE A NIPPY CHEESE SIMILAR TO CHEDDAR. GOOD SERVED HOT OR AT ROOM TEMPERATURE. TIP - IF YOU'RE IN A HURRY, USE A FROZEN PIE CRUST!

## SHORTCRUST PASTRY

| | | |
|---|---|---|
| 1/2 CUP | BUTTER, ICE COLD | 125 ML |
| 1/4 CUP | VEGETABLE SHORTENING, ICE COLD | 60 ML |
| 1 1/2 CUPS | FLOUR | 375 ML |
| 1 | EGG YOLK | 1 |
| 1/4 CUP | ICE WATER | 60 ML |

## CHEDDAR FILLING

| | | |
|---|---|---|
| 1 TBSP. | BUTTER | 15 ML |
| 1 | LARGE ONION, THINLY SLICED | 1 |
| 3/4 CUP | GRATED SHARP CHEDDAR CHEESE | 175 ML |
| 3 TBSP. | CHOPPED CHIVES | 45 ML |
| 1 | WHOLE EGG PLUS 1 EGG YOLK | 1 |
| 1/4 CUP | CREAM OR MILK | 60 ML |
| 1 TSP. | SALT | 5 ML |
| 1/2 TSP. | PEPPER | 2 ML |
| 6 OZ. | LARGE FRESH MUSHROOMS | 170 G |

PREHEAT OVEN TO 400°F (200°C). CUT BUTTER AND SHORTENING INTO FLOUR WITH PASTRY CUTTER UNTIL MIXTURE IS CRUMBLY. ADD EGG YOLK AND SPRINKLE WITH WATER. COMBINE TO MAKE A SOFT DOUGH. ROLL OUT DOUGH ON A LIGHTLY FLOURED SURFACE. LINE A 9" (23 CM) PIE PLATE OR QUICHE PAN WITH DOUGH AND

# COTSWOLD CHEESE FLAN

CONTINUED FROM PAGE 26.

PRICK WITH A FORK. BAKE UNTIL CRUST IS JUST SET, ABOUT 15 MINUTES. MELT BUTTER IN A LARGE FRYING PAN OVER MEDIUM-LOW HEAT AND SAUTÉ ONION UNTIL GOLDEN. COMBINE GRATED CHEESE, CHIVES, EGG AND YOLK, CREAM, SALT AND PEPPER IN A MIXING BOWL. REMOVE MUSHROOM STEMS AND PLACE WHOLE MUSHROOM CAPS, STEM SIDE UP, IN THE PREPARED CRUST.

DISTRIBUTE SAUTÉED ONIONS OVER MUSHROOMS. POUR CHEESE MIXTURE OVER ALL. RETURN TO OVEN FOR 15-20 MINUTES, OR UNTIL FILLING IS SET AND BROWN. LET COOL 10 MINUTES BEFORE CUTTING. BRUNCH FOR 8.

HELP WANTED: TELEPATH.
YOU KNOW WHERE TO APPLY.

YOU DON'T HAVE TO BE A PASTRY CHEF TO MAKE A PERFECT QUICHE.

| | | |
|---|---|---|
| 1/2 | 14 OZ. (397 G) PKG. FROZEN PUFF PASTRY | 1/2 |
| 2 TSP | BUTTER | 10 ML |
| 1 | LARGE ONION, CHOPPED | 1 |
| 12 | SLICES BACON, CHOPPED | 12 |
| 4 | EGGS | 4 |
| 2 CUPS | WHIPPING CREAM | 500 ML |
| 1/2 TSP. | SALT | 2 ML |
| PINCH | NUTMEG | OUCH! |
| PINCH | PEPPER | OUCH! |
| PINCH | CAYENNE PEPPER | OUCH! |
| 1 CUP | GRATED SWISS CHEESE | 250 ML |

ROLL OUT PASTRY TO FIT A 9" (23 CM) DEEP PIE PLATE. IN A FRYING PAN, MELT BUTTER AND SAUTÉ ONION UNTIL SOFT. FRY BACON UNTIL CRISP. COMBINE EGGS, CREAM AND SPICES IN A LARGE BOWL AND BEAT UNTIL WELL MIXED. SPRINKLE PIE SHELL WITH ONION, BACON AND CHEESE. CAREFULLY POUR EGG MIXTURE ON TOP. BAKE AT 425°F (220°C) FOR 15 MINUTES. REDUCE HEAT TO 300°F (150°C); BAKE ABOUT 40 MINUTES OR UNTIL KNIFE INSERTED IN CENTER COMES OUT CLEAN. SERVES 6-8.

# VEGETARIAN FIESTA CASSEROLE

GREAT FOR BRUNCH OR DINNER.

| | | |
|---|---|---|
| 1 TBSP. | VEGETABLE OIL | 15 ML |
| 1 | MEDIUM ONION, DICED | 1 |
| 2 | LARGE EGGS, BEATEN | 2 |
| 1 CUP | RICOTTA OR COTTAGE CHEESE | 250 ML |
| 2 | 4 OZ. (115 G) CANS DICED GREEN CHILIES, DRAINED | 2 |
| 2 TBSP. | CHOPPED FRESH CILANTRO | 30 ML |
| 1/2 TSP. | GROUND CUMIN | 2 ML |
| 1/4 TSP. | SALT | 1 ML |
| | FRESHLY GROUND PEPPER TO TASTE | |
| 8 | CORN TORTILLAS, IN 1/2" (1.3 CM) STRIPS | 8 |
| 14 OZ. | CAN REFRIED BEANS | 398 ML |
| 3 | MEDIUM TOMATOES, CHOPPED | 3 |
| 2 CUPS | GRATED MONTEREY JACK | 500 ML |
| 2 CUPS | GRATED CHEDDAR CHEESE | 500 ML |

TOPPINGS

CHOPPED PITTED BLACK OLIVES
SLICED GREEN ONIONS
LIGHT SOUR CREAM

PREHEAT OVEN TO 350°F (180°C). HEAT OIL AND SAUTÉ ONION UNTIL SOFT. IN A MEDIUM BOWL, COMBINE ONION, EGGS, RICOTTA CHEESE, CHILIES, CILANTRO, CUMIN, SALT AND PEPPER.

SPRAY A 9 X 13" (23 X 33 CM) BAKING DISH. LAYER HALF THE TORTILLA STRIPS, RICOTTA MIXTURE, BEANS, TOMATOES AND CHEESES. REPEAT LAYERS. BAKE, UNCOVERED, UNTIL BUBBLY, 30-40 MINUTES. LET STAND 10 MINUTES BEFORE SERVING. PASS THE TOPPINGS.

# VEGETARIAN TEXAS TACOS

| | | |
|---|---|---|
| 1 TBSP. | VEGETABLE OIL | 15 ML |
| 1 | MEDIUM ONION, MINCED | 1 |
| 3 | GARLIC CLOVES, MINCED | 3 |
| 4 TSP. | GROUND CUMIN | 20 ML |
| 4 TSP. | CHILI POWDER | 20 ML |
| 2 | 19 OZ. (540 ML) CANS BLACK OR PINTO BEANS, DRAINED, RINSED | 2 |
| 3/4 CUP | MEDIUM SALSA | 175 ML |
| 1/2 CUP | FROZEN KERNEL CORN | 125 ML |
| | SALT & PEPPER TO TASTE | |
| 1/2-1 TSP. | CRUSHED RED PEPPER | 2-5 ML |
| 3/4 CUP | GRATED MONTEREY JACK CHEESE | 175 ML |
| 1/4 CUP | GRATED CHEDDAR CHEESE | 60 ML |
| | ABOUT 10 FLOUR TORTILLAS | 410 G |
| | TOPPINGS (USE 3 OR MORE PLUS SALSA) | |

## TOPPINGS

| | | |
|---|---|---|
| 1 | MEDIUM DICED ZUCCHINI | 1 |
| | SHREDDED LETTUCE | |
| 2 | SMALL AVOCADOS, DICED & TOSSED WITH A SPLASH OF LIME JUICE | 2 |
| | GRATED CHEDDAR CHEESE | |
| | CHOPPED ONION | |
| | DICED RED OR YELLOW PEPPER | |
| | DICED FRESH TOMATOES | |
| | SALSA | |

PREHEAT OVEN TO 350°F (180°C). HEAT OIL IN A LARGE FRYING PAN OVER MEDIUM HEAT. ADD ONION AND GARLIC AND COOK, STIRRING OCCASIONALLY, UNTIL ONION IS TRANSLUCENT, ABOUT 5 MINUTES.

# VEGETARIAN TEXAS TACOS

CONTINUED FROM PAGE 30.

ADD CUMIN AND CHILI POWDER AND STIR UNTIL THEY ARE AROMATIC, ABOUT 1-2 MINUTES LONGER. ADD BEANS AND SALSA AND MASH WITH A POTATO MASHER TO A CONSISTENCY THAT IS TO YOUR LIKING. ADD CORN AND SEASON WITH SALT, PEPPER AND CRUSHED RED PEPPER.

PUT MIXTURE IN A CASSEROLE AND SPRINKLE CHEESES ON TOP. BAKE FOR 15-20 MINUTES OR UNTIL CHEESE MELTS. WARM TORTILLAS IN OVEN AND LET YOUR FAMILY DO THEIR OWN WRAPPING AND TOPPING. PASS THE SALSA. (PICTURED OPPOSITE PAGE 54.)

I DECIDED TO TAKE AN AEROBICS CLASS. I BENT, TWISTED, GYRATED AND JUMPED UP AND DOWN FOR AN HOUR. BUT, BY THE TIME I GOT MY LEOTARD ON, THE CLASS WAS OVER.

# CHILIES RELLENOS
# WITH SAGE CHEESE

OLÉ - A MAKE-AHEAD.

### SAGE CHEESE

| | | |
|---|---|---|
| 8 OZ. | CREAM CHEESE, SOFTENED | 250 G |
| 4 OZ. | CHÈVRE, (GOAT CHEESE) SOFTENED | 125 G |
| 3 TBSP. | MINCED GREEN ONIONS | 45 ML |
| 2 TBSP. | FINELY CHOPPED FRESH SAGE | 30 ML |
| 1 | EGG | 1 |
| 1 | GARLIC CLOVE, MINCED | 1 |
| | SALT & PEPPER TO TASTE | |

### SOUFFLÉ

| | | |
|---|---|---|
| 2 | 7 OZ. (200 G) CANS WHOLE GREEN CHILIES, DRAINED | 2 |
| 8 | EGGS | 8 |
| 2 CUPS | MILK | 500 ML |
| ½ CUP | FLOUR | 125 ML |
| ⅓ CUP | GRATED PARMESAN CHEESE | 75 ML |

TO MAKE SAGE CHEESE: IN A SMALL BOWL, BEAT ALL INGREDIENTS TOGETHER. SET ASIDE.

TO MAKE SOUFFLÉ: HALVE CHILIES LENGTHWISE; PAT DRY. SPREAD 1-2 TBSP. (15-30 ML) SAGE CHEESE ON CUT-SIDE OF CHILIES. TOP WITH REMAINING CHILI HALVES. ARRANGE IN A SINGLE LAYER IN A GREASED 9 X 13" (23 X 33 CM) BAKING DISH. REFRIGERATE OVERNIGHT IF MAKING AHEAD. PREHEAT OVEN TO 375°F (190°C). COMBINE EGGS, MILK, FLOUR AND PARMESAN; BEAT UNTIL SMOOTH. POUR OVER CHILIES. BAKE FOR 45 MINUTES, OR UNTIL LIGHT BROWN. SERVE IMMEDIATELY WITH SALSA, SAUSAGES, FRUIT AND CORN BREAD. SERVES 8.

# RENE'S SANDWICH LOAF

PUTTIN' ON THE RITZ!

| 8 OZ. | PKG. CREAM CHEESE | 250 G |
| I TBSP. | MILK | 15 ML |
| | UNSLICED SANDWICH LOAF, SLIGHTLY FROZEN | |

HAM FILLING

| I CUP | GROUND COOKED HAM | 250 ML |
| 2 TBSP. | PICKLE RELISH, DRAINED | 30 ML |
| ½ TSP. | HORSERADISH | 2 ML |
| ⅓ CUP | FINELY CHOPPED CELERY | 75 ML |
| ¼ CUP | MAYONNAISE | 60 ML |

ASPARAGUS TIP FILLING

| I | CAN ASPARAGUS TIPS, DRAINED | I |
| | CHEESE WHIZ | |

EGG FILLING

| 4 | HARD-BOILED EGGS, CHOPPED | 4 |
| 2 TBSP. | FINELY CHOPPED GREEN ONIONS | 30 ML |
| ½ TSP. | PREPARED MUSTARD | 5 ML |
| ¼ CUP | MAYONNAISE | 50 ML |
| | SALT & PEPPER TO TASTE | |
| | CHOPPED FRESH PARSLEY | |
| | PIMIENTO-STUFFED OLIVES | |

IN A SMALL BOWL, BEAT CREAM CHEESE WITH MILK UNTIL FLUFFY. SET ASIDE. TRIM CRUSTS FROM SANDWICH LOAF AND SLICE BREAD LENGTHWISE IN 4 EQUAL LAYERS. BUTTER EACH SLICE. SPREAD FIRST LAYER WITH HAM FILLING, SECOND LAYER WITH CHEESE WHIZ; TOP WITH ASPARAGUS, AND THIRD LAYER WITH EGG FILLING. FROST TOP SLICE AND SIDES OF LOAF WITH CREAM CHEESE. SPRINKLE WITH PARSLEY AND GARNISH WITH OLIVES. SERVES 8-10.

# ROAST BEEF SANDWICHES
## WITH BRIE AND CARAMELIZED ONIONS

A BIG HIT !

| | | |
|---|---|---|
| 2/3 CUP | SOUR CREAM | 150 ML |
| 2-3 TBSP. | HORSERADISH, DRAINED | 30-45 ML |
| 1/2 TSP. | GRATED LEMON ZEST | 2 ML |
| | SALT & PEPPER TO TASTE | |
| 3 TBSP. | BUTTER | 45 ML |
| 1 | RED ONION, THINLY SLICED | 1 |
| 4 | KAISER ROLLS, CUT IN HALF | 4 |
| 1 LB. | MEDIUM-RARE BEEF, THINLY SLICED | 500 G |
| 4" | ROUND OF BRIE (ABOUT 8 1/4 OZ/ 235 G), RIND REMOVED | 10 CM |
| 1 | BUNCH ARUGULA (LETTUCE) | 1 |

IN A SMALL BOWL, MIX TOGETHER SOUR CREAM, HORSERADISH, LEMON ZEST, SALT AND PEPPER. IN A HEAVY FRYING PAN, MELT BUTTER OVER LOW HEAT AND STIR IN ONIONS. COOK ABOUT 35 MINUTES, STIRRING OCCASIONALLY, UNTIL CARAMELIZED. REMOVE FROM HEAT AND COOL. SPREAD HORSERADISH MIXTURE ON EACH BUN HALF. LAYER THE ROAST BEEF, BRIE AND ARUGULA. TOP WITH CARAMELIZED ONIONS AND – LUNCH IS READY!

SERVES 4 – YOU MAY WANT TO MAKE MORE!!

## BEVERAGES

Hot Buttered Rum
Hot Rum Canadienne
Lifesaver Punch
Pink Party Punch

## OTHER GOOD THINGS

Terrific Turkey Stuffing
Dill Pickles
Processing Pickles
Bread and Butter Pickles
Piccalilli
Crab Apple Chutney
Hot Pepper Orange Chutney
Microwave Peanut Brittle
Peppermint Brittle
Sinfully Rich Low-Fat Fudge Sauce

# HOT BUTTERED RUM

STORE IN YOUR FREEZER IN SMALL CONTAINERS. VERY GIFTABLE.

## HOT RUM BASE

| | | |
|---|---|---|
| 1 LB. | BUTTER, ROOM TEMPERATURE | 500 G |
| 4 CUPS | VANILLA ICE CREAM, SOFTENED | 1 L |
| 3½ CUPS | ICING (CONFECTIONER'S) SUGAR | 875 ML |
| 2 CUPS | BROWN SUGAR | 500 ML |
| 1½ TSP. | CINNAMON | 7 ML |
| ½ TSP. | ALLSPICE | 2 ML |

IN A LARGE BOWL, MIX BUTTER AND ICE CREAM TOGETHER. BLEND IN ALL OTHER INGREDIENTS. STORE IN FREEZER.

## TO ENJOY ONE SERVING

| | | |
|---|---|---|
| 2 TBSP. | HOT RUM BASE | 30 ML |
| 1½ OZ. | DARK RUM | 45 ML |
| | CINNAMON STICK | |

IN A LARGE MUG, ADD HOT RUM BASE AND DARK RUM. FILL MUG WITH BOILING WATER AND STIR WITH CINNAMON STICK UNTIL MIXTURE IS BLENDED.

I'D STOP DRINKING BUT I'M NO QUITTER.

Berry Best Muffins, page 8

Puffy Hot Pepper Jack Cheese Omelet, page 20

# HOT RUM CANADIENNE

MARVELOUS AFTER SKIING, AFTER FOOTBALL GAMES, AFTER TOBOGGANING, AFTER ANYTHING!

| 2 OZ.   | DARK RUM                     | 60 ML |
| 2 TBSP. | MAPLE SYRUP                  | 30 ML |
|         | SQUIRT OF LEMON JUICE        |       |
|         | NUTMEG                       |       |
|         | CINNAMON (A STICK IS BEST)   |       |
|         | BOILING WATER                |       |
|         | DAB OF BUTTER                |       |

COMBINE FIRST 5 INGREDIENTS, TOP OFF WITH BOILING WATER AND A SMALL DAB OF BUTTER. MAKES 1 STEAMING MUG.

# LIFESAVER PUNCH

PERFECT FOR POOL PARTIES. IF YOU ADD VODKA, ADD A LIFEGUARD!

| 8 OZ.      | CAN FROZEN STRAWBERRY DACQUIRI MIX | 250 ML |
| 12½ OZ.    | CAN FROZEN PINK LEMONADE           | 355 ML |
| 4 CUPS     | SODA WATER (OR GINGER ALE)         | 1 L    |
|            | LOTS OF ICE                        |        |
|            | FRESH STRAWBERRIES, SLICED         |        |
|            | VODKA, OPTIONAL                    |        |

THAW AND COMBINE DACQUIRI MIX AND LEMONADE. ADD SODA WATER AND ICE. FLOAT FRESH STRAWBERRY SLICES ON TOP.

# PINK PARTY PUNCH

PERFECT FOR LUNCH WITH LITTLE SQUIRTS.

| | | |
|---|---|---|
| 8 CUPS | PINK LEMONADE | 2 L |
| 4 CUPS | LEMON-LIME SODA OR 7-UP | 1 L |
| 2 QTS. | RASPBERRY SHERBET | 2 L |

<u>GARNISH</u>

LEMON OR ORANGE SLICES

MIX PINK LEMONADE AND SODA IN A LARGE BOWL. ADD
HALF OF THE SHERBET. STIR TO MAKE A CREAMY, FROTHY
MIXTURE. FOR GARNISH, ADD SCOOPS OF REMAINING
SHERBET AND LEMON OR ORANGE SLICES. SERVES 20.

INTAXICATION: EUPHORIA AT GETTING A TAX REFUND, WHICH
LASTS UNTIL YOU REALIZE IT WAS YOUR MONEY TO START
WITH.

# TERRIFIC TURKEY STUFFING

## FINALLY SOMETHING THAT'S GOOD FOR YOUR CAVITIES!

| | | |
|---|---|---|
| 3 CUPS | COOKED WILD RICE | 750 ML |
| 2 CUPS | FRESH BREAD CRUMBS | 500 ML |
| 1 LB. | BULK PORK SAUSAGE | 500 G |
| 2 | STALKS CELERY, FINELY CHOPPED | 2 |
| 1 | MEDIUM ONION, FINELY CHOPPED | 1 |
| | SALT & PEPPER, TO TASTE | |
| 1-2 TSP. | SAGE | 5-10 ML |
| ½ CUP | DRIED CRANBERRIES | 125 ML |

PLACE COOKED RICE AND BREAD CRUMBS IN A LARGE
BOWL. FRY SAUSAGE, CELERY AND ONION UNTIL SAUSAGE
IS BROWN. DRAIN AND ADD TO RICE MIXTURE. ADD
SEASONINGS AND DRIED CRANBERRIES AND TOSS.
MIXTURE SHOULD BE MOIST BUT NOT STICKY. ADD MORE
BREAD CRUMBS IF NECESSARY. SPOON, BUT DON'T PACK,
INTO NECK CAVITY AND BREAST CAVITY OF TURKEY. BE
SURE TO REMOVE STUFFING FROM BIRD IMMEDIATELY
AFTER REMOVING TURKEY FROM OVEN. KEEP WARM IN
A SMALL CASSEROLE.

BEAUTY IS IN THE EYE OF THE BEER HOLDER.

# DILL PICKLES

PUCKER UP!

BRINE

| 1 CUP | PICKLING SALT | 250 ML |
| 1 QT. | VINEGAR (GOOD QUALITY - HEINZ) | 1 L |
| 12 CUPS | WATER | 3 L |

PICKLES

| 22 LBS. | PICKLING CUCUMBERS | 10 KG |
| | FRESH DILL SPRIGS | |
| 3-4 | BULBS GARLIC | 3-4 |
| | WHOLE PEPPERCORNS | |
| 18-20 | GLASS 1-QUART (1 L) JARS | 18-20 |
| | WITH LIDS | |

TO MAKE BRINE: IN A LARGE CANNER OR BROTH POT, COMBINE AND BRING PICKLING SALT, VINEGAR AND WATER TO A BOIL. SET ASIDE.

TO MAKE PICKLES: WASH CUCUMBERS AND PLACE IN STERILIZED JARS. TO EACH JAR ADD 1-2 SPRIGS OF FRESH DILL, 1-2 PEELED GARLIC CLOVES AND A FEW PEPPERCORNS. LADLE HOT BRINE INTO EACH JAR UP TO 1/2" (1.3 CM) FROM THE TOP AND PUT LIDS ON IMMEDIATELY (DON'T TIGHTEN COMPLETELY). TO PROCESS SEE OPPOSITE PAGE. ALLOW AT LEAST A WEEK TO LET THE FLAVORS COMMINGLE.

## PROCESSING PICKLES

TO PROCESS: PLACE FILLED JARS IN A DEEP POT OR CANNER WITH A WIRE RACK IN THE BOTTOM. MAKE SURE THE JARS ARE NOT TOUCHING. POUR IN HOT WATER TO ABOUT 1" (2.5 CM) OVER TOP OF JARS. BRING TO A BOIL AND PROCESS FOR 20 MINUTES. REMOVE JARS AND SET ASIDE. LIDS SHOULD POP AND HAVE A SMALL DIP IN THE MIDDLE AS THEY COOL. LIDS MAY NOW BE TIGHTENED. ALWAYS STORE IN A COOL PLACE. HAPPY CANNING!

A GOOD FRIEND WILL COME AND BAIL YOU OUT OF JAIL, BUT – A TRUE FRIEND WILL BE SITTING NEXT TO YOU SAYING "DAMN . . . THAT WAS FUN!"

# BREAD AND BUTTER PICKLES

HOMEMADE ARE THE BEST!!

| | | |
|---|---|---:|
| 10 CUPS | PICKLING CUCUMBERS, UNPEELED, THINLY SLICED | 2.5 L |
| 2 | GREEN PEPPERS, DICED | 2 |
| 2 | CLOVES GARLIC, MINCED | 2 |
| 3 | LARGE ONIONS, THINLY SLICED | 3 |
| 1/3 CUP | PICKLING SALT | 75 ML |
| 12 CUPS | ICE CUBES | 3 L |
| 3 CUPS | WHITE VINEGAR | 750 ML |
| 4 CUPS | SUGAR | 1 L |
| 1 1/2 TSP. | TURMERIC | 7 ML |
| 1 1/2 TSP. | CELERY SEED | 7 ML |
| 1 1/2 TSP. | MUSTARD SEED | 7 ML |

COMBINE CUCUMBERS, PEPPERS, GARLIC AND ONIONS IN CANNER OR LARGE POT. MIX IN SALT AND ICE CUBES. LET STAND IN A COOL PLACE FOR AT LEAST 4 HOURS. DRAIN AND DISCARD ANY LEFTOVER ICE. SET VEGETABLES ASIDE. IN A LARGE POT COMBINE VINEGAR, SUGAR, TURMERIC, CELERY SEED AND MUSTARD SEED. BRING TO A BOIL AND COOK FOR 3-5 MINUTES. MIX IN VEGETABLES AND BRING TO A BOIL AGAIN. REMOVE FROM HEAT, SPOON INTO STERILIZED JARS AND PUT LIDS ON IMMEDIATELY (DON'T TIGHTEN COMPLETELY) AND PROCESS, PAGE 41. MAKES TEN 8-OZ. (250 ML) JARS.

# PICCALILLI

PICK THIS ONE – IT'S EASIER THAN TRYING TO PICK ANYTHING ELSE – A ROSE, A MAN, A DRESS . . .

| | | |
|---|---|---|
| 10–12 | MEDIUM GREEN TOMATOES | 10–12 |
| 6 | MEDIUM GREEN PEPPERS | 6 |
| 6 | MEDIUM RED PEPPERS | 6 |
| 4 | MEDIUM ONIONS | 4 |
| 6 CUPS | VINEGAR | 1.5 L |
| 3½ CUPS | SUGAR | 825 ML |
| ¼ CUP | MUSTARD SEED | 60 ML |
| ¼ CUP | SALT | 60 ML |
| 1 TBSP. | CELERY SEED | 15 ML |
| 2 TSP. | ALLSPICE | 10 ML |
| 1 TSP. | CINNAMON | 5 ML |

GRIND OR FINELY CHOP ALL VEGETABLES AND PLACE IN A LARGE DUTCH OVEN. ADD 4 CUPS (1 L) VINEGAR AND BRING TO A FULL BOIL OVER HIGH HEAT. REDUCE HEAT AND SIMMER FOR 30 MINUTES, STIRRING OCCASIONALLY. DRAIN AND RETURN TO POT. ADD 2 CUPS (500 ML) VINEGAR AND REMAINING INGREDIENTS AND BRING MIXTURE TO BOIL OVER HIGH HEAT. SIMMER FOR 3 MINUTES. LADLE INTO STERILIZED JARS, PUT ON LIDS IMMEDIATELY (DON'T TIGHTEN COMPLETELY) AND PROCESS (SEE PAGE 41). THIS MAKES NINE 12-OZ. (340 ML) JARS.

# CRAB APPLE CHUTNEY

MORE FUN THAN CRAB APPLE JELLY! GREAT SERVED WITH "NOTTA CHEESE BALL" ON PAGE 51.

| | | |
|---|---|---|
| 12 CUPS | QUARTERED CRAB APPLES | 3 L |
| 8 CUPS | SUGAR | 2 L |
| 3 | LARGE ORANGES, PEELED & CHOPPED | 3 |
| 1 LB. | RAISINS | 500 G |
| 1 TBSP. | CINNAMON | 15 ML |
| 1 TBSP. | GROUND CLOVES | 15 ML |
| 2 CUPS | CIDER VINEGAR | 500 ML |

IN A LARGE POT, MIX INGREDIENTS TOGETHER AND LET STAND OVERNIGHT. NEXT DAY BRING TO A BOIL, REDUCE HEAT AND COOK UNTIL CRAB APPLES ARE SOFT AND MIXTURE IS DARK IN COLOR (APPROXIMATELY 3/4-1 HOUR). POUR INTO 8-OZ. (250 ML) STERILIZED JARS, PUT LIDS ON IMMEDIATELY (DON'T TIGHTEN COMPLETELY) AND PROCESS (PAGE 41). MAKES ABOUT 12 JARS. RECIPE CAN BE DOUBLED.

LAST NIGHT I LAY IN BED LOOKING UP AT THE STARS IN THE SKY AND I THOUGHT TO MYSELF, WHERE THE HECK IS THE CEILING?

# HOT PEPPER ORANGE CHUTNEY

A SPICY CHUTNEY FOR HAM OR PORK OR SERVE AS AN APPETIZER WITH CREAM CHEESE AND CRACKERS.

| | | |
|---|---|---|
| 8 | LARGE ORANGES | 8 |
| 3 CUPS | CHOPPED RED PEPPER | 750 ML |
| 1/2 CUP | CHOPPED JALAPEÑO PEPPERS | 125 ML |
| 1 CUP | CHOPPED ONION | 250 ML |
| 1 CUP | RAISINS | 250 ML |
| 1 CUP | MIXED GLACÉ PEEL | 250 ML |
| 1 1/2 CUPS | WHITE WINE VINEGAR | 375 ML |
| 2 CUPS | BROWN SUGAR | 500 ML |
| 1/4 TSP. | CAYENNE PEPPER | 1 ML |
| 1 TSP. | CINNAMON | 5 ML |
| 1/2 TSP. | NUTMEG | 2 ML |

PEEL ALL BUT 3 ORANGES. SLICE THE 3 UNPEELED ORANGES THINLY AND CUT EACH SLICE IN HALF. CUT PEELED ORANGES IN 1/2" (1.3 CM) CHUNKS. PLACE ALL INGREDIENTS IN A LARGE POT OVER MEDIUM-HIGH HEAT AND BRING TO A BOIL. REDUCE HEAT AND SIMMER UNTIL THICKENED. POUR INTO 8-OZ. (250 ML) STERILIZED JARS AND PUT LIDS ON IMMEDIATELY (DON'T TIGHTEN COMPLETELY). PROCESS (SEE PAGE 41). MAKES 12 JARS.

# MICROWAVE PEANUT BRITTLE

GIFTABLE AND TRAVELS WELL.

| | | |
|---|---|---|
| I CUP | SALTED PEANUTS, PECANS OR CASHEWS | 250 ML |
| I CUP | SUGAR | 250 ML |
| 1/2 CUP | CORN SYRUP | 125 ML |
| PINCH | SALT | PINCH |
| I TSP. | BUTTER | 5 ML |
| I TSP. | VANILLA | 5 ML |
| I TSP. | BAKING SODA | 5 ML |

STIR FIRST 4 INGREDIENTS TOGETHER IN AN 8 CUP (2 L) MEASURING CUP, OR VERY LARGE "MICROWAVE SAFE" BOWL. COOK ON HIGH 3-4 MINUTES. STIR WELL. COOK 4 MORE MINUTES. STIR IN BUTTER AND VANILLA. COOK I MINUTE MORE. ADD BAKING SODA AND GENTLY STIR UNTIL LIGHT AND FOAMY. SPREAD MIXTURE QUICKLY ON LIGHTLY GREASED COOKIE SHEET. COOL FOR A HOUR. BREAK INTO PIECES.

A JOURNEY OF A THOUSAND MILES BEGINS WITH A CASH ADVANCE.

# PEPPERMINT BRITTLE

WHIP UP A BATCH FOR CHRISTMAS GIFTING. GREAT FOR STOCKING STUFFERS AND FOR KIDS HELPING MOMS COOK!

| 2 LBS. | GOOD-QUALITY WHITE CHOCOLATE | 1 KG |
| 1-1½ CUPS | CRUSHED CANDY CANES | 250-375 ML |

LINE A 10 X 15" (25 X 38 CM) EDGED COOKIE SHEET WITH HEAVY-DUTY FOIL. IN A HEAVY SAUCEPAN, MELT CHOCOLATE OVER LOW HEAT – BE VERY CAREFUL NOT TO BURN. ADD CRUSHED CANDY TO CHOCOLATE, POUR ONTO COOKIE SHEET AND CHILL UNTIL SET (ABOUT 1 HOUR). BREAK INTO PIECES BY SLAMMING PAN ON COUNTER (THAT'S FUN!). GOOD COOKING MRS. CLAUS!

WHEN YOU HAVE A HEADACHE – DO WHAT THEY SAY ON THE ASPIRIN BOTTLE: "TAKE 2 ASPIRIN" AND "KEEP AWAY FROM CHILDREN".

# SINFULLY RICH LOW-FAT
## FUDGE SAUCE

SERVE OVER FRUIT, ANGEL FOOD CAKE OR LOW-FAT FROZEN YOGURT. THE BEST!

| | | |
|---|---|---|
| 1/2 CUP | SUGAR | 125 ML |
| 1/4 CUP | COCOA | 60 ML |
| 4 TSP. | CORNSTARCH | 20 ML |
| 1/2 CUP | EVAPORATED SKIM MILK | 125 ML |
| 2 TSP. | VANILLA | 10 ML |

IN SMALL SAUCEPAN, COMBINE SUGAR, COCOA AND CORNSTARCH. STIR IN MILK AND WHISK OVER LOW HEAT FOR 3 MINUTES, OR UNTIL MIXTURE BOILS. WHISK 1-2 MINUTES LONGER, UNTIL THICKENED AND SMOOTH. REMOVE FROM HEAT AND STIR IN VANILLA. SERVE WARM OR COLD. REFRIGERATE LEFTOVER SAUCE. MAKES 1 CUP (250 ML).

CELL PHONES ARE SUCH A STATUS SYMBOL. I DON'T HAVE ONE, SO I JUST CARRY AROUND MY GARAGE DOOR OPENER.

# APPETIZERS

Grape Tomatoes Au Vodka
Cool Cocktail Grapes
Notta Cheese Ball
Cheese Wheel with Mango Chutney
Ginger Curry Dip with Mango Chutney
Peachy Cheese Dip
Mexican Dip
Cocktail Spread
Potted Pecan Shrimp
Caramelized Onion Dip
White Bean and Artichoke Dip with Pita Chips
Brandied Blue Cheese, Walnut and Pear Crostini
Bomb Shelter Croustades
Seasoned Flatbread
Bruschetta
Cheddar Chutney Tarts
Wonton Crispies
Dilled Cocktail Crackers
Nuts and Bolts
Cheddar-Cayenne Coins
Sesame Coins
Flatbread with Caramelized Onions and Cheese
Jalapeño Poppers
Phyllo Bundles with Two Cheese Fillings
Asian Vegetable Rolls with Dipping Sauce
Wrapped Brie with Caramelized Onions and Pepper
Jelly
Chicken Roca
Chicken Lettuce Wraps
Peanut-Curry Chicken in Wonton Cups
Asparagus Chicken Puffs
Curried Seafood Cocktail Puffs
Smoked Salmon Cheesecake

## GRAPE TOMATOES AU VODKA

THIS WOULD GET DR. ATKIN'S VOTE!

BASKET OF GRAPE TOMATOES
CITRUS VODKA (LEMON)
COARSE SEA SALT
FANCY TOOTHPICKS

WASH TOMATOES AND PRICK THEM WITH A SMALL SKEWER. PLACE TOMATOES IN A LARGE SEALABLE BAG AND POUR ENOUGH VODKA OVER THEM TO COVER. MARINATE OVERNIGHT IN REFRIGERATOR. TO SERVE, PLACE TOMATOES WITH SOME OF THE MARINADE IN A LARGE STEMMED GLASS. POUR SEA SALT IN A SEPARATE SMALL DISH. SPEAR A TOMATO WITH A TOOTHPICK, DIP IN SEA SALT - ET VOILA! (PICTURED OPPOSITE PAGE 108.)

## COOL COCKTAIL GRAPES

MAKE LOTS - THEY WON'T LAST!!

BLUE CHEESE, SOFTENED
SEEDLESS GRAPES, GREEN OR RED
TOASTED PISTACHIO NUTS,
FINELY CHOPPED

FORM SOFTENED CHEESE AROUND EACH GRAPE, THEN ROLL (NOT YOU - THE GRAPES!) IN CRUSHED PISTACHIO NUTS. REFRIGERATE UNTIL SERVING TIME.

THESE CAN BE PREPARED THE NIGHT BEFORE.

# NOTTA CHEESE BALL

| | | |
|---|---|---|
| ½ CUP | CHOPPED PECANS, TOASTED | 125 ML |
| 8 OZ. | PKG. IMPERIAL CHEESE | 250 G |
| | (COLD PACK CHEDDAR) | |
| ½ CUP | MAYONNAISE | 125 ML |
| ½ CUP | CHOPPED RED ONION | 125 ML |
| 3 | GARLIC CLOVES, MINCED | 3 |
| ½ TSP. | TABASCO | 2 ML |
| | CHUTNEY | |

TO TOAST PECANS: PLACE WHOLE NUTS ON A COOKIE SHEET AND BAKE AT 350°F (180°C) FOR 5-7 MINUTES. SET ASIDE, COOL AND CHOP.

IN A MEDIUM BOWL, CREAM CHEESE AND MAYONNAISE UNTIL SMOOTH. MIX IN ONION, GARLIC AND TABASCO. CHOP PECANS AND MIX INTO CHEESE MIXTURE. ON A SERVING PLATE, MAKE A DOUGHNUT SHAPE WITH CHEESE MIXTURE AND POUR SOME CHUTNEY INTO THE CENTER. SERVE WITH CRACKERS. SEE CRAB APPLE CHUTNEY PAGE 44.

AN INVISIBLE MAN MARRIES AN INVISIBLE WOMAN. THE KIDS WERE NOTHING TO LOOK AT EITHER.

# CHEESE WHEEL
## WITH MANGO CHUTNEY

| | | |
|---|---|---|
| 8 OZ. | PKG. CREAM CHEESE, SOFTENED | 250 G |
| 4 OZ. | SHARP CHEDDAR CHEESE, GRATED | 115 G |
| 1/2 TSP. | CURRY POWDER | 2 ML |
| 1/3 CUP | MANGO CHUTNEY OR CRAB APPLE CHUTNEY (PG. 48) | 75 ML |
| 1/4 CUP | TOASTED SLIVERED ALMONDS (OPTIONAL) | 60 ML |
| 3 | GRANNY SMITH APPLES | 3 |
| | WATER BISCUITS | |

COMBINE CREAM CHEESE, CHEDDAR CHEESE AND CURRY POWDER. BEAT BY HAND UNTIL SMOOTH. SHAPE INTO A 5 1/2" (14 CM) DIAMETER WHEEL ABOUT 1" (2.5 CM) THICK. CHILL UNTIL FIRM (ABOUT 45 MINUTES).

TO SERVE: PLACE CHEESE ON A SERVING DISH AND SPREAD CHUTNEY ON TOP. SPRINKLE WITH TOASTED ALMONDS IF DESIRED. CUT APPLES INTO THIN WEDGES. ARRANGE WEDGES AND WATER BISCUITS AROUND CHEESE.

THE CHEESE WHEEL MAY BE MADE UP TO 2 DAYS IN ADVANCE. COVER AND CHILL UNTIL READY TO SERVE.

# GINGER CURRY DIP
## WITH MANGO CHUTNEY

| | | |
|---|---|---|
| 8 OZ. | PKG. CREAM CHEESE, SOFTENED | 250 G |
| 1/2 CUP | SOUR CREAM | 125 ML |
| 1 CUP | MANGO CHUTNEY, DRAINED & CHOPPED | 250 ML |
| 1 TSP. | CURRY POWDER | 5 ML |
| 3 | PIECES CANDIED GINGER, FINELY CHOPPED | 3 |
| 1/2 CUP | CHOPPED SALTED CASHEWS | 125 ML |

CREAM INGREDIENTS TOGETHER EXCEPT NUTS. MIX IN NUTS JUST BEFORE SERVING (SAVING SOME TO SPRINKLE ON TOP). TO ENJOY THE BEST FLAVOR, MAKE SEVERAL HOURS AHEAD, COVER AND REFRIGERATE. SERVE AT ROOM TEMPERATURE WITH CRACKERS.

DEAR GOD:

DO YOU REALLY MEAN DO UNTO OTHERS AS THEY DO UNTO YOU, BECAUSE IF YOU DID THEN I'M GOING TO FIX MY BROTHER.

# PEACHY CHEESE DIP

| | | |
|---|---|---|
| 8 OZ. | PKG. CREAM CHEESE, SOFTENED | 250 G |
| 8 OZ. | PKG. IMPERIAL CHEESE (OR COLD PACK SHARP CHEDDAR) | 250 G |
| 2 TBSP. | SHERRY | 30 ML |
| 1 TSP. | CURRY POWDER | 5 ML |
| 3/4 CUP | PEACH JAM | 175 ML |
| | PEACH CHUTNEY | |
| | CHIVES | |

USING A FOOD PROCESSOR OR ELECTRIC MIXER, BLEND CHEESES TOGETHER. ADD SHERRY, CURRY AND JAM, MIXING UNTIL SMOOTH. POUR INTO STERILIZED JARS AND KEEP REFRIGERATED. TO SERVE, GARNISH WITH CHUTNEY AND CHIVES AND SET OUT WITH CRACKERS. MAKES ABOUT TWO 8-OZ. (250 ML) JARS.

# MEXICAN DIP

YOU HAVE TO MAKE THIS!

| | | |
|---|---|---|
| 1 LB. | VELVEETA CHEESE, CUBED | 500 G |
| 8 OZ. | OLD CHEDDAR CHEESE, GRATED | 250 G |
| 3-4 | JALAPEÑO PEPPERS, SEEDS REMOVED, FINELY CHOPPED | 3-4 |
| 4 | LARGE TOMATOES, FINELY CHOPPED | 4 |
| 1 | MEDIUM ONION, FINELY CHOPPED | 1 |
| 4 | GARLIC CLOVES, MINCED | 4 |

CONTINUED ON PAGE 55.

Vegetarian Texas Tacos, page 30

Flatbread with Caramelized Onions and Cheese, page 69

## MEXICAN DIP

CONTINUED FROM PAGE 54.

PREHEAT OVEN TO 350°F (180°C). FOR EASIER MIXING, SOFTEN CHEESES IN MICROWAVE. COMBINE INGREDIENTS AND SPOON INTO AN OVENPROOF SERVING DISH. BAKE 40 MINUTES, OR UNTIL BUBBLY. SERVE WITH CORN OR TORTILLA CHIPS.

## COCKTAIL SPREAD

GUESTS WILL ASK FOR A SPOON. JIMMY DID!

| | | |
|---|---|---|
| 8 OZ. | PKG. CREAM CHEESE, SOFTENED | 250 ML |
| 1/2 CUP | SOUR CREAM | 125 ML |
| 1/4 CUP | MAYONNAISE | 60 ML |
| 3 | 4 OZ. (125 ML) CANS BROKEN SHRIMP, RINSED & DRAINED OR 1 1/2 CUPS (375 ML) FRESH BABY SHRIMP | 3 |
| 1 CUP | SEAFOOD COCKTAIL SAUCE | 250 ML |
| 2 CUPS | GRATED MOZZARELLA CHEESE | 500 ML |
| 3 | GREEN ONIONS, CHOPPED | 3 |
| 1 | TOMATO, DICED | 1 |
| 1 | GREEN PEPPER, CHOPPED | 1 |

COMBINE CHEESE, SOUR CREAM AND MAYONNAISE. SPREAD IN A 12" (30 CM) DISH OR PIE PLATE. SCATTER SHRIMP OVER CHEESE. LAYER SEAFOOD SAUCE, THEN MOZZARELLA, GREEN ONIONS, TOMATO AND GREEN PEPPER. COVER UNTIL READY TO SERVE. SERVE WITH CRACKERS.

# POTTED PECAN SHRIMP

THIS IS SO EASY – AND SOOO GOOD!

| | | |
|---|---|---|
| 1/2 CUP | PECANS, TOASTED | 125 ML |
| 8 OZ. | PKG. CREAM CHEESE, SOFTENED | 250 G |
| 1/4 CUP | FINELY CHOPPED CELERY | 60 ML |
| 1/4 CUP | BEER | 60 ML |
| 4 TSP. | GRATED ONION | 20 ML |
| 1/2 TSP. | WORCESTERSHIRE SAUCE | 2 ML |
| 1/4 TSP. | DRY MUSTARD | 1 ML |
| 1 1/2 CUPS | CHOPPED COOKED FRESH SHRIMP | 375 ML |

TO TOAST PECANS: BAKE AT 350°F (180°C) FOR 5-7 MINUTES. SET ASIDE, COOL AND CHOP.

IN A MEDIUM BOWL, COMBINE CREAM CHEESE, CELERY, BEER, ONION, WORCESTERSHIRE AND MUSTARD. BLEND WELL. STIR IN SHRIMP AND PECANS. PACK THE MIXTURE INTO A CROCK OR OTHER SERVING CONTAINER. COVER AND REFRIGERATE AT LEAST 1 HOUR. SERVE WITH CRACKERS.

ALWAYS READ STUFF THAT WILL MAKE YOU LOOK GOOD IF YOU DIE IN THE MIDDLE OF IT.

# CARAMELIZED ONION DIP

TASTES TERRIFIC ON A HAMBURGER TOO!

| | | |
|---|---|---|
| ¼ CUP | VEGETABLE OIL | 60 ML |
| ¼ CUP | BUTTER | 60 ML |
| I | LARGE YELLOW ONION, HALVED & THINLY SLICED | I |
| ¼ TSP. | CAYENNE PEPPER | I ML |
| I TSP. | SALT | 5 ML |
| ½ TSP. | GROUND PEPPER | 2 ML |
| 4 OZ. | PKG. CREAM CHEESE, SOFTENED | 115 G |
| ½ CUP | SOUR CREAM | 125 ML |
| ½ CUP | MAYONNAISE | 125 ML |

HEAT OIL AND BUTTER IN A LARGE FRYING PAN OVER MEDIUM HEAT. ADD ONION, CAYENNE, SALT AND PEPPER AND SAUTÉ FOR 10 MINUTES. REDUCE HEAT TO MEDIUM-LOW AND COOK, STIRRING OCCASIONALLY, FOR 20 MINUTES MORE, UNTIL ONIONS ARE BROWNED AND CARAMELIZED. COOL. BEAT CHEESE, SOUR CREAM AND MAYONNAISE UNTIL SMOOTH. ADD ONIONS AND MIX WELL. SERVE WITH POTATO CHIPS OR CRACKERS.

NEVER BUY A PURSE FROM A MAN WHO IS OUT OF BREATH.

# WHITE BEAN AND
# ARTICHOKE DIP WITH PITA CHIPS

TASTES FINE!! VERY FINE!!

<u>PITA CHIPS</u>

| | | |
|---|---|---|
| 4 | 8″ (20 CM) PITA ROUNDS, SLICED INTO 8 TRIANGLES, SEPARATED INTO 2 PIECES EACH | 4 |
| 3 TBSP. | OLIVE OIL | 45 ML |
| | CAYENNE PEPPER | |
| | SEA SALT & FRESHLY GROUND PEPPER | |

<u>DIP</u>

| | | |
|---|---|---|
| 19 OZ. | CAN WHITE KIDNEY BEANS, DRAINED & RINSED | 540 ML |
| 2 | 6 OZ. (170 ML) JARS MARINATED ARTICHOKE HEARTS, DRAINED, RINSED OR | 2 |
| 14 OZ. | CAN ARTICHOKE HEARTS, DRAINED & CHOPPED | 398 ML |
| 1 | SMALL GARLIC CLOVE, CHOPPED | 1 |
| 2 TBSP. | FRESH LEMON JUICE | 30 ML |
| 3 TBSP. | FRESHLY GRATED PARMESAN CHEESE | 45 ML |
| 1 TSP. | CHOPPED FRESH ROSEMARY | 5 ML |
| | SALT & PEPPER | |
| | CAYENNE | |

TO MAKE CHIPS: PUT OVEN RACK TO UPPER-MIDDLE OF OVEN AND HEAT BROILER. TOSS PITA PIECES WITH OIL, PINCH OF CAYENNE AND A GENEROUS AMOUNT OF SALT AND PEPPER. LAY PIECES FLAT ON 2 BAKING SHEETS AND BROIL ON BOTH SIDES UNTIL GOLDEN. WATCH CAREFULLY. REMOVE AND COOL.

# WHITE BEAN DIP

CONTINUED FROM PAGE 58.

TO MAKE BEAN DIP: BLEND BEANS, ARTICHOKE HEARTS, GARLIC AND LEMON JUICE IN A FOOD PROCESSOR TO FORM A SMOOTH PASTE. IF NECESSARY, WHILE MACHINE IS RUNNING, DRIZZLE WATER FOR A SMOOTH CONSISTENCY. BLEND IN CHEESE AND ROSEMARY; SEASON WITH SALT AND PEPPER. POUR DIP INTO SERVING BOWL AND SPRINKLE WITH CAYENNE. SERVE WITH PITA CHIPS. MAKES ABOUT 2 CUPS (500 ML).

# BRANDIED BLUE CHEESE, WALNUT AND PEAR CROSTINI

| 4 OZ. | BLUE CHEESE, CRUMBLED | 125 G |
| 2 TBSP. | BUTTER | 30 ML |
| 2 TBSP. | BRANDY | 30 ML |
| 1/4 CUP | COARSELY CHOPPED WALNUTS | 60 ML |
| 16 | 1/2" (1.3 CM) BAGUETTE SLICES | 16 |
| 1 | RIPE PEAR, THINLY SLICED | 1 |

SOFTEN CHEESE AND BUTTER. MASH WITH FORK UNTIL SMOOTH. STIR BRANDY AND WALNUTS INTO CHEESE MIXTURE. PLACE BAGUETTE SLICES ON COOKIE SHEET. TOAST 1 SIDE UNDER BROILER. TURN AND PLACE PEAR SLICE ON UNTOASTED SIDE. TOP WITH TEASPOONFUL OF CHEESE MIXTURE. BROIL 4-5" (10-13 CM) FROM HEAT FOR ABOUT 2 MINUTES, OR UNTIL CHEESE IS BUBBLY. SERVES 8.

## CROUSTADES

| 24 | SLICES WHITE BREAD, THINLY ROLLED | 24 |
|---|---|---|
| 2 TBSP. | BUTTER | 30 ML |

## MUSHROOM FILLING

| 1/4 CUP | BUTTER | 60 ML |
|---|---|---|
| 3 TBSP. | FINELY CHOPPED, ONION | 45 ML |
| 1/2 LB. | FINELY CHOPPED MUSHROOMS | 250 G |
| 2 TBSP. | FLOUR | 30 ML |
| I CUP | WHIPPING CREAM | 250 ML |
| 3 TBSP. | DRY WHITE WINE | 45 ML |
| 1/2 TSP. | SALT | 2 ML |
| PINCH | CAYENNE PEPPER | PINCH |
| I TBSP. | FINELY CHOPPED PARSLEY | 15 ML |
| 1 1/2 TBSP. | FINELY CHOPPED GREEN ONION | 22 ML |
| 3 TBSP. | GRATED PARMESAN CHEESE | 45 ML |

PREHEAT OVEN TO 400°F (200°C).

TO MAKE CROUSTADES: GENEROUSLY BUTTER SMALL
TART TINS. CUT A 3" (8 CM) ROUND FROM EACH SLICE
OF BREAD. CAREFULLY FIT INTO TART TINS. BAKE FOR
10 MINUTES, OR UNTIL RIMS ARE LIGHTLY BROWNED.
REMOVE FROM TINS AND COOL. (MAY BE FROZEN AT
THIS POINT.)

TO MAKE FILLING: MELT BUTTER IN A FRYING
PAN AND SAUTÉ ONION AND MUSHROOMS. STIR AND COOK
UNTIL MOISTURE EVAPORATES. SPRINKLE WITH FLOUR.
STIR THOROUGHLY AND ADD CREAM, STIRRING UNTIL IT
BOILS. ADD WINE, REDUCE HEAT AND SIMMER A FEW

# BOMB SHELTER CROUSTADES

CONTINUED FROM PAGE 60.

MINUTES LONGER. REMOVE FROM HEAT, STIR IN SALT, CAYENNE, PARSLEY AND GREEN ONION. TRANSFER TO A BOWL. COVER AND REFRIGERATE.

TO SERVE: PREHEAT OVEN TO 350°F (180°C). SPOON MUSHROOM FILLING INTO CROUSTADES; LIGHTLY SPRINKLE WITH PARMESAN AND PLACE ON COOKIE SHEET. HEAT IN OVEN FOR 10 MINUTES, THEN BRIEFLY UNDER THE BROILER.

# SEASONED FLATBREAD

IS THERE A CARPENTER IN THE HOUSE?

| 8 OZ. | PKG. KAVLI THIN FLATBREAD | 250 G |
|---|---|---|
| 1/2 CUP | BUTTER, SOFTENED | 125 ML |
| 2 | LARGE GARLIC CLOVES, MINCED | 2 |
| 1/3 CUP | GRATED PARMESAN CHEESE | 75 ML |
| 1 TBSP. | FINELY CHOPPED, FRESH PARSLEY | 15 ML |

PREHEAT OVEN TO 325°F (160°C). USING A BREAD KNIFE, SAW STACKED FLATBREAD IN HALVES OR THIRDS. COMBINE BUTTER, GARLIC, CHEESE AND PARSLEY; MIX WELL. SPREAD BUTTER MIXTURE ON FLATBREAD PIECES; PLACE ON A COOKIE SHEET. BAKE FOR ABOUT 5 MINUTES. LET COOL. STORE IN COVERED CONTAINER OR FREEZE.

# BRUSCHETTA

USE FIRM, RIPE, RED ROMA TOMATOES.

| | | |
|---|---|---|
| 2 | LARGE GARLIC CLOVES, CHOPPED | 2 |
| | SALT & PEPPER TO TASTE | |
| 1/3 CUP | OLIVE OIL | 75 ML |
| 6-8 | ROMA TOMATOES, COARSELY CHOPPED | 6-8 |
| | HANDFUL OF CHOPPED FRESH BASIL | |
| 24" | BAGUETTE | 61 CM |
| | GRATED PROVOLONE, FONTINA OR | |
| | MOZZARELLA CHEESE (OPTIONAL) | |

IN A SHALLOW BOWL, COMBINE GARLIC, SALT, PEPPER AND A FEW DROPS OF OIL. MASH WITH THE BACK OF A WOODEN SPOON TO MAKE A PASTE. STIR IN OLIVE OIL. ADD TOMATOES AND BASIL. TOSS GENTLY AND SET ASIDE. CUT BREAD IN HALF, LENGTHWISE. BRUSH EACH HALF WITH ADDITIONAL OIL AND PLACE UNDER A PREHEATED BROILER UNTIL GOLDEN BROWN. SPOON TOMATO MIXTURE ONTO EACH HALF AND DRIZZLE WITH REMAINING OIL. (IF DESIRED, SPRINKLE WITH GRATED CHEESE.) BROIL – WATCH CAREFULLY! CUT AND SERVE IMMEDIATELY.

A TRULY HAPPY PERSON IS ONE WHO CAN ENJOY THE SCENERY ON A DETOUR.

# CHEDDAR CHUTNEY TARTS

THIS RECIPE WAS DEVELOPED BY AWARD-WINNING CANADIAN FOODIE AND COOKBOOK AUTHOR ROSE MURRAY FOR HER DAUGHTER'S WEDDING. WE LOVE IT!

| | | |
|---|---|---|
| 8 OZ. | PKG. CREAM CHEESE, SOFTENED | 250 G |
| I CUP | GRATED SHARP CHEDDAR CHEESE | 250 ML |
| I | GARLIC CLOVE, MINCED | I |
| I TSP. | CURRY POWDER | 5 ML |
| 1/3 CUP | MANGO CHUTNEY | 75 ML |
| 4 | GREEN ONIONS, FINELY CHOPPED | 4 |
| PINCH | CAYENNE PEPPER | PINCH |
| DASH | WORCESTERSHIRE SAUCE | DASH |
| 14 OZ. | PKG. FROZEN PUFF PASTRY, THAWED | 397 G |

IN A LARGE BOWL, MIX CREAM CHEESE UNTIL SMOOTH. ADD CHEDDAR, GARLIC AND CURRY; MIX WELL. CHOP LARGE PIECES OF CHUTNEY AND ADD TO CHEESE MIXTURE ALONG WITH REMAINING CHUTNEY, ONIONS, CAYENNE AND WORCESTERSHIRE. MIX WELL. FILLING MAY BE MADE SEVERAL DAYS AHEAD, COVERED AND REFRIGERATED. ON A LIGHTLY FLOURED SURFACE, ROLL HALF THE PASTRY AT A TIME INTO A 12" (30 CM) SQUARE. CUT INTO 2" (5 CM) SQUARES. PRESS INTO SMALL TART TINS AND PRICK WITH A FORK. SPOON I TSP. (5 ML) FILLING INTO EACH TART. BAKE IN CENTER OF A 400°F (200°C) OVEN FOR ABOUT 15 MINUTES, OR UNTIL PASTRY IS GOLDEN. THESE CAN BE FROZEN IN AN AIRTIGHT CONTAINER AND REHEATED IN A 350°F (180°C) OVEN FOR 5-7 MINUTES. SERVE HOT. MAKES 6 DOZEN.

# WONTON CRISPIES

ADDICTIVE - YOU'LL WANT TO DOUBLE THIS!

| | | |
|---|---|---|
| 1/4 CUP | BUTTER | 60 ML |
| 20 | WONTON WRAPPERS | 20 |
| 1/4 CUP | PARMESAN CHEESE | 60 ML |

MELT BUTTER AND BRUSH SOME ON AN EDGED BAKING
SHEET. CUT EACH WONTON DIAGONALLY TO MAKE
TRIANGLES. PLACE CLOSE TOGETHER AND BRUSH TOPS
WITH BUTTER. SPRINKLE WITH CHEESE. BAKE AT 375°F
(190°C) FOR 5 MINUTES. REPEAT UNTIL ALL ARE BAKED.
IF YOU'RE INTO EXPERIMENTING, ADD HERBS OR CHOPPED
GREEN ONIONS TO THE CHEESE. MAKES 40.

# DILLED COCKTAIL CRACKERS

ALL-TIME FAVORITE - GREAT HOSTESS GIFT.

| | | |
|---|---|---|
| 8 OZ. | BOX MINI RITZ ORIGINAL CRACKERS OR OYSTER CRACKERS | 250 G |
| I OZ. | PKG. RANCH STYLE SALAD DRESSING MIX | 28 G |
| I TBSP. | DILLWEED | 15 ML |
| 1/2 CUP | VEGETABLE OIL | 125 ML |
| I TSP. | GARLIC POWDER | 5 ML |

COMBINE ALL INGREDIENTS IN A PLASTIC CONTAINER.
SEAL. SHAKE OFTEN. LET STAND OVERNIGHT OR AT LEAST
6 HOURS.

# NUTS AND BOLTS

FOR THOSE WHO ARE MECHANICALLY DECLINED! – AND
JUST ABOUT ANYONE ELSE!

| | | |
|---|---|---|
| 1 LB. | BUTTER | 500 G |
| 2 TBSP. | WORCESTERSHIRE SAUCE | 30 ML |
| 1 TBSP. | GARLIC POWDER | 15 ML |
| 1½ TSP. | ONION SALT | 7 ML |
| 1½ TSP. | CELERY SALT | 7 ML |
| 4 CUPS | 'CHEERIOS' | 1 L |
| 4 CUPS | 'LIFE' CEREAL | 1 L |
| 4 CUPS | 'SHREDDIES' OR 'WHEAT CHEX' | 1 L |
| 2 | 16 OZ. (454 G) BOXES PRETZELS | 2 |
| 2 CUPS | PEANUTS, SALTED (IF YOU INSIST) | 500 ML |
| 5½ OZ. | BOX 'BUGLES' | 150 G |
| 8 OZ. | BOX 'CHEESE NIPS' OR 'CHEESE BITES' | 250 G |

PREHEAT OVEN TO 250°F (120°C). PLACE BUTTER IN A VERY
LARGE ROASTER. PLACE IN OVEN TO MELT WHILE OVEN IS
PREHEATING. REMOVE ROASTER AND ADD SPICES; STIR.
ADD REMAINING INGREDIENTS, MIXING WELL TO COAT
EVENLY WITH BUTTER MIXTURE. BAKE FOR 1½ HOURS.
STIR AND TURN EVERY ½ HOUR.

MY PHILOSOPHY IS: NO PAIN . . . GOOD.

# CHEDDAR-CAYENNE COINS

GREAT FREEZER FARE!

| | | |
|---|---|---|
| 1 1/3 CUPS | FLOUR | 325 ML |
| 1 1/4 CUPS | GRATED SHARP CHEDDAR CHEESE | 300 ML |
| 1 TSP. | SALT | 5 ML |
| 1/8-1/4 TSP. | CAYENNE PEPPER | 0.5-1 ML |
| 1/2 CUP | BUTTER CUT INTO 1/2" (1.3 CM) PIECES, CHILLED | 125 ML |
| 1 | LARGE EGG YOLK | 1 |
| 2 TBSP. | WATER | 30 ML |
| 1 1/3 CUPS | CHOPPED WALNUTS OR PECANS | 325 ML |
| | COARSE SALT FOR SPRINKLING (OPTIONAL) | |

IN A LARGE MIXING BOWL COMBINE FLOUR, CHEESE, SALT AND CAYENNE. ADD BUTTER PIECES AND BLEND UNTIL DOUGH RESEMBLES COARSE CRUMBS. STIR EGG YOLK AND WATER TOGETHER AND DRIZZLE OVER DOUGH. MIX UNTIL DOUGH BEGINS TO FORM SMALL MOIST CRUMBS. ADD CHOPPED NUTS AND MIX BRIEFLY, UNTIL CRUMBS BEGIN TO COME TOGETHER. PILE CRUMBS ON AN UNFLOURED WORK SURFACE. WORK CRUMBS WITH YOUR HANDS UNTIL THEY START TO COME TOGETHER AND FORM INTO A 14" (36 CM) LOG 1 1/4" (3.5 CM) IN DIAMETER. WRAP IN PLASTIC AND REFRIGERATE UNTIL FIRM, ABOUT 4 HOURS.

# CHEDDAR-CAYENNE COINS

CONTINUED FROM PAGE 66.

(DOUGH MAY ALSO BE FROZEN FOR UP TO A MONTH AND THAWED FOR AN HOUR AT ROOM TEMPERATURE OR IN REFRIGERATOR OVERNIGHT).

PREHEAT OVEN TO 375°F (190°C). LINE 2 LARGE BAKING SHEETS WITH PARCHMENT. CUT THE LOG INTO 1/4" (6 MM) SLICES. BAKE IN CENTER OF OVEN UNTIL GOLDEN BROWN AROUND THE EDGES, 15-20 MINUTES. SPRINKLE A LITTLE COARSE SALT OVER TOP AS SOON AS THEY COME OUT OF THE OVEN. PLACE ON A RACK TO COOL. STORE IN AN AIRTIGHT CONTAINER. MAKES 4 DOZEN.

KID'S LETTER TO GOD:

DEAR GOD:

THANK YOU FOR THE BABY BROTHER BUT WHAT I ASKED FOR WAS A PUPPY. I NEVER ASKED FOR ANYTHING BEFORE. YOU CAN LOOK THAT UP.

# SESAME COINS

| | | |
|---|---|---|
| 1 1/4 CUPS | FLOUR | 300 ML |
| 1 TSP. | SALT | 5 ML |
| 1/4 TSP. | COARSELY GROUND BLACK PEPPER | 1 ML |
| 1/2 CUP | BUTTER, CUT INTO 1/2" (1.3 CM) PIECES, CHILLED | 125 ML |
| 1 | LARGE EGG YOLK | 1 |
| 1 TBSP. | WATER | 15 ML |
| 1 TBSP. | DIJON MUSTARD | 15 ML |
| 2 TBSP. | SESAME SEEDS, TOASTED | 30 ML |
| | COARSE SALT FOR SPRINKLING (OPTIONAL) | |

IN A MIXING BOWL, COMBINE FLOUR, SALT AND PEPPER UNTIL JUST BLENDED. ADD BUTTER AND MIX UNTIL DOUGH RESEMBLES COARSE CRUMBS. STIR YOLK, WATER AND MUSTARD TOGETHER AND DRIZZLE OVER MIXTURE. MIX UNTIL DOUGH BEGINS TO CLUMP TOGETHER. ADD SESAME SEEDS AND MIX BRIEFLY. PILE ON AN UNFLOURED WORK SURFACE. USING YOUR HANDS, GENTLY WORK TO FORM A 12" (30 CM) LOG 1 1/4" (3.5 CM) IN DIAMETER. WRAP IN PLASTIC AND REFRIGERATE FOR AT LEAST 4 HOURS. PREHEAT OVEN TO 375°F (190°C). PLACE PARCHMENT PAPER ON 2 LARGE BAKING SHEETS. USING A SHARP KNIFE, SLICE LOG INTO 1/4" (6 MM) PIECES AND PLACE ON BAKING SHEETS. BAKE IN CENTER OF OVEN UNTIL EDGES ARE GOLDEN BROWN, ABOUT 15 MINUTES. REMOVE AND SPRINKLE WITH COARSE SALT. COOL ON RACK; STORE IN AIRTIGHT CONTAINER. MAKES 3 DOZEN COINS.

# FLATBREAD WITH CARAMELIZED ONIONS AND CHEESE

IT'S DEAD EASY AND ABSOLUTELY DELICIOUS!

| 3 | LARGE ONIONS, THINLY SLICED | 3 |
|---|---|---|
| 2 TBSP. | OLIVE OIL | 30 ML |
| 1 TBSP. | BROWN SUGAR | 15 ML |
| 2 TSP. | BALSAMIC VINEGAR | 10 ML |
| | SALT & PEPPER TO TASTE | |
| 14 OZ. | PKG. FROZEN PUFF PASTRY | 397 G |
| 6 OZ. | BRIE (RIND REMOVED), DICED | 170 G |
| 6 OZ. | MILD BLUE CHEESE, CRUMBLED | 170 G |
| 2 TBSP. | CHOPPED FRESH PARSLEY | 30 ML |

HEAT OIL IN LARGE DEEP FRYING PAN ON MEDIUM-HIGH, ADD ONIONS; COOK UNTIL WILTED AND STARTING TO BROWN, ABOUT 10 MINUTES. ADD SUGAR, VINEGAR, SALT AND PEPPER. REDUCE HEAT TO MEDIUM-LOW; COOK FOR 15-25 MINUTES, UNTIL ONIONS ARE CARAMELIZED AND GOLDEN. COOL. PUFF PASTRY PACKAGE HAS 2 POUCHES. PINCH BOTH TOGETHER AND ROLL OUT TO A 12 X 16" (30 X 40 CM) RECTANGLE. PLACE PASTRY ON BAKING SHEET LINED WITH PARCHMENT PAPER. SPREAD ONIONS OVER PASTRY. DOT WITH CHEESE. SPRINKLE WITH PARSLEY AND REFRIGERATE IF NOT BAKING IMMEDIATELY. BAKE IN PREHEATED 400°F (200°C) OVEN FOR 20-25 MINUTES, UNTIL CHEESE IS MELTED AND PASTRY IS CRISP. COOL FOR 5 MINUTES. CUT INTO 20 SQUARES; CUT SQUARES IN HALF DIAGONALLY TO MAKE 40 TRIANGLES. (PICTURED OPPOSITE PAGE 55.)

# JALAPEÑO POPPERS

HOT STUFF FOR THE ADVENTUROUS PALATE.

PARMESAN GARLIC FILLING

| | | |
|---|---|---:|
| 2 TSP. | VEGETABLE OIL | 10 ML |
| 3 TBSP. | FINELY MINCED RED ONION | 45 ML |
| 3 | GARLIC CLOVES, MINCED | 3 |
| 4 OZ. | SPREADABLE LIGHT CREAM CHEESE | 115 G |
| 2 TBSP. | FINELY GRATED FRESH PARMESAN CHEESE | 30 ML |
| 1/8 TSP. | SALT | 0.5 ML |
| | FRESHLY GROUND BLACK PEPPER TO TASTE | |
| 8 | JALAPEÑO PEPPERS | 8 |
| 4 | LARGE EGG WHITES | 4 |
| I CUP | FINE DRY BREAD CRUMBS | 250 ML |
| | COOKING SPRAY | |
| 1/2 CUP | PREPARED SALSA | 125 ML |

FILLING: HEAT OIL IN A SMALL FRYING PAN. ADD ONION AND GARLIC AND SAUTÉ UNTIL SOFT, ABOUT 5 MINUTES. DO NOT BROWN. TRANSFER TO A SMALL BOWL AND ADD CREAM CHEESE, PARMESAN, SALT AND PEPPER. STIR TO BLEND. SET ASIDE.

WEARING RUBBER GLOVES, CUT PEPPERS IN HALF, LENGTHWISE. SCRAPE OUT MEMBRANES AND SEEDS. FILL PEPPER HALVES WITH CHEESE FILLING AND SMOOTH SURFACE WITH A SMALL KNIFE. AT THIS POINT, PEPPERS CAN BE COVERED AND REFRIGERATED OVERNIGHT.

# JALAPEÑO POPPERS

CONTINUED FROM PAGE 70.

PREHEAT OVEN TO 350°F (180°C). LINE A 12 X 15" (30 X 38 CM) BAKING SHEET WITH PARCHMENT PAPER. WHISK EGG WHITES IN A BOWL UNTIL FROTHY. PLACE BREAD CRUMBS IN A SEPARATE SHALLOW BOWL. DIP PEPPER HALVES, 1 AT A TIME IN EGG WHITES AND THEN DIP INTO BREAD CRUMBS, COATING EVENLY. PLACE PEPPERS CUT SIDE UP ON PREPARED BAKING SHEET. LIGHTLY SPRAY PEPPERS WITH COOKING SPRAY AND BAKE ABOUT 20 MINUTES, OR UNTIL CRISP AND GOLDEN. SPOON SALSA ON TOP AND SERVE PDQ! (PICTURED OPPOSITE PAGE 108.)

CHILDREN'S OBSERVATIONS:

NO MATTER HOW HARD YOU TRY, YOU CAN'T BAPTIZE CATS.

WHEN YOUR MOM IS MAD AT YOUR DAD, DON'T LET HER BRUSH YOUR HAIR.

# PHYLLO BUNDLES WITH
## TWO CHEESE FILLINGS

YOU CAN MAKE THESE ATTRACTIVE BITE-SIZED APPETIZERS THE SAME DAY – OR BETTER YET, DO A MAKE-AHEAD. FREEZE THEM AND BAKE 10 MINUTES BEFORE SERVING.

## THE BUNDLES

| | | |
|---|---|---|
| 3 | SHEETS PHYLLO PASTRY | 3 |
| 1/4 CUP | BUTTER | 60 ML |

TO THAW PASTRY: FOLLOW PACKAGE INSTRUCTIONS.

MELT BUTTER. WORKING ON A FLAT SURFACE, GENEROUSLY BRUSH A SHEET OF PHYLLO WITH BUTTER. TOP WITH SECOND AND THIRD SHEETS, BRUSHING EACH WITH BUTTER. CUT PHYLLO INTO 20, 3" (8 CM) SQUARES. PLACE A DOLLOP OF FILLING IN THE CENTER OF EACH SQUARE. PULL UP THE EDGES, PINCH TOGETHER AND PLACE ON PARCHMENT-PAPER-LINED COOKIE SHEET. IF REFRIGERATING, COVER WITH A DAMP, CLEAN CLOTH OR PLASTIC WRAP. IF FREEZING, COVER WITH PLASTIC WRAP AND SEAL. PREHEAT OVEN TO 400°F (200°C). BAKE REFRIGERATED BUNDLES FOR 8 MINUTES, FROZEN BUNDLES FOR 10 MINUTES, OR UNTIL GOLDEN. SERVE WARM.

### CONTINUED FROM PAGE 72.

## BLUE CHEESE, WALNUT AND ROASTED RED PEPPER FILLING

| | | |
|---|---|---|
| I CUP | CHOPPED TOASTED WALNUTS | 250 ML |
| 8 OZ. | BLUE CHEESE, CRUMBLED | 250 ML |
| ½ CUP | CHOPPED BOTTLED ROASTED RED PEPPERS | 125 ML |

MIX INGREDIENTS TOGETHER AND REFRIGERATE UNTIL NEEDED. MAKES ENOUGH FILLING FOR 20 BUNDLES.

## CHÈVRE WITH CRANBERRY AND ORANGE ZEST

| | | |
|---|---|---|
| 8 OZ. | CHÈVRE (GOAT CHEESE) | 250 G |
| ½ CUP | DRIED CRANBERRIES | 125 ML |
| 2 TSP. | GRATED ORANGE ZEST | IO ML |
| 2 TSP. | CHOPPED FRESH CHIVES | IO ML |

MIX INGREDIENTS TOGETHER AND REFRIGERATE UNTIL NEEDED. MAKES ENOUGH FILLING FOR 20 BUNDLES.

WHAT'S ANOTHER WORD FOR THESAURUS?

# ASIAN VEGETABLE ROLLS WITH DIPPING SAUCE

GREAT CRUNCH! TANGY SAUCE! MAKE AHEAD; FREEZE AND COOK THE DAY OF YOUR PARTY.

| | | |
|---|---|---|
| 2 TBSP. | SOY SAUCE | 30 ML |
| I TSP. | CORNSTARCH | 5 ML |
| I TSP. | SUGAR | 5 ML |
| 1/2 TSP. | SESAME OIL | 2 ML |
| 1/4 TSP. | PEPPER | I ML |
| I TBSP. | BUTTER | 15 ML |
| 2 TSP. | FRESHLY GRATED GINGER ROOT | 10 ML |
| 1 1/2 CUPS | CHOPPED FRESH SHIITAKE OR CREMINI MUSHROOMS | 375 ML |
| I CUP | SHREDDED CARROT | 250 ML |
| 1/2 CUP | THINLY SLICED GREEN ONION | 125 ML |
| 1/4 CUP | CHOPPED CILANTRO | 60 ML |
| 4 CUPS | FINELY SHREDDED SUEY CHOY (OR NAPA CABBAGE), WHITE CORE REMOVED | I L |
| 1/3 CUP | COARSELY CHOPPED SALTED PEANUTS | 75 ML |
| 6-8 | SHEETS PHYLLO PASTRY, THAWED | 6-8 |
| 1/3 CUP | MELTED BUTTER | 75 ML |

## DIPPING SAUCE

| | | |
|---|---|---|
| | JUICE OF 2 LIMES (3 TBSP./45 ML) | |
| 3 TBSP. | RICE VINEGAR | 45 ML |
| 3 TBSP. | SESAME OIL | 45 ML |
| I TBSP. | LIQUID HONEY | 15 ML |
| I TBSP. | GRATED GINGER ROOT | 15 ML |
| 2 | GARLIC CLOVES, MINCED | 2 |
| 3/4 CUP | HOISIN SAUCE | 175 ML |
| I TBSP. | CHOPPED CILANTRO | 15 ML |

# ASIAN VEGETABLE ROLLS

CONTINUED FROM PAGE 74.

STIR SOY, CORNSTARCH, SUGAR, SESAME OIL AND PEPPER TOGETHER IN A BOWL. SET ASIDE.

IN A LARGE FRYING PAN, MELT BUTTER; STIR-FRY GINGER ABOUT 15 SECONDS. ADD MUSHROOMS, CARROT, ONION AND CILANTRO; STIR-FRY 2 MINUTES. STIR SOY MIXTURE AND ADD TO VEGETABLES. SAUCE WILL THICKEN IMMEDIATELY. STIR CABBAGE AND PEANUTS INTO VEGETABLES AND REMOVE FROM HEAT. SET ASIDE.

LAY 1 SHEET OF PHYLLO VERTICALLY ON COUNTER; BRUSH BOTTOM HALF WITH BUTTER. FOLD TOP HALF DOWN; PRESS DOWN SO IT STICKS TOGETHER. SPOON VEGETABLE MIXTURE ACROSS SHORT END OF PHYLLO, FORMING A 1½" (4 CM) ROLL. ROLL PHYLLO TIGHTLY AROUND MIXTURE, FOLDING IN SIDES AS YOU GO. SEAL WITH MELTED BUTTER. PLACE ON A COOKIE SHEET, SEALED SIDE DOWN. BRUSH TOP LIGHTLY WITH BUTTER AND SCORE ON DIAGONAL (NOT TOO DEEP) ABOUT 1" (2.5 CM) APART. CONTINUE WITH REMAINING SHEETS AND FILLING. WRAP EACH ROLL IN PLASTIC WRAP AND FREEZE ON A COOKIE SHEET. KEEPS UP TO 2 WEEKS. BAKE AT 375°F (190°C) FOR 15 MINUTES. COOL SLIGHTLY AND CUT AT SCORED INTERVALS. TRIM BROWN ENDS. MAKES 3 DOZEN. COMBINE DIPPING SAUCE INGREDIENTS. REFRIGERATE UNTIL NEEDED.

# WRAPPED BRIE WITH CARAMELIZED ONIONS AND PEPPER JELLY

DISAPPEARS IMMEDIATELY!

| | | |
|---|---|---:|
| 1 TBSP. | BUTTER | 15 ML |
| 1/2 | SWEET ONION, THINLY SLICED | 1/2 |
| | SALT & PEPPER TO TASTE | |
| 1/4 CUP | SHERRY | 60 ML |
| 2 TBSP. | CHOPPED PECANS | 30 ML |
| 2 | SHEETS PHYLLO PASTRY | 2 |
| 2 TBSP. | BUTTER, MELTED | 30 ML |
| 7 OZ. | ROUND OF BRIE | 190 G |
| 3 TBSP. | RED OR GREEN PEPPER JELLY | 45 ML |

PREHEAT OVEN TO 350°F (180°C). MELT BUTTER IN FRYING PAN OVER MEDIUM HEAT. ADD ONIONS, SALT AND PEPPER; COOK UNTIL ONIONS ARE GOLDEN. ADD SHERRY, BRING TO A BOIL, REDUCE HEAT AND SIMMER UNTIL LIQUID IS EVAPORATED. COOL. STIR IN PECANS. BRUSH EACH PHYLLO SHEET WITH MELTED BUTTER, FOLD IN HALF AND PLACE ONE ON TOP OF THE OTHER. PLACE ON BAKING SHEET, SET BRIE IN CENTER AND TOP WITH PEPPER JELLY. GATHER PHYLLO UP AROUND SIDES OF BRIE TO CREATE A RAISED, RUFFLED EDGE. SPOON ONIONS INTO MIDDLE, AND BRUSH SIDES OF PHYLLO WITH REMAINING MELTED BUTTER. BAKE FOR 15 MINUTES. SERVE WARM WITH WATER BISCUITS. SERVES 8.

# CHICKEN ROCA

THE PEOPLE FROM SOUTH BEACH WOULD APPROVE . . . SO WOULD THE REST OF THE BEACHES!

## MUSTARD DIPPING SAUCE

| | | |
|---|---|---|
| 1 CUP | WHIPPING CREAM | 250 ML |
| 1 TBSP. | DIJON MUSTARD | 15 ML |
| 1 TBSP. | GRAINY DIJON MUSTARD | 15 ML |
| 1 TSP. | HONEY | 5 ML |
| | | |
| 3 | CHICKEN BREAST HALVES | 3 |
| 3/4 CUP | DIJON MUSTARD | 175 ML |
| 1 1/2 CUPS | GROUND PECANS | 375 ML |
| | SMALL WOODEN SKEWERS, SOAKED IN WATER FOR 1/2 HOUR | |

TO MAKE THE SAUCE: IN A SMALL HEAVY POT, BRING CREAM TO A BOIL. LOWER HEAT TO SIMMER AND REDUCE CREAM TO HALF, ABOUT 15-20 MINUTES. WHISK MUSTARDS AND HONEY INTO CREAM. STORE IN REFRIGERATOR.

PREHEAT OVEN TO 350°F (180°C). CUT CHICKEN IN STRIPS 1/2" (1.3 CM) WIDE BY 4" (10 CM) LONG. THREAD CHICKEN ONTO WOODEN SKEWERS. BRUSH WITH MUSTARD AND ROLL IN GROUND NUTS UNTIL COMPLETELY COVERED. PLACE SKEWERS ON A COOKIE SHEET COVERED WITH PARCHMENT PAPER AND BAKE ABOUT 10 MINUTES. TO SERVE, LET GUESTS SPOON ON A LITTLE MUSTARD DIPPING SAUCE.

# CHICKEN LETTUCE WRAPS

### SAUCE

| | | |
|---|---|---|
| 3/4 CUP | HOISIN SAUCE | 175 ML |
| 1 1/2 TSP. | RICE VINEGAR | 7 ML |
| 1 TBSP. | LIQUID HONEY | 15 ML |
| 2 TBSP. | WATER | 30 ML |
| 1 TBSP. | FRESH LIME JUICE | 15 ML |
| 2 TSP. | SESAME OIL | 10 ML |
| 1 | LARGE GARLIC CLOVE, MINCED | 1 |
| 1 TSP. | FRESHLY GRATED GINGER | 5 ML |

### WRAPS

| | | |
|---|---|---|
| 2 | BONELESS CHICKEN BREASTS | 2 |
| 1/3 CUP | GRATED CARROT | 75 ML |
| 2 | GREEN ONIONS, DIAGONALLY SLICED | 2 |
| 1 CUP | DRY STEAM-FRIED NOODLES | 250 ML |
| 1/2 CUP | UNSALTED PEANUTS, CHOPPED | 125 ML |
| 1 | HEAD ICEBURG LETTUCE, SEPARATED INTO WHOLE LEAVES, CORE REMOVED | 1 |

IN A SMALL SAUCEPAN, OVER MEDIUM-LOW HEAT, BLEND
SAUCE INGREDIENTS. SET ASIDE TO COOL. POACH
CHICKEN IN A SMALL AMOUNT OF WATER UNTIL NO
LONGER PINK. COOL. CUT EACH BREAST IN HALF
HORIZONTALLY AND THEN DICE TO ABOUT 1/4" (6 MM).
IN MEDIUM BOWL, TOSS CHICKEN, CARROTS AND
ONION WITH ENOUGH SAUCE TO COAT. LET STAND FOR
15 MINUTES. ADD NOODLES AND PEANUTS, GENTLY TOSS
WITH MORE SAUCE TO COAT.

TO SERVE: SET OUT LETTUCE AND CHICKEN MIXTURE.
LET GUESTS WRAP THEIR OWN. SERVE EXTRA SAUCE ON
THE SIDE. (PICTURED OPPOSITE PAGE 109.)

# PEANUT-CURRY CHICKEN IN WONTON CUPS

DEE-LISH!!

| | | |
|---|---|---|
| 12 | WONTON WRAPPERS | 12 |
| | OIL | |
| 3 | BONELESS, SKINLESS CHICKEN BREAST HALVES | 3 |
| ½ CUP | MANGO CHUTNEY | 125 ML |
| ¼ CUP | PLUS 2 TBSP. PLAIN YOGURT | 90 ML |
| 3 TBSP. | CRUNCHY PEANUT BUTTER | 45 ML |
| I TBSP. | FRESH LIME JUICE | 15 ML |
| 4 TSP. | CURRY PASTE | 20 ML |
| I TSP. | CURRY POWDER | 5 ML |
| | CHIVES, CHOPPED | |

PREHEAT OVEN TO 325°F (160°C). PLACE WRAPPERS ON CUTTING SURFACE AND BRUSH TOP WITH OIL. CUT INTO 4 SQUARES. USING MINI MUFFIN TINS, PLACE EACH SQUARE, OILED SIDE UP, INTO A MUFFIN CUP, PRESSING INTO PAN TO FORM A CUP. BAKE UNTIL LIGHT BROWN (5-7 MINUTES). COOL AND REMOVE. IN A FRYING PAN, POACH CHICKEN IN WATER WITH A LITTLE SALT UNTIL JUST COOKED THROUGH (DON'T OVERCOOK!). TRANSFER TO PAPER TOWEL AND COOL. DICE CHICKEN AND SET ASIDE. IN A MEDIUM BOWL, COMBINE CHUTNEY, YOGURT, PEANUT BUTTER, LIME JUICE, CURRY PASTE AND CURRY POWDER. STIR IN CHICKEN AND CHECK SEASONING. PLACE I TSP. (5 ML) OF FILLING INTO EACH CUP AND GARNISH WITH CHIVES. MAKES ABOUT 48 HOT AND SPICY BITES.

# ASPARAGUS CHICKEN PUFFS

| 1 | LARGE BONELESS CHICKEN BREAST, COOKED & CUBED | 1 |
|---|---|---|
| 2 TBSP. | MAYONNAISE | 30 ML |
| 1/2-1 TSP. | CURRY POWDER | 2-5 ML |
| | SALT & PEPPER TO TASTE | |
| 14 OZ. | PKG. PUFF PASTRY | 397 G |
| 12 OZ. | CAN ASPARAGUS, WELL-DRAINED OR 12 FRESH SMALL ASPARAGUS, BLANCHED | 341 ML |
| 1 | EGG, BEATEN | 1 |
| | SESAME SEEDS | |

IN A FOOD PROCESSOR, PURÉE CHICKEN, MAYONNAISE, CURRY, SALT AND PEPPER UNTIL SMOOTH. ROLL PASTRY INTO RECTANGULAR SHAPE, 10 X 14" (25 X 36 CM). CUT LENGTHWISE INTO 3 EVEN STRIPS. SPREAD CHICKEN MIXTURE ALONG 1 SIDE OF EACH STRIP OF PASTRY. PLACE ASPARAGUS SPEARS LENGTHWISE BESIDE CHICKEN MIXTURE. BRUSH EDGES OF PASTRY WITH EGG. ROLL PASTRY OVER TO CLOSE COMPLETELY. BRUSH TOP WITH EGG, CUT ROLLS DIAGONALLY INTO 1" (2.5 CM) PIECES AND SPRINKLE WITH SESAME SEEDS. PLACE ON GREASED COOKIE SHEET AND BAKE AT 450°F (230°C) FOR 10 MINUTES. LOWER TEMPERATURE TO 350°F (180°C); BAKE FOR ANOTHER 10 MINUTES, OR UNTIL GOLDEN BROWN. MAKES 48 APPETIZERS.

# CURRIED SEAFOOD COCKTAIL PUFFS

THESE ELEGANT PUFFS CAN BE MADE AHEAD, FROZEN THEN FILLED AT SERVING TIME.

## PUFFS (CHOUX PASTRY)

| | | |
|---|---|---|
| 1 CUP | WATER | 250 ML |
| 1/2 CUP | BUTTER | 125 ML |
| 1 CUP | FLOUR | 250 ML |
| 1/2 TSP. | SALT | 2 ML |
| 4 | EGGS | 4 |

## SEAFOOD FILLING

| | | |
|---|---|---|
| 7 OZ. | CRAB OR SHRIMP | 200 G |
| 1/3 CUP | MAYONNAISE | 75 ML |
| 1 TSP. | CURRY POWDER | 5 ML |
| 2 TBSP. | CHOPPED GREEN ONION | 30 ML |

PREHEAT OVEN TO 400°F (200°C).

TO MAKE PUFFS: IN A MEDIUM SAUCEPAN, BOIL WATER. ADD BUTTER AND STIR UNTIL MELTED. TURN HEAT TO LOW, ADD FLOUR AND SALT, STIRRING VIGOROUSLY UNTIL MIXTURE FORMS A SMOOTH BALL. REMOVE FROM HEAT. ADD EGGS 1 AT A TIME, BEATING WELL WITH A SPOON AFTER EACH ADDITION. DROP BY TEASPOONFULS ONTO LIGHTLY GREASED COOKIE SHEET; BAKE 20-25 MINUTES, UNTIL GOLDEN. COOL, CUT IN HALF.

TO MAKE FILLING: MIX FILLING INGREDIENTS TOGETHER. FILL PUFFS, REPLACING TOPS. HEAT BEFORE SERVING. MAKES ABOUT 2 DOZEN.

# SMOKED SALMON CHEESECAKE

GREAT FOR A CROWD! THIS FREEZES WELL FOR UP TO 1 MONTH.

## BASE

| | | |
|---|---|---|
| 1/2 CUP | FINE, DRY BREAD CRUMBS | 125 ML |
| 2 TBSP. | BUTTER, MELTED | 30 ML |
| 1 TSP. | DRIED DILL | 5 ML |

## FILLING

| | | |
|---|---|---|
| 1 TBSP. | BUTTER | 15 ML |
| 1 | SMALL ONION, FINELY CHOPPED | 1 |
| 3 | 8 OZ. (250 G) PKGS CREAM CHEESE | 3 |
| 3 | EGGS | 3 |
| 1/3 CUP | LIGHT CREAM | 75 ML |
| 1/2 LB. | SMOKED SALMON, CHOPPED | 250 G |
| 1 CUP | GRATED SWISS CHEESE | 250 ML |

TO MAKE BASE: COMBINE BREAD CRUMBS, BUTTER AND DILL. PRESS INTO A 9" (23 CM) SPRINGFORM PAN. BAKE AT 350°F (180°C) FOR 5-7 MINUTES, OR UNTIL GOLDEN.

TO MAKE FILLING: MELT BUTTER AND SAUTÉ ONION; COOL. BEAT CREAM CHEESE WITH EGGS AND CREAM. MIX IN SALMON, SWISS CHEESE AND SAUTÉED ONION. POUR FILLING OVER BASE.

BAKE FOR 75 MINUTES AT 350°F (180°C). TURN OVEN OFF AND OPEN DOOR SLIGHTLY. ALLOW PAN TO COOL IN OVEN FOR 1 HOUR. REFRIGERATE AT LEAST 2 HOURS BEFORE REMOVING SIDES AND BOTTOM OF PAN. SERVE AT ROOM TEMPERATURE WITH SMALL BAGELS OR WATER BISCUITS.

# SALADS

Grilled Feta with Tomatoes
Layered Mozzarella and Tomato Salad (Caprese)
Watermelon with Feta
Pomegranate & Feta Salad
Spinach Salad with Pears, Brie and Raspberries
Warm Spinach Salad with Apples and Brie
Pear and Stilton Salad
Mixed Greens with Apples and Cider Vinaigrette
Cucumber Fruit Salad
Super Salad
Patrick's Salad
Napa Cabbage Salad
Thai Noodle Salad
Show-Off Tortellini Salad
Asparagus Pasta Salad
Mediterranean Orzo & Vegetable Salad
Chicken Atlanta
Chicken and Mixed Rice Salad
with Orange Vinaigrette
Asian Chicken Salad
Mango and Spicy Shrimp Salad

# GRILLED FETA WITH TOMATOES

BUY SOME FRESH TOMATOES AT THE FARMER'S MARKET AND CREATE THIS SUPERB SALAD.

| | | |
|---|---|---|
| I LB. | MIXTURE OF YELLOW, GREEN & RED TOMATOES | 500 G |
| | BUTTER LETTUCE | |
| I LB. | CHUNK FETA CHEESE | 500 G |
| 2 TBSP. | EXTRA-VIRGIN OLIVE OIL | 30 ML |
| | BUNCH OF FRESH BASIL LEAVES | |
| 1/4 CUP | EXTRA-VIRGIN OLIVE OIL | 60 ML |
| | FRESHLY GROUND PEPPER | |

SLICE TOMATOES AND ARRANGE ON SERVING PLATES WITH LETTUCE. CUT FETA INTO 6 EVEN SLICES AND PLACE ON LIGHTLY OILED COOKIE SHEET. DRIZZLE WITH OIL AND HEAT UNDER BROILER UNTIL LIGHTLY BROWNED. PLACE WARM FETA ON TOP OF TOMATOES. CHOP BASIL AND SPRINKLE OVER SALAD. DRIZZLE WITH OIL AND SPRINKLE WITH FRESHLY GROUND PEPPER. SERVES 6.

A NICE BOX OF CHOCOLATES PROVIDES YOUR TOTAL DAILY INTAKE OF CALORIES IN ONE PLACE. ISN'T THAT HANDY?

# LAYERED MOZZARELLA AND TOMATO SALAD (CAPRESE)

AN ATTRACTIVE BUFFET PLATTER.

| | | |
|---|---|---|
| 10 | ROMA TOMATOES | 10 |
| 2 LBS. | BOCCONCINI (FRESH MOZZARELLA) | 1 KG |
| | CUT INTO 1/4" (6 MM) SLICES | |
| 1/4 CUP | CHOPPED FRESH BASIL | 60 ML |
| 1/4 CUP | CHOPPED FRESH PARSLEY | 60 ML |

## VINAIGRETTE

| | | |
|---|---|---|
| 3/4 CUP | OLIVE OIL | 175 ML |
| 1/4 CUP | WINE VINEGAR | 60 ML |
| | FRESHLY GROUND PEPPER | |

ARRANGE SLICED TOMATOES AND CHEESE ALTERNATELY ON A PLATTER. SPRINKLE WITH BASIL, PARSLEY AND VINAIGRETTE.

TO MAKE VINAIGRETTE: COMBINE ALL INGREDIENTS.

# WATERMELON WITH FETA

QUICK & DELICIOUS

| | | |
|---|---|---|
| 1/2 | SMALL RED ONION | 1/2 |
| 3 CUPS | WATERMELON BALLS | 750 ML |
| 1/2 CUP | CRUMBLED FETA CHEESE | 125 ML |
| | BALSAMIC VINEGAR, FOR DRIZZLING | |

SLICE ONION INTO THIN RINGS. TO MAKE MELON BALLS, USE A MELON BALLER; PLACE IN MEDIUM BOWL. ADD ONION AND FETA CHEESE AND DRIZZLE WITH BALSAMIC VINEGAR. TOSS GENTLY. CHILL IN REFRIGERATOR UNTIL READY TO SERVE.

# POMEGRANATE AND FETA SALAD

THE POMEGRANATE SEEDS ADD SPARKLE TO THIS SALAD!

| | | |
|---|---|---|
| I | HEAD ROMAINE LETTUCE, WASHED & TORN | I |
| I | BUNCH SPINACH, STEMS REMOVED, WASHED & TORN | I |
| 1/2 CUP | DRIED CRANBERRIES OR SEEDS OF I POMEGRANATE | 125 ML |
| 1/4 CUP | TOASTED PINE NUTS | 60 ML |
| 1/2 CUP | CRUMBLED FETA CHEESE | 125 ML |

## DRESSING

| | | |
|---|---|---|
| 1/3 CUP | OLIVE OIL | 75 ML |
| I TBSP. | RED WINE VINEGAR | 15 ML |
| 2 TBSP. | MAPLE SYRUP | 30 ML |
| I TSP. | DIJON MUSTARD | 5 ML |
| 1/2 TSP. | OREGANO | 2 ML |
| | SALT & FRESHLY GROUND PEPPER | |

TOSS LETTUCE AND SPINACH TOGETHER IN A LARGE SALAD BOWL. ADD DRIED CRANBERRIES OR POMEGRANATE SEEDS, PINE NUTS AND FETA. WHISK DRESSING INGREDIENTS TOGETHER; STORE IN REFRIGERATOR. TOSS WITH SALAD INGREDIENTS JUST BEFORE SERVING. SERVES 6.

I HAVE A DEGREE IN LIBERAL ARTS. DO YOU WANT FRIES WITH THAT?

# SPINACH SALAD WITH
## PEARS, BRIE AND RASPBERRIES

YOUR NEXT FAVORITE SUMMER SALAD.

### DRESSING

| | | |
|---|---|---|
| 3 TBSP. | RASPBERRY VINEGAR | 45 ML |
| 1/3 CUP | VEGETABLE OIL | 75 ML |
| 1 TBSP. | SUGAR | 15 ML |
| 1/4 CUP | FRESH RASPBERRIES, MASHED | 60 ML |

### SALAD

| | | |
|---|---|---|
| 10 OZ. | BAG BABY SPINACH | 283 G |
| 2 | RIPE PEARS, CORED & THINLY SLICED | 2 |
| 1/2 LB. | BRIE CHEESE, ROOM TEMPERATURE, SLICED | 250 G |

### GARNISH

RASPBERRIES
SLIVERED ALMONDS, TOASTED

TO MAKE DRESSING: WHISK INGREDIENTS TOGETHER AND REFRIGERATE UNTIL READY TO SERVE.

WASH SPINACH AND REMOVE ANY LONG STEMS. DIVIDE AMONG 4 PLATES. GARNISH WITH PEARS, CHEESE, RASPBERRIES AND A SPRINKLE OF ALMONDS. DRIZZLE WITH DRESSING. A GREAT ACCOMPANIMENT TO BALSAMIC HONEY TENDERLOIN PAGE 208. SERVES 4.

# WARM SPINACH SALAD WITH APPLES AND BRIE

A WINNER!

| | | |
|---|---|---|
| 4 | LARGE GRANNY SMITH APPLES | 4 |
| 1/4 CUP | MAPLE SYRUP | 60 ML |
| 8 CUPS | WASHED SPINACH LEAVES | 2 L |
| 1/2 LB. | BRIE, CUT IN SMALL PIECES | 250 G |
| 1/2 CUP | TOASTED PECANS | 125 ML |

DRESSING

| | | |
|---|---|---|
| 1/4 CUP | APPLE CIDER OR APPLE JUICE | 60 ML |
| 3 TBSP. | CIDER VINEGAR | 45 ML |
| 1 TSP. | DIJON MUSTARD | 5 ML |
| 1 | GARLIC CLOVE, MINCED | 1 |
| 1/4 CUP | OLIVE OIL | 60 ML |
| | SALT & PEPPER TO TASTE | |

PEEL AND CORE APPLES; CUT INTO 1/2" (1.3 CM) SLICES. ARRANGE ON BAKING SHEET AND BRUSH WITH SYRUP. BROIL UNTIL GOLDEN; TURN, BRUSH SYRUP ON OTHER SIDE AND BROIL. PLACE SPINACH IN A LARGE BOWL. WHISK DRESSING INGREDIENTS TOGETHER IN A SMALL SAUCEPAN AND HEAT UNTIL SIMMERING. POUR OVER SPINACH; TOSS AND ADD CHEESE, APPLES AND NUTS. DEE-LISH!

MY MIND NOT ONLY WANDERS, IT SOMETIMES LEAVES COMPLETELY.

# PEAR AND STILTON SALAD

SHOP AHEAD FOR THIS SALAD SO YOU CAN RIPEN THE PEARS!

## DRESSING

| | | |
|---|---|---|
| ¼ CUP | FRESH LEMON JUICE | 60 ML |
| ¼ CUP | CANOLA OIL | 60 ML |
| 1 TBSP. | LIQUID HONEY | 15 ML |
| 2 TSP. | GRAINY OR DIJON MUSTARD | 10 ML |
| | | |
| | BUTTER LETTUCE | |
| 2 | FRESH, RIPE PEARS, CORED & SLICED | 2 |
| 4 OZ. | STILTON CHEESE, CRUMBLED, OR ASIAGO CHEESE, SHAVED | 125 G |
| ¼ CUP | FRESH PINE NUTS, TOASTED | 60 ML |

TO MAKE DRESSING: WHISK INGREDIENTS TOGETHER AND REFRIGERATE UNTIL READY TO SERVE.

PLACE LETTUCE LEAVES ON INDIVIDUAL PLATES. ARRANGE SLICED PEARS ON TOP AND SPRINKLE WITH STILTON AND PINE NUTS.

DRIZZLE DRESSING OVER TOP. A DELICIOUS STARTER SALAD FOR 4.

SEEN UPSIDE DOWN ON A JEEP: IF YOU CAN READ THIS, PLEASE FLIP ME OVER.

# MIXED GREENS WITH APPLES AND CIDER VINAIGRETTE

A DELICIOUS SIMPLE SALAD – THIS DRESSING IS ABOUT TO BECOME YOUR NEW HOUSE FAVORITE.

## CIDER VINAIGRETTE

| | | |
|---|---|---|
| ¼ CUP | APPLE CIDER VINEGAR | 60 ML |
| 3 TBSP. | MINCED SHALLOTS | 45 ML |
| 2 TSP. | DIJON MUSTARD | 10 ML |
| 2 TSP. | HONEY | 10 ML |
| ½ CUP | LIGHT OLIVE OIL | 125 ML |
| 1 | CRISP RED-SKINNED APPLE, CORED AND THINLY SLICED | 1 |
| | MIXED GREENS FOR 6 | |

TO MAKE VINAIGRETTE: WHISK TOGETHER INGREDIENTS AND REFRIGERATE UNTIL READY TO SERVE.

TOSS APPLES AND MIXED GREENS WITH DRESSING, USING JUST ENOUGH TO LIGHTLY COAT GREENS.

THE HARDNESS OF BUTTER IS PROPORTIONAL TO THE SOFTNESS OF THE BREAD.

# CUCUMBER FRUIT SALAD

YEAR-ROUND PARTNER FOR CHICKEN OR FISH.

| | | |
|---|---|---|
| 1/2 CUP | SOUR CREAM | 125 ML |
| 1 TBSP. | SUGAR | 15 ML |
| 1 | MEDIUM ENGLISH CUCUMBER, PEELED & DICED | 1 |
| 1 | GRANNY SMITH APPLE, CHOPPED | 1 |
| 1 CUP | SEEDLESS GREEN GRAPES, CUT IN HALF | 250 ML |
| 1 CUP | SEEDLESS RED GRAPES, CUT IN HALF | 250 ML |
| 1 TSP. | FRESH PARSLEY, MINCED | 5 ML |
| 1/2 CUP | WALNUTS, CHOPPED | 125 ML |

IN A MEDIUM BOWL, COMBINE SOUR CREAM AND SUGAR.
ADD REMAINING INGREDIENTS AND MIX THOROUGHLY.
REFRIGERATE.

TYPICAL SYMPTOMS OF STRESS: EATING TOO MUCH, IMPULSE
BUYING AND DRIVING TOO FAST. ARE YOU KIDDING? THAT'S MY
IDEA OF A PERFECT DAY!

# SUPER SALAD

GREAT FOR BUFFETS AND BARBECUES.

| | | |
|---|---|---:|
| 1 | HEAD ROMAINE LETTUCE | 1 |
| 1 | HEAD BUTTER LETTUCE | 1 |
| 1 | HEAD ICEBERG LETTUCE | 1 |
| ½ CUP | GRATED PARMESAN CHEESE | 125 ML |
| 2 OZ. | BLUE CHEESE, CRUMBLED | 55 G |
| 3 | AVOCADOS, PEELED & SLICED | 3 |
| 1 | LARGE CUCUMBER, PEELED & DICED | 1 |
| 1½ CUPS | CHERRY TOMATOES, HALVED | 375 ML |
| 6 | SLICES OF BACON, COOKED CRISP & CRUMBLED | 6 |
| 1 | RED PEPPER, SLICED | 1 |
| 1 | GREEN PEPPER, SLICED | 1 |
| ½ CUP | SLICED RIPE OLIVES | 125 ML |
| 8 OZ. | BOTTLE ITALIAN DRESSING | 250 ML |
| | FRESH PARSLEY, CHOPPED | |

WASH, DRY AND TEAR SALAD GREENS INTO A LARGE SALAD BOWL. SPRINKLE WITH CHEESES. ARRANGE REMAINING INGREDIENTS ON TOP, TOSS WITH DRESSING AND SPRINKLE WITH PARSLEY. SERVES 12-14.

THE BEST WAY TO FORGET ALL YOUR TROUBLES IS TO WEAR TIGHT SHOES.

# PATRICK'S SALAD

GOES WITH EVERYTHING - THANKS PATRICK!

## DRESSING

| | | |
|---|---|---|
| 1/2 CUP | OLIVE OIL | 125 ML |
| 1/4 CUP | VINEGAR (RED OR WHITE WINE) | 60 ML |
| | JUICE OF HALF A SMALL LIME | |
| 2 TSP. | SOY SAUCE | 10 ML |
| | PINCH OF CAYENNE PEPPER | |
| 1 | LARGE GARLIC CLOVE, MINCED | 1 |
| | SALT & PEPPER TO TASTE | |
| 3 TBSP. | CHOPPED FRESH PARSLEY | 45 ML |
| 2 TBSP. | MINCED RED ONION | 30 ML |
| 3-4 TBSP. | SUGAR | 45-60 ML |

## SALAD

| | | |
|---|---|---|
| | ROMAINE LETTUCE | |
| 1 | LARGE RED PEPPER | 1 |
| | SNOW PEAS | |
| | SLIVERED ALMONDS, TOASTED | |

TO MAKE DRESSING: COMBINE INGREDIENTS IN A BLENDER
AND BLEND WELL. POUR INTO A JAR AND REFRIGERATE.

WASH AND TEAR ROMAINE INTO BITE-SIZED PIECES.
CUT RED PEPPER AND PEA PODS INTO LONG STRIPS.
ADD TOASTED ALMONDS. TOSS WITH DRESSING JUST
BEFORE SERVING.

# NAPA CABBAGE SALAD

ALWAYS A HIT AT PICNICS, BUFFETS – AND THE FAMILY BUN FIGHT!

| | | |
|---|---|---|
| 1 | LARGE NAPA CABBAGE (SUEY CHOY), CHOPPED | 1 |
| 2 | BUNCHES GREEN ONIONS, CHOPPED | 2 |
| 1 | RED BELL PEPPER, SEEDED & DICED | 1 |
| 1/4 CUP | BUTTER | 60 ML |
| 1 CUP | SLIVERED ALMONDS | 250 ML |
| 2 | PKGS. CHICKEN-FLAVORED ORIENTAL SOUP NOODLES WITH SEASONING MIX | 2 |

### DRESSING

| | | |
|---|---|---|
| 1 CUP | VEGETABLE OIL | 250 ML |
| 1/2 CUP | RED WINE VINEGAR | 125 ML |
| 2 | GARLIC CLOVES, MINCED | 2 |
| 2 TSP. | SOY SAUCE | 10 ML |
| 1/3 CUP | SUGAR | 75 ML |

PLACE CABBAGE, GREEN ONIONS AND RED PEPPER IN LARGE SALAD BOWL. MELT BUTTER IN FRYING PAN AND SAUTÉ ALMONDS, BROKEN NOODLES AND SEASONINGS UNTIL GOLDEN. ADD TO CABBAGE MIXTURE AND TOSS. SHAKE DRESSING INGREDIENTS IN A JAR. POUR OVER SALAD AND TOSS AT LEAST A HOUR BEFORE SERVING. YOU WILL HAVE EXTRA DRESSING, REFRIGERATE AND USE AGAIN. SERVES 10-12.

# THAI NOODLE SALAD

SERVE WITH THAI GRILLED CHICKEN PAGE 183.

## VINAIGRETTE

| | | |
|---|---|---|
| ¼ CUP | FRESH LIME JUICE | 60 ML |
| 3 TBSP. | VEGETABLE OIL | 45 ML |
| 3 TBSP. | SOY SAUCE | 45 ML |
| 2 TBSP. | BROWN SUGAR | 30 ML |
| 1 TBSP. | SESAME OIL | 15 ML |
| 1 TBSP. | MINCED GARLIC | 15 ML |
| 1 TBSP. | GRATED ORANGE OR LIME ZEST | 15 ML |
| 1 TBSP. | MINCED JALAPEÑO PEPPER | 15 ML |
| | SALT & PEPPER TO TASTE | |
| | | |
| ½ LB. | GREEN BEANS OR ASPARAGUS SPEARS, TRIMMED | 250 G |
| 8 OZ. | CHINESE EGG NOODLES, FRESH OR DRIED | 250 G |
| 2 CUPS | PEELED, SHREDDED CARROTS | 500 ML |
| ½ CUP | SLIVERED RED PEPPER | 125 ML |
| 1 CUP | THINLY SLICED GREEN ONIONS | 250 ML |

TO MAKE VINAIGRETTE: WHISK INGREDIENTS TOGETHER AND SET ASIDE. CUT GREEN BEANS OR ASPARAGUS DIAGONALLY INTO ½" (1.3 CM) PIECES. COOK IN BOILING WATER UNTIL TENDER-CRISP. PLUNGE INTO COLD WATER (TO RETAIN COLOR); DRAIN AND SET ASIDE. COOK NOODLES ACCORDING TO PACKAGE DIRECTIONS. DRAIN. TOSS NOODLES WITH VEGETABLES AND VINAIGRETTE. COVER AND REFRIGERATE AT LEAST 2 HOURS OR OVERNIGHT. GARNISH WITH GREEN ONIONS BEFORE SERVING. SERVES 6.

# SHOW-OFF TORTELLINI SALAD

YOU'LL BE A HIT AT THE NEXT POTLUCK. HOPE THE OTHER PEOPLE BRING THEIR SHARE.

| | | |
|---|---|---|
| 12 OZ. | PKG. HERB TORTELLINI WITH CHEESE | 340 G |
| 12 OZ. | PKG. SPINACH TORTELLINI WITH CHEESE | 340 G |
| 2 CUPS | BROCCOLI FLORETS | 500 ML |
| 14 OZ. | CAN ARTICHOKE HEARTS, QUARTERED | 398 ML |
| 12 OZ. | PITTED BLACK OLIVES, SLICED | 341 ML |
| 1 LB. | SHRIMP, COOKED & TAILS REMOVED | 500 G |
| 16 OZ. | BOTTLE GOLDEN CAESAR DRESSING OR SPICY ITALIAN DRESSING | 455 ML |
| 2 CUPS | HALVED CHERRY TOMATOES | 500 ML |
| 1 CUP | FRESHLY GRATED PARMESAN CHEESE | 250 ML |

COOK TORTELLINI ACCORDING TO PACKAGE DIRECTIONS. DRAIN WELL. IN A LARGE BOWL, TOSS TORTELLINI, BROCCOLI, ARTICHOKES, OLIVES AND SHRIMP WITH DRESSING. MARINATE OVERNIGHT IN REFRIGERATOR. PRIOR TO SERVING, TOSS WITH TOMATOES AND PARMESAN CHEESE. SERVES 8.

THE FOUR BASIC FOOD GROUPS: CANNED, FROZEN, CARRY-OUT AND DELIVERED.

# ASPARAGUS PASTA SALAD

A TASTY AND ATTRACTIVE LUNCHEON, SPRINGTIME PICNIC OR BUFFET DISH!

## DRESSING

| | | |
|---|---|---|
| 1 | GARLIC CLOVE, MINCED | 1 |
| 2 | ANCHOVY FILLETS, RINSED | 2 |
| 2 TSP. | DIJON MUSTARD | 10 ML |
| 1/2 TSP. | SALT | 2 ML |
| 1/2 TSP. | GROUND PEPPER | 2 ML |
| 1/2 TSP. | WORCESTERSHIRE SAUCE | 2 ML |
| 1 | EGG YOLK | 1 |
| 2 TBSP. | FRESH LEMON JUICE | 30 ML |
| 1 TBSP. | WHITE WINE VINEGAR | 15 ML |
| 1/2 CUP | OLIVE OIL | 125 ML |
| 1/4 CUP | GRATED PARMESAN CHEESE | 60 ML |

## SALAD

| | | |
|---|---|---|
| 2 CUPS | SMALL PASTA SHELLS, COOKED, DRAINED & COOLED | 500 ML |
| 1 LB. | ASPARAGUS, CUT INTO 2" (5 CM) PIECES, COOKED TENDER-CRISP & COOLED | 500 G |
| 1 | MEDIUM RED PEPPER, CHOPPED | 1 |
| 1 CUP | SLICED MUSHROOMS | 250 ML |
| 1 CUP | SLICED GREEN ONION | 250 ML |
| 1/4 CUP | CHOPPED PARSLEY | 60 ML |
| 2 TBSP. | CHOPPED FRESH BASIL | 30 ML |
| 2 TBSP. | SLIVERED ALMONDS | 30 ML |

TO MAKE DRESSING: PLACE ALL INGREDIENTS IN BLENDER AND BLEND WELL. ASSEMBLE SALAD INGREDIENTS IN A LARGE BOWL, TOSS WITH DRESSING AND REFRIGERATE AT LEAST 1 HOUR BEFORE SERVING. SERVES 6.

# MEDITERRANEAN ORZO AND VEGETABLE SALAD

THIS IS GREAT WITH GRILLED LAMB OR CHICKEN.

| | | |
|---|---|---|
| I CUP | UNCOOKED ORZO | 250 ML |
| 12 | ASPARAGUS SPEARS, CHOPPED IN 1-2" (2.5-5 CM) PIECES | 12 |

## DRESSING

| | | |
|---|---|---|
| 3 TBSP. | WHITE WINE VINEGAR | 45 ML |
| I TBSP. | GRAINY DIJON MUSTARD | 15 ML |
| I TBSP. | MAPLE SYRUP OR HONEY | 15 ML |
| 2 TBSP. | COARSELY CHOPPED FRESH DILL | 30 ML |
| I TSP. | FINELY CHOPPED CAPERS | 5 ML |
| I | GARLIC CLOVE, PEELED & SLICED | I |
| | SALT & PEPPER TO TASTE | |
| 1/3 CUP | EXTRA-VIRGIN OLIVE OIL | 75 ML |
| I CUP | HALVED RED CHERRY OR GRAPE TOMATOES | 250 ML |
| 1/4 CUP | PITTED & COARSELY CHOPPED KALAMATA OLIVES | 60 ML |
| I TBSP. | TOASTED PINE NUTS | 15 ML |

BRING A MEDIUM-LARGE POT OF SALTED WATER TO A BOIL AND ADD ORZO. COOK ORZO FOR ABOUT 10 MINUTES, UNTIL AL DENTE, ADDING ASPARAGUS TO POT DURING LAST 2 MINUTES. DRAIN ORZO AND ASPARAGUS IN COLANDER, RINSE WITH COLD WATER AND SET ASIDE.

# MEDITERRANEAN ORZO AND VEGETABLE SALAD

CONTINUED FROM PAGE 98.

TO MAKE DRESSING: IN BLENDER OR FOOD PROCESSOR, COMBINE VINEGAR, MUSTARD, MAPLE SYRUP, DILL, CHOPPED CAPERS, GARLIC, SALT AND PEPPER. SLOWLY ADD OIL AND CONTINUE TO BLEND UNTIL MIXTURE EMULSIFIES.

PLACE ORZO AND ASPARAGUS IN A LARGE BOWL AND TOSS WITH DRESSING. REFRIGERATE, COVERED, FOR 1 HOUR. REMOVE SALAD FROM REFRIGERATOR 30 MINUTES BEFORE SERVING AND GENTLY TOSS IN TOMATOES, OLIVES AND PINE NUTS. SERVES 4-6. (PICTURED OPPOSITE PAGE 126.)

HUSBAND: WHAT'S FOR DINNER?

WIFE STANDING IN FRONT OF THE FREEZER: THAT DEPENDS. WILL YOU BE HUNGRY IN 10-12 MINUTES OR 18-20 MINUTES?

# CHICKEN ATLANTA

WE WERE GIFTED WITH THIS RECIPE WHILE ON A PROMOTIONAL TRIP TO ATLANTA. MINT JULEPS, ANYONE?

## ORANGE SOUFFLÉ

| | | |
|---|---|---:|
| 2 | 1/4 OZ. (7 G) ENVELOPES (1 TBSP./15 ML EACH) GELATIN | 2 |
| 2 CUPS | SUGAR | 500 ML |
| | DASH OF SALT | |
| 4 | EGG YOLKS | 4 |
| 2 1/2 CUPS | ORANGE JUICE, DIVIDED | 625 ML |
| 1 1/2 TSP. | GRATED ORANGE ZEST | 5 ML |
| 1 TSP. | GRATED LEMON ZEST | 5 ML |
| 3 TBSP. | LEMON JUICE | 45 ML |
| 1 CUP | HALVED ORANGE SECTIONS | 250 ML |
| 2 CUPS | WHIPPING CREAM, WHIPPED | 500 ML |

## CHICKEN SALAD

| | | |
|---|---|---:|
| 1 CUP | MAYONNAISE | 250 ML |
| | DASH OF WHITE VINEGAR | |
| 1/2 CUP | WHIPPING CREAM, WHIPPED | 125 ML |
| | SALT & PEPPER TO TASTE | |
| 3 CUPS | DICED COOKED CHICKEN BREAST OR TURKEY | 750 ML |
| 1/2 CUP | DICED CELERY | 125 ML |
| 1/2 CUP | SLIVERED ALMONDS, TOASTED | 125 ML |

TO MAKE SOUFFLÉ: MIX GELATIN, SUGAR AND SALT IN A SAUCEPAN. BEAT TOGETHER EGG YOLKS AND 1 CUP (250 ML) OF ORANGE JUICE. STIR INTO GELATIN MIXTURE; COOK OVER MEDIUM HEAT, STIRRING CONSTANTLY, UNTIL MIXTURE COMES TO A BOIL. REMOVE FROM HEAT AND STIR

# CHICKEN ATLANTA

CONTINUED FROM PAGE 100.

IN ORANGE AND LEMON ZEST AND REMAINING JUICES. CHILL, STIRRING OCCASIONALLY, UNTIL MIXTURE MOUNDS WHEN DROPPED FROM A SPOON. STIR IN ORANGE SECTIONS. FOLD IN WHIPPED CREAM AND POUR INTO A 2-QUART (2 L) RING MOLD. COVER AND CHILL OVERNIGHT.

TO MAKE SALAD: COMBINE MAYONNAISE AND VINEGAR. FOLD IN WHIPPED CREAM, SALT AND PEPPER. ADD CHICKEN AND CELERY. REFRIGERATE UNTIL READY TO ASSEMBLE.

TO SERVE: UNMOLD SOUFFLÉ ONTO A GLASS PLATE AND MOUND CHICKEN IN CENTER. GARNISH WITH ALMONDS. SERVES 8.

HUSBAND PACKING LUNCHBOX FOR 6-YEAR-OLD: "WHAT ELSE SHOULD I PUT IN?"

WIFE: "WHAT WOULD YOU PUT IN IF I WASN'T HERE?"

HUSBAND: "FIVE DOLLARS."

# CHICKEN AND MIXED RICE SALAD
## WITH ORANGE VINAIGRETTE

SALAD

| | | |
|---|---|---|
| 4 CUPS | CHICKEN BROTH | 1 L |
| 1 CUP | WILD RICE, UNCOOKED | 250 ML |
| 1 CUP | LONG-GRAIN BROWN RICE, UNCOOKED | 250 ML |
| 4 | CHICKEN BREAST HALVES, COOKED & CUBED | 4 |
| 1 CUP | PECANS, TOASTED | 250 ML |
| 3 | GREEN ONIONS, SLICED | 3 |
| 1/2 CUP | GOLDEN RAISINS | 125 ML |
| 1/2 CUP | CHOPPED CELERY | 125 ML |
| 2 TSP. | GRATED ORANGE ZEST | 10 ML |

ORANGE VINAIGRETTE

| | | |
|---|---|---|
| 1/4 CUP | RICE WINE VINEGAR | 60 ML |
| 1/4 CUP | ORANGE JUICE, FRESHLY SQUEEZED | 60 ML |
| 2 TBSP. | DIJON MUSTARD | 30 ML |
| 2 TBSP. | MANGO CHUTNEY | 30 ML |
| 1/2 TSP. | SALT | 2 ML |
| 1/4 TSP. | WHITE PEPPER | 1 ML |
| 1/2 CUP | CANOLA OR VEGETABLE OIL | 125 ML |

GARNISH

| | | |
|---|---|---|
| 2 TBSP. | FRESH CHIVES, MINCED | 30 ML |

TO MAKE SALAD: IN A LARGE SAUCEPAN, BRING CHICKEN BROTH TO A BOIL. STIR IN WILD RICE AND SIMMER, COVERED, FOR 10 MINUTES. ADD BROWN RICE; SIMMER MIXTURE, COVERED, FOR 30-35 MINUTES, UNTIL LIQUID IS ABSORBED. REMOVE FROM HEAT, COOL TO ROOM TEMPERATURE.

# CHICKEN AND MIXED RICE SALAD
## WITH ORANGE VINAIGRETTE

CONTINUED FROM PAGE 102.

IN A LARGE BOWL: COMBINE RICE, CHICKEN, PECANS, GREEN ONIONS, RAISINS, CELERY AND ORANGE ZEST.

TO MAKE VINAIGRETTE: IN A SMALL BOWL, COMBINE VINEGAR, ORANGE JUICE, MUSTARD, CHUTNEY, SALT AND PEPPER. ADD OIL IN A SLOW, STEADY STREAM, WHISKING CONSTANTLY, UNTIL SLIGHTLY THICKENED AND THOROUGHLY COMBINED. ADD TO RICE MIXTURE, TOSSING GENTLY TO MIX. SPRINKLE WITH CHIVES AND SERVE AT ROOM TEMPERATURE.

EMPLOYEE: THE AMOUNT OF MY PAYCHECK SEEMS LOWER THAN USUAL.

BOSS: IT'S NOT AS LOW AS IT SEEMS - I'VE JUST STARTED PAYING YOU IN CENTIGRADE.

# ASIAN CHICKEN SALAD

IT'S A HOT SUMMER'S NIGHT AND DINNER'S READY!

## DRESSING

| | | |
|---|---|---|
| 1/2 CUP | OLIVE OIL | 125 ML |
| 2 TBSP. | APPLE CIDER VINEGAR | 30 ML |
| 2-3 TBSP. | SOY SAUCE | 30-45 ML |
| 1 1/2 TBSP. | DARK SESAME OIL | 22 ML |
| 1/2 TBSP. | HONEY | 7 ML |
| 1 | GARLIC CLOVE, MINCED | 1 |
| 1/2 TSP. | MINCED FRESH GINGER | 2 ML |
| 1/2-1 TSP. | SALT (SEA SALT IF POSSIBLE) | 2-5 ML |
| | GROUND PEPPER TO TASTE | |
| 2 TBSP. | SESAME SEEDS, TOASTED | 30 ML |

## SALAD

| | | |
|---|---|---|
| 4 | CHICKEN BREAST HALVES | 4 |
| | SALT & PEPPER TO TASTE | |
| 12 | ASPARAGUS SPEARS | 12 |
| 1 | RED PEPPER, CHOPPED | 1 |
| 2 CUPS | SUGAR SNAP PEAS, | 500 ML |
| 2 | GREEN ONIONS, CUT DIAGONALLY | 2 |
| | INTO 1/2" (1.3 CM) PIECES | |
| 1 TBSP. | SESAME SEEDS, TOASTED | 15 ML |

TO MAKE DRESSING: IN A SCREW-TOP JAR, COMBINE ALL
INGREDIENTS. SHAKE VIGOROUSLY.

AH, THE PRAIRIES. . . WHERE YOU CAN WATCH YOUR DOG RUN
AWAY FOR A WEEK.

## ASIAN CHICKEN SALAD

CONTINUED FROM PAGE 104.

TO MAKE SALAD: SALT AND PEPPER CHICKEN AND SAUTÉ UNTIL NO LONGER PINK. (DO NOT OVER COOK.) COOL CHICKEN AND CUT INTO CUBES. BLANCH ASPARAGUS FOR 2 MINUTES AND RUN UNDER COLD WATER. CUT EACH SPEAR DIAGONALLY INTO 1" (2.5 CM) PIECES. IN A LARGE BOWL, COMBINE CHICKEN, ASPARAGUS, RED PEPPERS, PEAS, GREEN ONIONS AND SESAME SEEDS. POUR DRESSING OVER SALAD AND TOSS. SERVE WITH PITA CRISPS ON PAGE 14.

VARIATION: ADD SOME COOKED RICE VERMICELLI. (PICTURED OPPOSITE PAGE 127.)

TEACHER: GIVE ME A SENTENCE USING THE TERM "CAESARIAN SECTION".

CHILD: THE CAESARIAN SECTION IS A DISTRICT IN ROME.

# MANGO AND SPICY SHRIMP SALAD

AN ELEGANT STARTER OR MAIN-COURSE SALAD.

## HONEY-CHIVE SALAD DRESSING

| | | |
|---|---|---|
| 1 | EGG YOLK | 1 |
| 2 TBSP. | WHITE WINE VINEGAR | 30 ML |
| 1 TSP. | FRESH LEMON JUICE | 5 ML |
| 1¼ CUPS | CANOLA OIL | 300 ML |
| 3 TBSP. | SNIPPED FRESH CHIVES | 45 ML |
| 1 TBSP. | MINCED FRESH PARSLEY | 15 ML |
| 1 TBSP. | LIQUID HONEY | 15 ML |
| 1 | GARLIC CLOVE, MINCED | 1 |
| | PINCH OF SALT | |
| 3 | MANGOES, PEELED & SLICED | 3 |
| | JUICE OF 1 LIME | |
| 24 | LARGE, RAW SHRIMP, PEELED & DEVEINED | 24 |
| 1 TBSP. | CAJUN SEASONING | 15 ML |
| 1 TBSP. | CANOLA OIL | 15 ML |
| 1 | MEDIUM JICAMA, PEELED & SLICED | 1 |
| ¼ | ENGLISH CUCUMBER, PEELED & CUT IN STRIPS | ¼ |
| 2 | RADISHES, THINLY SLICED | 2 |
| 1 | PKG. MIXED LETTUCE | 1 |

TO MAKE DRESSING: WHISK EGG YOLK, GRADUALLY ADDING VINEGAR AND LEMON JUICE. WHISK IN OIL. ADD REMAINING INGREDIENTS, SHAKE WELL AND REFRIGERATE. TOSS MANGO WITH LIME JUICE. COAT SHRIMP WITH CAJUN SEASONING AND QUICKLY PAN-FRY IN OIL UNTIL JUST COOKED (PINK). DIVIDE LETTUCE AMONG 6 PLATES. ARRANGE MANGO AND VEGETABLES ON LETTUCE. DRIZZLE WITH HONEY-CHIVE DRESSING AND PLACE SHRIMP ON EACH SALAD. SERVES 6.

# SOUPS

Avocado Soup with Tomato-Cucumber Salsa
Pear & Watercress Soup
Forest Mushroom Chowder
Tomato Basil Soup
Cream of Tomato Soup
Cheddar Cheese Soup
Broccoli Soup
Carrot Fennel Soup with Maple Crème Fraîche
Roasted Squash Soup with Apple and Brie
Red Lentil Soup
Garlicky Tortellini, Spinach and Tomato Soup
Baked Potato and Leek Soup with
Cheddar and Bacon
Zuppa Du Jour
Crab and Corn Chowder
Chicken, Apple and Curry Soup
Turkey Soup
Beef and Barley Soup

# AVOCADO SOUP WITH TOMATO-CUCUMBER SALSA

AN IDEAL SUMMER SOUP THAT DOESN'T REQUIRE COOKING.

## SOUP

| | | |
|---|---|---|
| 2 | LARGE RIPE AVOCADOS | 2 |
| 3 CUPS | CHICKEN BROTH | 750 ML |
| 2 TBSP. PLUS 1 TSP. | FRESH LEMON JUICE | 35 ML |
| 2 TBSP. | FINELY CHOPPED FRESH CHIVES | 30 ML |
| 1/2 TSP. | CHILI POWDER | 2 ML |
| | SALT TO TASTE | |
| 1/4 CUP | SOUR CREAM | 60 ML |

TO MAKE SOUP: PEEL AVOCADOS AND CUT INTO LARGE PIECES. PLACE IN A FOOD PROCESSOR OR BLENDER WITH A SMALL AMOUNT OF BROTH. PROCESS UNTIL SMOOTH. ADD REMAINING BROTH, LEMON JUICE, CHIVES, CHILI POWDER AND SALT TO TASTE AND PROCESS UNTIL SMOOTH. COVER AND REFRIGERATE UNTIL CHILLED, AT LEAST 4 HOURS OR OVERNIGHT.

TO SERVE: LADLE SOUP INTO BOWLS AND GARNISH WITH A DOLLOP OF SOUR CREAM AND TOMATO-CUCUMBER SALSA (SEE PAGE 109). SERVES 4.

Grape Tomatoes au Vodka, page 50
Jalapeño Poppers, page 70

Chicken Lettuce Wraps, page 78

# TOMATO-CUCUMBER SALSA

| | | |
|---|---|---|
| 2 | LARGE TOMATOES, PEELED, SEEDED & FINELY CHOPPED | 2 |
| 1/2 CUP | PEELED, SEEDED & FINELY CHOPPED ENGLISH CUCUMBER | 125 ML |
| 1 | MEDIUM JALAPEÑO CHILI, SEEDED & FINELY CHOPPED* | 1 |
| 1 TBSP. | FINELY CHOPPED FRESH CILANTRO | 15 ML |
| 1 TBSP. | FRESH LEMON JUICE | 15 ML |
| 1 | MEDIUM GARLIC CLOVE, MINCED | 1 |
| | SALT TO TASTE | |

TO MAKE SALSA: COMBINE INGREDIENTS IN A MEDIUM BOWL AND MIX WELL. TASTE FOR SEASONING. COVER AND REFRIGERATE. THIS CAN BE PREPARED 3 DAYS IN ADVANCE.

*REMEMBER TO WEAR RUBBER GLOVES WHEN DEALING WITH JALAPEÑO CHILIES.

A LOT OF MONEY IS TAINTED – IT TAINT YOURS AND IT TAINT MINE.

# PEAR AND WATERCRESS SOUP

DELICIOUS HOT OR COLD.

| | | |
|---|---|---:|
| 3 TBSP. | BUTTER | 45 ML |
| 2 | MEDIUM POTATOES, PEELED & CUBED | 2 |
| 4 | GREEN ONIONS, SLICED | 4 |
| 14 OZ. | CAN PEARS, DRAINED & COARSELY CHOPPED, RESERVE JUICE | 398 ML |
| 2 TSP. | GRATED LEMON ZEST | 10 ML |
| 1/2 TSP. | DRIED TARRAGON | 2 ML |
| 2 CUPS | CHICKEN BROTH | 500 ML |
| 1 BUNCH | WATERCRESS, COARSELY CHOPPED, ENDS REMOVED | |
| 1/2 CUP | LIGHT CREAM | 125 ML |
| | SALT & FRESHLY GROUND PEPPER | |
| | WATERCRESS OR GREEN ONIONS, FINELY SLIVERED FOR GARNISH | |

IN A SAUCEPAN OVER MEDIUM HEAT, MELT BUTTER. ADD POTATOES AND COOK 5-8 MINUTES, STIRRING FREQUENTLY. ADD GREEN ONIONS, PEARS, LEMON ZEST AND TARRAGON. STIR, COVER AND SIMMER 3-5 MINUTES. CAREFULLY POUR IN BROTH AND RESERVED PEAR JUICE. BRING SOUP JUST TO A BOIL AND ADD WATERCRESS. COVER AND REDUCE HEAT. SIMMER UNTIL POTATOES ARE TENDER AND WATERCRESS IS SLIGHTLY WILTED. REMOVE SOUP FROM HEAT. PURÉE SOUP IN BLENDER IN SMALL BATCHES. RETURN SOUP TO SAUCEPAN AND SLOWLY STIR IN CREAM. HEAT OVER MEDIUM-LOW HEAT UNTIL WARMED THROUGH. SEASON AND GARNISH. SERVES 4-6.

# FOREST MUSHROOM CHOWDER

A SOUP MADE WITH CARE IS A DELIGHT TO THE SOUL. (SO THERE!)

| | | |
|---|---|---:|
| 2 TBSP. | VEGETABLE OIL | 30 ML |
| 1 | GARLIC CLOVE, MINCED | 1 |
| ½ CUP | SLICED ONIONS | 125 ML |
| ½ CUP | DICED CARROTS | 125 ML |
| 3 CUPS | SLICED WILD MUSHROOMS | 750 ML |
| | (CHANTERELLE, MOREL, | |
| | SHIITAKE, OYSTER) | |
| 3 CUPS | CHICKEN BROTH | 750 ML |
| 2 CUPS | WHIPPING CREAM | 500 ML |
| ¼ CUP | DICED POTATOES | 60 ML |
| ¼ CUP | FROZEN CORN NIBLETS | 60 ML |
| ½ | APPLE, PEELED & DICED | ½ |
| 2 | BAY LEAVES | 2 |
| 3 TBSP. | SHERRY | 45 ML |
| 2 TBSP. | CHOPPED PARSLEY | 30 ML |
| | SALT & FRESHLY GROUND PEPPER | |

IN LARGE SAUCEPAN OR DUTCH OVEN, HEAT OIL AND SAUTÉ GARLIC, ONIONS, CARROTS AND MUSHROOMS. DO NOT BROWN.

ADD BROTH AND CREAM TO VEGETABLE MIXTURE. BRING TO A BOIL AND REDUCE HEAT TO SIMMER.

ADD POTATOES, CORN, APPLE, BAY LEAVES, SHERRY AND PARSLEY TO SOUP. SIMMER ABOUT ½ HOUR. REMOVE BAY LEAVES AND SEASON WITH SALT AND PEPPER. SERVES 6.

# TOMATO BASIL SOUP

SIMPLE, QUICK, DELICIOUS AND LOADED WITH NUTRITION.

| | | |
|---|---|---|
| 2 TBSP. | BUTTER | 30 ML |
| 1 | CARROT, CHOPPED | 1 |
| 1 | LARGE ONION, CHOPPED | 1 |
| 5 | LARGE TOMATOES, CHOPPED | 5 |
| 3/4 TSP. | SUGAR | 3 ML |
| 2 CUPS | CHICKEN BROTH | 500 ML |
| 1 CUP | CHOPPED FRESH BASIL | 250 ML |
| | SALT & PEPPER TO TASTE | |

MELT BUTTER IN A LARGE FRYING PAN AND SAUTÉ CARROT AND ONION. ADD TOMATOES, SUGAR AND BROTH. SIMMER FOR 15 MINUTES. PROCESS BASIL IN FOOD PROCESSOR, ADD TOMATO-BROTH MIXTURE AND PROCESS AGAIN. ADD SALT AND PEPPER AND REHEAT FOR SERVING. SPRINKLE WITH GARLIC CROÛTONS, IF YOU'RE NOT ON THE SOUTH BEACH DIET!

## GARLIC CROÛTONS

| | | |
|---|---|---|
| 1 | LOAF DAY-OLD SOURDOUGH BREAD | 1 |
| 1/4 CUP | OLIVE OIL | 60 ML |
| 1 TSP. | GARLIC POWDER | 5 ML |
| 1 TSP. | CRUSHED DRIED PARSLEY | 5 ML |
| 3/4 TSP. | PAPRIKA | 3 ML |
| | SALT & PEPPER | |

CUT BREAD INTO 1/2" (1.3 CM) CUBES. COMBINE OIL, GARLIC POWDER, PARSLEY, PAPRIKA, SALT AND PEPPER. WORK GARLIC-OIL MIXTURE INTO BREAD. SPREAD CUBES IN SHALLOW PAN AND BAKE AT 325°F (160°C) FOR 25 MINUTES.

# CREAM OF TOMATO SOUP

THIS IS SO DARN GOOD, YOU'LL WISH YOU'D DOUBLED THE RECIPE!

| | | |
|---|---|---|
| 2 | 19 OZ. (540 ML) CANS TOMATOES | 2 |
| 1 | LARGE ONION, FINELY CHOPPED | 1 |
| 1 CUP | CHOPPED CELERY | 250 ML |
| 10 OZ. | CAN CHICKEN BROTH | 284 ML |
| ½ CUP | SPICY CLAMATO JUICE | 125 ML |
| 1 TSP. | DILL | 5 ML |
| ¼ CUP | BUTTER | 60 ML |
| ½ CUP | FLOUR | 125 ML |
| 4 CUPS | MILK | 1 L |
| 1 CUP | CHEESE WHIZ | 250 ML |
| | CHOPPED PARSLEY FOR GARNISH | |

SIMMER TOMATOES, ONION, CELERY, BROTH, CLAMATO JUICE AND DILL UNTIL VEGGIES ARE COOKED, ABOUT 20 MINUTES. PURÉE IN BLENDER IF SMOOTH CONSISTENCY IS DESIRED. IN A MEDIUM-SIZED PAN, MELT BUTTER AND BLEND IN FLOUR TO MAKE A PASTE. ADD MILK SLOWLY, STIRRING CONSTANTLY, TO MAKE A THICK WHITE SAUCE. STIR IN TOMATO SOUP. FOLD IN CHEESE WHIZ AND GARNISH WITH PARSLEY. SERVES 4-6.

IN MY DAY, WE DIDN'T NEED ALL THIS THERAPY. WE HAD A LITTLE THING CALLED THE MARTINI.

# CHEDDAR CHEESE SOUP

BEST SERVED THE DAY IT'S MADE.

| | | |
|---|---|---|
| 2 TBSP. | BUTTER | 30 ML |
| 1/2 | LARGE RED PEPPER, CUT INTO MATCHSTICKS | 1/2 |
| 1/2 | LARGE YELLOW PEPPER, CUT INTO MATCHSTICKS | 1/2 |
| 3/4 CUP | CHOPPED ONION | 175 ML |
| 2 | GARLIC CLOVES, MINCED | 2 |
| 1/4 CUP | FLOUR | 60 ML |
| 1 1/2 CUPS | CHICKEN BROTH | 375 ML |
| 1 CUP | WHOLE MILK | 250 ML |
| 1 CUP | WHIPPING CREAM | 250 ML |
| 2 CUPS | GRATED SHARP WHITE CHEDDAR CHEESE | 500 ML |
| | SALT & PEPPER TO TASTE | |

IN HEAVY LARGE POT OVER MEDIUM HEAT, MELT BUTTER. ADD PEPPERS, ONION AND GARLIC AND SAUTÉ UNTIL TENDER. ADD FLOUR AND STIR FOR 2 MINUTES. WHISK IN BROTH, THEN MILK AND CREAM. SIMMER UNTIL SLIGHTLY THICKENED, STIRRING CONSTANTLY. GRADUALLY ADD CHEESE 1/2 CUP (125 ML) AT A TIME, STIRRING AFTER EACH ADDITION UNTIL MELTED AND SMOOTH. ADD SALT AND PEPPER. SERVES 4-6.

TEACHER: HOW CAN YOU DELAY MILK TURNING SOUR?
CHILD: KEEP IT IN THE COW.

# BROCCOLI SOUP

OK – IT'S THE MIDDLE OF WINTER AND YOU HAVE NOTHING PLANNED FOR DINNER. TRY THIS!

| | | |
|---|---|---|
| 6 CUPS | CHOPPED BROCCOLI FLORETS | 1.5 L |
| 1/4 CUP | FINELY CHOPPED ONION | 60 ML |
| 2 CUPS | CHICKEN BROTH | 500 ML |
| 2 TBSP. | BUTTER | 30 ML |
| 1 TBSP. | FLOUR | 15 ML |
| 1 TSP. | SALT | 5 ML |
| | PEPPER TO TASTE | |
| | PINCH OF MACE | |
| 2 CUPS | HALF & HALF CREAM | 500 ML |
| 2 CUPS | GRATED CHEDDAR CHEESE (OPTIONAL) | 500 ML |

IN A LARGE SAUCEPAN, COMBINE BROCCOLI WITH ONION AND BROTH. BRING TO A BOIL, REDUCE HEAT AND SIMMER FOR 10 MINUTES. BLENDERIZE FOR A SMOOTH CONSISTENCY. IN A LARGE SAUCEPAN, MELT BUTTER, ADD FLOUR, SALT, PEPPER AND MACE. SLOWLY ADD CREAM AND STIR UNTIL SMOOTH. ADD BROCCOLI AND CHEESE, IF USING, AND WARM UNTIL CHEESE IS MELTED. SERVES 4-6.

I GAVE HIM THE SKINNIEST YEARS OF MY LIFE.

# CARROT FENNEL SOUP WITH MAPLE CRÈME FRAÎCHE

FENNEL – AN INSPIRED CHOICE.

## SOUP

| | | |
|---|---|---|
| 3 TBSP. | OLIVE OIL | 45 ML |
| I | MEDIUM RED ONION, DICED | I |
| 2 | SMALL FENNEL BULBS, TRIMMED & CHOPPED | 2 |
| 5 | MEDIUM CARROTS, PEELED, CHOPPED | 5 |
| 1/4 CUP | CHOPPED FRESH DILL | 60 ML |
| 8 CUPS | CHICKEN BROTH | 2 L |
| | SALT & PEPPER TO TASTE | |

## MAPLE CRÈME FRAÎCHE

| | | |
|---|---|---|
| 1/3 CUP | SOUR CREAM | 75 ML |
| I TSP. | MAPLE SYRUP | 5 ML |

## GARNISH

FRESH DILL SPRIGS

TO MAKE SOUP: HEAT OIL IN A MEDIUM SAUCEPAN, SAUTÉ ONION AND FENNEL FOR 2-3 MINUTES. ADD CARROTS AND SAUTÉ ANOTHER 2-3 MINUTES. ADD DILL AND BROTH; BRING TO A BOIL. SIMMER 10-12 MINUTES, UNTIL CARROTS ARE TENDER. SEASON WITH SALT AND PEPPER. PURÉE SOUP UNTIL SMOOTH, ADDING MORE BROTH IF IT'S TOO THICK.

TO MAKE CRÈME FRAÎCHE: WHISK SOUR CREAM AND MAPLE SYRUP TOGETHER IN A SMALL BOWL; SET ASIDE. SERVE SOUP WITH A DOLLOP OF CRÈME FRAÎCHE AND A DILL SPRIG. SERVES 6-8.

# ROASTED SQUASH SOUP WITH APPLE AND BRIE

| | | |
|---|---|---|
| 1 | LARGE BUTTERNUT SQUASH | 1 |
| 1 | CARROT | 1 |
| 1 | MEDIUM ONION | 1 |
| 1 | LEEK, WHITE PORTION ONLY | 1 |
| 2 TBSP. | BUTTER | 30 ML |
| 8 CUPS | CHICKEN BROTH | 2 L |
| 1 | APPLE, PEELED & CHOPPED | 1 |
| 1 | BAY LEAF | 1 |
| 1 TSP. | SUGAR | 5 ML |
| | SALT & FRESHLY GROUND PEPPER | |
| 8 OZ. | BRIE CHEESE | 250 G |
| | SNIPPED CHIVES | |

CUT SQUASH IN HALF LENGTHWISE AND REMOVE SEEDS. PLACE CUT-SIDE DOWN ON PAN AND BAKE AT 350°F (180°C) UNTIL TENDER, ABOUT 45 MINUTES (OR MICROWAVE CUT-SIDE DOWN IN A SMALL AMOUNT OF WATER, COVERED, ABOUT 10 MINUTES). CHOP CARROT, ONION AND LEEK INTO 1" (2.5 CM) PIECES AND PLACE IN A LARGE POT. GENTLY SAUTÉ IN BUTTER. DO NOT BROWN. ADD COOKED SQUASH TO VEGETABLES. ADD BROTH AND BRING TO A BOIL. ADD APPLE, BAY LEAF AND SUGAR. SIMMER, UNCOVERED, FOR 40 MINUTES. REMOVE BAY LEAF AND PURÉE SOUP IN BATCHES. SEASON WITH SALT AND PEPPER TO TASTE. SLICE OFF RIND OF BRIE AND CUT BRIE INTO 1/2" (1.3 CM) PIECES. PLACE CHEESE IN BOTTOM OF SOUP BOWLS AND FILL WITH HOT SOUP. GARNISH WITH CHIVES. SERVES 6-8.

# RED LENTIL SOUP

THIS VARIATION OF LENTIL SOUP IS LIGHT, BRIGHT AND PACKED WITH FRESH VEGETABLES.

| | | |
|---|---|---|
| 1½ TBSP. | OLIVE OIL | 22 ML |
| 1 | LARGE ONION, CHOPPED | 1 |
| 3 | GARLIC CLOVES, CHOPPED | 3 |
| 2 | LARGE CARROTS, CHOPPED | 2 |
| ½ CUP | CHOPPED FRESH OR CANNED TOMATOES | 125 ML |
| 1 | CELERY STALK, CHOPPED | 1 |
| 1¼ TSP. | GROUND CUMIN | 6 ML |
| ½ TSP. | SALT | 2 ML |
| 1 CUP | DRIED RED LENTILS | 250 ML |
| 4 CUPS | WATER | 1 L |
| 1½ CUPS | CHICKEN BROTH | 375 ML |
| 2 TBSP. | CHOPPED FRESH PARSLEY | 30 ML |
| | SALT & PEPPER TO TASTE | |

HEAT OIL IN A 4-5-QUART (4-5 L) HEAVY SAUCEPAN OVER MODERATELY HIGH HEAT. SAUTÉ ONION, STIRRING UNTIL GOLDEN. ADD GARLIC, CARROT, TOMATOES, CELERY, CUMIN AND SALT AND SAUTÉ, STIRRING, FOR ABOUT 2 MINUTES. ADD LENTILS, WATER AND BROTH AND SIMMER, UNCOVERED, STIRRING OCCASIONALLY, UNTIL LENTILS ARE TENDER, ABOUT 20 MINUTES. STIR IN PARSLEY AND SEASON WITH SALT AND PEPPER. MAKES APPROXIMATELY 7 CUPS (1.75 L).

# GARLICKY TORTELLINI, SPINACH AND TOMATO SOUP

BADDA BOOM - BADDA BING - IF SOUP IS YOUR THING!

| | | |
|---|---|---|
| I TBSP. | BUTTER | 15 ML |
| 6-8 | CLOVES GARLIC, CHOPPED (USE IT ALL - HONEST!) | 6-8 |
| 4 CUPS | CHICKEN BROTH | I L |
| 6 OZ. | CHEESE TORTELLINI | 170 G |
| 14 OZ. | CAN DICED TOMATOES, WITH LIQUID OR 2½ CUPS (625 ML) SKINNED, CHOPPED FRESH RIPE TOMATOES | 398 ML |
| 10 OZ. | BAG OF SPINACH, STEMS REMOVED | 300 G |
| 8-10 | FRESH BASIL LEAVES, COARSELY CHOPPED | 8-10 |
| | PARMESAN CHEESE, GRATED | |

MELT BUTTER IN A LARGE SAUCEPAN OVER MEDIUM-HIGH HEAT. ADD GARLIC AND SAUTÉ ABOUT 2 MINUTES. ADD BROTH AND BRING TO A BOIL. ADD TORTELLINI AND COOK HALFWAY (ABOUT 5 MINUTES IF FROZEN, LESS IF USING FRESH). ADD TOMATOES AND THEIR LIQUID; REDUCE HEAT TO SIMMER AND COOK JUST UNTIL PASTA IS TENDER. STIR IN SPINACH AND BASIL AND COOK UNTIL WILTED, 1-2 MINUTES. TO SERVE, SPRINKLE WITH PARMESAN CHEESE. SERVES 4. (PICTURED OPPOSITE PAGE 144.)

# BAKED POTATO AND LEEK SOUP WITH CHEDDAR AND BACON

A SUPERB DINNER FOR A WINTER'S NIGHT – SERVE WITH SALAD AND CRUSTY ROLLS.

| | | |
|---|---|---|
| 2 | MEDIUM BAKER POTATOES | 2 |
| 1/4 CUP | BUTTER | 60 ML |
| 2 1/2 CUPS | SLICED LEEKS (WHITE & LIGHT GREEN PARTS), WELL RINSED | 625 ML |
| 2 | GARLIC CLOVES, MINCED | 2 |
| | SALT & FRESHLY GROUND PEPPER TO TASTE | |
| 2 CUPS | CHICKEN BROTH | 500 ML |
| 2 CUPS | WATER | 500 ML |
| 4 | SLICES BACON, CUT INTO 1/2" (1.3 CM) PIECES | 4 |
| 1/2 CUP | MILK | 125 ML |
| 1/2 CUP | SOUR CREAM | 125 ML |
| I CUP | GRATED SHARP CHEDDAR CHEESE | 250 ML |
| 2 TBSP. | SLICED GREEN ONIONS OR CHIVES | 30 ML |

WASH POTATOES AND BAKE UNTIL TENDER. SET ASIDE TO COOL. MELT BUTTER IN DUTCH OVEN OVER MEDIUM-LOW HEAT. ADD LEEKS AND GARLIC, SEASON WITH SALT AND PEPPER AND COOK, STIRRING OCCASIONALLY, UNTIL SOFTENED, ABOUT 10 MINUTES. ADD BROTH AND WATER. SIMMER OVER MEDIUM HEAT AND COOK UNTIL LEEKS ARE TENDER, ABOUT 20 MINUTES. COOK BACON UNTIL BROWN AND CRISP. DRAIN ON PAPER TOWEL.

# BAKED POTATO AND LEEK SOUP
## WITH CHEDDAR AND BACON

CONTINUED FROM PAGE 120.

CUT POTATOES IN HALF LENGTHWISE. USE A LARGE SPOON TO SCOOP PULP IN 1 PIECE FROM EACH HALF. CUT PULP INTO $\frac{1}{2}$" (1.3 CM) CUBES AND SET ASIDE. COARSELY CHOP POTATO SKIN AND ENTIRE REMAINING POTATO AND ADD TO POT WITH LEEKS.

IN A BLENDER OR FOOD PROCESSOR, PURÉE IN BATCHES. RETURN PURÉED SOUP TO A CLEAN POT AND REHEAT OVER MEDIUM-LOW. IN A SMALL BOWL, WHISK TOGETHER MILK AND SOUR CREAM UNTIL SMOOTH, THEN WHISK INTO SOUP WITH A CUP (125 ML) OF CHEDDAR. STIR IN DICED POTATO.

IF SOUP IS TOO THICK, IT MAY BE THINNED WITH A LITTLE WATER. SEASON TO TASTE AND GARNISH WITH REMAINING CHEDDAR, BACON AND CHIVES. SERVES 4. (PICTURED ON FRONT COVER.)

YOU NEVER FEEL MORE CLEVER THAN WHEN YOU KNOW THE ANSWER AND THE CONTESTANT DOESN'T.

# ZUPPA DU JOUR

A COLD WINTER'S NIGHT, HOMEMADE SOUP, A LOAF OF BREAD AND PERHAPS A VIDEO??

| | | |
|---|---|---|
| 6 | SLICES BACON, CHOPPED | 6 |
| 2 | MEDIUM ONIONS, CHOPPED | 2 |
| 3 | STALKS CELERY, CHOPPED | 3 |
| 3-4 | GARLIC CLOVES, MINCED | 3-4 |
| 1/4 TSP. | EACH MARJORAM, THYME | 1 ML |
| 1/2 TSP. | EACH OREGANO, ROSEMARY | 2 ML |
| 2 TBSP. | CHOPPED FRESH BASIL | 30 ML |
| | OR 2 TSP. (10 ML) DRIED BASIL | |
| 1/4 CUP | CHOPPED FRESH PARSLEY | 60 ML |
| 1/2 TSP. | HOT RED PEPPER FLAKES | 2 ML |
| 5 CUPS | CHICKEN BROTH | 1.25 L |
| 28 OZ. | CAN ITALIAN TOMATOES, CHOPPED | 798 ML |
| 2/3 CUP | BABY SHELL PASTA | 150 ML |
| 14 OZ. | CAN ARTICHOKE HEARTS (12-14 COUNT), DRAINED & CUT INTO WEDGES | 398 ML |
| | SALT & PEPPER TO TASTE | |
| | GRATED PARMESAN CHEESE TO SPRINKLE | |

IN A LARGE HEAVY POT, COOK BACON, ONIONS, CELERY, GARLIC, HERBS AND HOT PEPPER FLAKES, UNTIL ONIONS ARE SOFTENED. STIR IN BROTH AND TOMATOES. BRING TO BOIL. ADD PASTA. REDUCE HEAT AND SIMMER, UNCOVERED, 10 MINUTES, OR UNTIL PASTA IS JUST TENDER. STIR IN ARTICHOKES AND SEASON TO TASTE. SERVE WITH A SPRINKLING OF PARMESAN CHEESE. SERVES 6.

# CRAB AND CORN CHOWDER

WHAT COULD BE BETTER THAN CHOWDER, FRENCH BREAD AND WINE AFTER A DAY'S SKIING – OR A DAY OF ANYTHING!

| | | |
|---|---|---|
| 4 | SLICES BACON | 4 |
| ¼ CUP | BUTTER | 60 ML |
| I | SMALL ONION, CHOPPED | I |
| ⅓ CUP | FLOUR | 75 ML |
| 3 CUPS | MILK | 750 ML |
| 2 | MEDIUM POTATOES, PEELED & DICED & SET IN COLD WATER | 2 |
| I | SMALL GREEN PEPPER, SEEDED & CHOPPED | I |
| I | STALK CELERY, DICED | I |
| I | BAY LEAF | I |
| I CUP | HALF & HALF CREAM | 250 ML |
| 10 OZ. | CRABMEAT | 305 G |
| 12 OZ. | CAN WHOLE KERNEL CORN | 341 ML |
| | SALT & PEPPER TO TASTE | |
| I TBSP. | CHOPPED PARSLEY | 15 ML |

FRY BACON UNTIL CRISP. COOL AND CRUMBLE. SET ASIDE. IN A LARGE SAUCEPAN, MELT BUTTER AND SAUTÉ ONION UNTIL SOFT. ADD FLOUR, STIR AND COOK GENTLY FOR I MINUTE. GRADUALLY ADD MILK, STIRRING CONSTANTLY UNTIL THICKENED. DRAIN POTATOES AND ADD TO SAUCE WITH PEPPER, CELERY, BAY LEAF AND CREAM. SIMMER 35-40 MINUTES. ADD CRAB, CORN AND BACON; HEAT THROUGH. SEASON WITH SALT AND PEPPER. GARNISH EACH BOWL WITH PARSLEY. SERVES 6.

# CHICKEN, APPLE AND CURRY SOUP

FEELS LIKE AUTUMN!

| | | |
|---|---|---|
| 2 TBSP. | OLIVE OIL | 30 ML |
| 2 CUPS | CHOPPED CELERY | 500 ML |
| I CUP | CHOPPED CARROTS | 250 ML |
| 1/2 CUP | CHOPPED ONION | 125 ML |
| 4 CUPS | CHICKEN BROTH | I L |
| I CUP | CHOPPED APPLE | 250 ML |
| 1/4 CUP | UNCOOKED LONG-GRAIN RICE | 60 ML |
| 2 TSP. | CURRY POWDER | 10 ML |
| 1/8 TSP. | DRIED THYME | 0.5 ML |
| 1/2 CUP | HALF & HALF CREAM | 125 ML |
| 2 TBSP. | FLOUR | 30 ML |
| I CUP | CHOPPED COOKED CHICKEN | 250 ML |
| | SALT & PEPPER TO TASTE | |

IN A LARGE SAUCEPAN, HEAT OIL AND COOK CELERY, CARROTS AND ONION FOR 5 MINUTES. CAREFULLY ADD BROTH, APPLE, RICE, CURRY POWDER AND THYME. BRING TO A BOIL; REDUCE HEAT AND SIMMER, COVERED, FOR 15-20 MINUTES, OR UNTIL RICE IS TENDER.

IN A GLASS-MEASURING CUP, BLEND CREAM AND FLOUR. STIR INTO VEGETABLES IN SAUCEPAN. COOK AND STIR UNTIL THICKENED AND BUBBLY. STIR IN CHICKEN, SEASON TO TASTE AND HEAT THROUGH.

TO SERVE: LADLE SOUP INTO BOWLS, GARNISH EACH SERVING WITH AN APPLE SLICE. SERVES 4.

# TURKEY SOUP

AHHH – THE AROMA OF SOUP BUBBLING ON THE BACK BURNER – LIFE IS GOOD!

|  | LEFTOVER TURKEY CARCASS (BONES, SKIN, EVERYTHING!) |  |
|---|---|---|
| 8 CUPS | WATER | 2 L |
| 3 | CHICKEN BOUILLON CUBES | 3 |
| 1 TSP. | SALT | 5 ML |
| 1/4 TSP. | POULTRY SEASONING OR SAGE | 1 ML |
| 1 | BAY LEAF | 1 |
| 1/2 CUP | BARLEY | 125 ML |
| 2 CUPS | CHOPPED CARROTS | 500 ML |
| 1 CUP | CHOPPED ONION | 250 ML |
| 1 CUP | CHOPPED CELERY | 250 ML |
| 28 OZ. | CAN TOMATOES | 796 ML |
| 3 CUPS | CHOPPED TURKEY | 750 ML |
| 1 CUP | MACARONI OR NOODLES, UNCOOKED (OPTIONAL) | 250 ML |
| 1/4 CUP | CHOPPED FRESH PARSLEY | 60 ML |

IN A LARGE DUTCH OVEN, COMBINE TURKEY CARCASS, WATER, BOUILLON CUBES, SALT, POULTRY SEASONING AND BAY LEAF. BRING TO A BOIL. REDUCE HEAT, COVER AND SIMMER FOR 2 HOURS. STRAIN AND DISCARD BONES. PLACE BROTH IN REFRIGERATOR OVERNIGHT. SKIM FAT OFF SOLIDIFIED BROTH. SIMMER IN DUTCH OVEN WITH REMAINING INGREDIENTS FOR 2-3 HOURS. SERVE WITH FRESH BREAD AND A GREEN SALAD.

# BEEF AND BARLEY SOUP

"OH, THE WEATHER OUTSIDE IS FRIGHTFUL."

| | | |
|---|---|---|
| 1½ LBS. | BEEF ROUND STEAK, TRIMMED & CUT INTO ½" (1.3 CM) CUBES | 750 G |
| ¾ TSP. | SALT | 3 ML |
| ½ TSP. | PEPPER | 2 ML |
| 2 TBSP. | VEGETABLE OIL, DIVIDED | 30 ML |
| 2 CUPS | FINELY CHOPPED ONION | 500 ML |
| 1 CUP | DICED CARROT | 250 ML |
| ½ CUP | CHOPPED CELERY | 125 ML |
| 1 LB. | MUSHROOMS, SLICED | 500 G |
| 1 TSP. | MINCED GARLIC | 5 ML |
| ¼ TSP. | DRIED THYME | 1 ML |
| 2 CUPS | BEEF BROTH | 500 ML |
| 2 CUPS | CHICKEN BROTH | 500 ML |
| 2 CUPS | WATER | 500 ML |
| ½ CUP | PEARL BARLEY | 125 ML |
| 3 TBSP. | CHOPPED FRESH PARSLEY | 45 ML |

SPRINKLE BEEF WITH SALT AND PEPPER. PLACE 1 TBSP. (15 ML) OIL IN DUTCH OVEN AND BROWN BEEF UNTIL NO LONGER PINK. SET ASIDE. HEAT REMAINING OIL IN SAME POT AND ADD ONION, CARROT AND CELERY. COOK AND STIR UNTIL VEGETABLES ARE SOFTENED, ABOUT 5 MINUTES. STIR IN MUSHROOMS, GARLIC AND THYME, COOK 5 MINUTES MORE. ADD BEEF AND CHICKEN BROTHS WITH WATER, BARLEY AND BEEF; BRING TO A BOIL. REDUCE HEAT; COVER AND SIMMER UNTIL BEEF IS TENDER, ABOUT 1½ HOURS. ADD MORE WATER IF NECESSARY. SPRINKLE WITH PARSLEY JUST BEFORE SERVING. SERVES 8.

Mediterranean Orzo and Vegetable Salad, page 98

Asian Chicken Salad, page 104

# PASTA

Orzo With Parmesan and Basil
Pronto Primavera
Fresh Tomato and Cheese Pasta
Marinara Sauce and Rose Sauce
Pasta with Sausage and Mushrooms
Spinach Fettuccine Alfredo with
Chicken and Broccoli
Pad Thai
Roasted Vegetable Manicotti with Cheese Sauce
Crab Manicotti with Parmesan Cheese Sauce
Creamy Ravioli with Spinach
Vegetable Lasagne
Best Seafood Lasagne

# ORZO WITH PARMESAN & BASIL

THE PASTA THAT LOOKS LIKE RICE – GREAT
WITH CHICKEN OR FISH.

| | | |
|---|---|---|
| 3 TBSP. | BUTTER | 45 ML |
| 1½ CUPS | ORZO | 375 ML |
| 3 CUPS | CHICKEN BROTH | 750 ML |
| ½ CUP | GRATED PARMESAN CHEESE | 125 ML |
| 6 TBSP. | CHOPPED FRESH BASIL OR | 90 ML |
| | 2 TBSP. (30 ML) DRIED BASIL | |
| | SALT & PEPPER TO TASTE | |

MELT BUTTER IN A FRYING PAN OVER MEDIUM-HIGH HEAT.
ADD ORZO AND SAUTÉ FOR 2 MINUTES, UNTIL SLIGHTLY
BROWNED. ADD BROTH AND BRING TO A BOIL. REDUCE HEAT,
COVER AND SIMMER UNTIL ORZO IS TENDER AND LIQUID
IS ABSORBED, ABOUT 20 MINUTES. MIX IN PARMESAN AND
BASIL. SEASON WITH SALT AND PEPPER. TRANSFER TO
SHALLOW BOWL. SERVES 6.

VARIATION: FOR A CREAMIER PASTA DISH, TRY STIRRING
IN 2 TBSP. (30 ML) PLAIN YOGURT THINNED WITH A
LITTLE MILK.

A TINY FORTUNE TELLER WHO ESCAPES FROM PRISON IS A
SMALL MEDIUM AT LARGE.

# PRONTO PRIMAVERA

FAST AND FRESH – NEED WE SAY MORE!

| | | |
|---|---|---|
| 1 CUP | BROCCOLI FLORETS | 250 ML |
| 1 | SMALL ZUCCHINI, SLICED | 1 |
| 1 | SMALL RED PEPPER, CUT IN STRIPS | 1 |
| 1/2 CUP | SNOW PEAS | 125 ML |
| 1/4 CUP | BUTTER | 60 ML |
| 1 CUP | CREAM, WARMED | 250 ML |
| | FRESHLY GROUND PEPPER | |
| 1 LB. | LINGUINI, COOKED & DRAINED | 500 G |
| 1/4 CUP | CHOPPED FRESH BASIL | 60 ML |
| | GRATED PARMESAN CHEESE | |

IN A LARGE FRYING PAN, SAUTÉ BROCCOLI, ZUCCHINI, RED PEPPER AND SNOW PEAS IN BUTTER UNTIL TENDER-CRISP. ADD CREAM AND BLACK PEPPER. COOK UNTIL SLIGHTLY REDUCED. MIX WITH PASTA AND BASIL AND SPRINKLE WITH PARMESAN. SERVE IMMEDIATELY. SERVES 4.

MY WIFE WENT AWAY FOR THE WEEKEND AND LEFT ME TO MY OWN DEVICES – THE CAN OPENER AND THE MICROWAVE.

# FRESH TOMATO AND CHEESE PASTA

BOY, THIS IS GOOD!

BOW TIE PASTA FOR 4

| | | |
|---|---|---|
| 2 | GARLIC CLOVES, MINCED | 2 |
| 2 CUPS | QUARTERED, FRESH ROMA TOMATOES (6) | 500 ML |
| 2 TBSP. | OLIVE OIL | 30 ML |
| 1/2 CUP | FRESH BASIL, CHOPPED | 125 ML |
| 1/2 LB. | BRIE CHEESE, REMOVE RIND | 250 G |
| 1/2 CUP | PINE NUTS, TOASTED (OPTIONAL) | 125 ML |
| | FRESHLY GROUND SALT & PEPPER TO TASTE | |
| | CHOPPED PARSLEY | |
| | PARMESAN CHEESE | |

COOK PASTA ACCORDING TO PACKAGE DIRECTIONS. SAUTÉ GARLIC AND TOMATOES IN OIL. ADD BASIL AND PINCHED-OFF PIECES OF BRIE. STIR UNTIL BRIE IS PARTIALLY MELTED. ADD PINE NUTS. SPRINKLE WITH SALT AND PEPPER. ADD COOKED PASTA TO PAN AND MIX GENTLY. PLACE IN A PASTA BOWL AND SPRINKLE WITH PARSLEY AND PARMESAN. SERVE WITH A GREEN SALAD AND GARLIC TOAST.

MY IDEA OF CLEANING THE HOUSE IS SWEEPING THE ROOM WITH A GLANCE.

# MARINARA AND ROSE SAUCES

A STAPLE FOR ITALIAN CUISINE. DO TRY THE ROSE SAUCE - RICH AND WORTH IT!

| | | |
|---|---|---|
| 3 TBSP. | OLIVE OIL | 45 ML |
| 1 | ONION, DICED | 1 |
| 2 | GARLIC CLOVES, CHOPPED | 2 |
| 28 OZ. | CAN PLUM TOMATOES | 796 ML |
| 1/2 CUP | CHOPPED FRESH BASIL | 125 ML |
| | SALT & FRESH BLACK PEPPER | |
| 1 TBSP. | CHOPPED FRESH PARSLEY | 15 ML |

FOR MARINARA SAUCE: IN A LARGE FRYING PAN, HEAT OIL AND ADD ONION. SAUTÉ UNTIL SOFT AND TRANSLUCENT. ADD GARLIC AND COOK FOR 1 MINUTE; REMOVE FROM HEAT. PLACE TOMATOES IN A BLENDER AT THE LOWEST SPEED FOR A FEW SECONDS TO CHOP COARSELY. ADD TOMATOES TO FRYING PAN, STIR AND RETURN TO HEAT. ADD BASIL, SALT AND PEPPER AND SIMMER, COVERED, FOR 30 MINUTES.

FOR ROSE SAUCE: ADD 1/2 CUP (125 ML) WHIPPING CREAM TO MARINARA SAUCE AND HEAT GENTLY.

HOW'S YOUR DIET GOING?
THE ONLY THING GETTING SLIMMER IS MY CHANCE OF STICKING TO IT.

# PASTA WITH SAUSAGE AND MUSHROOMS

FREEZE EXTRA SAUCE - BE PREPARED!

| | | |
|---|---|---|
| 3 TBSP. | OLIVE OIL | 45 ML |
| 2½ LBS. | ITALIAN SWEET (OR SPICY) SAUSAGES, CASING REMOVED & CUT INTO BITE-SIZED PIECES | 1.25 KG |
| 1½ LBS. | FRESH MUSHROOMS, SLICED | 750 G |
| 1 | MEDIUM ONION, CHOPPED | 1 |
| 1½ CUPS | CHOPPED FRESH BASIL | 375 ML |
| ¼ CUP | CHOPPED FRESH OREGANO | 60 ML |
| 7 | GARLIC CLOVES, CHOPPED | 7 |
| 1 CUP | DRY WHITE WINE | 250 ML |
| 28 OZ. & 19 OZ. | CANS DICED TOMATOES | 1.3 L |
| 2 TBSP. | BUTTER | 30 ML |
| | SALT & PEPPER TO TASTE | |
| | BROAD NOODLES, COOKED | |
| | PARMESAN CHEESE TO GARNISH | |

IN A LARGE HEAVY POT, HEAT 1 TBSP. (15 ML) OIL; SAUTÉ SAUSAGE UNTIL NO LONGER PINK. TRANSFER TO A LARGE BOWL. ADD REMAINING OIL TO SAUSAGE DRIPPINGS. ADD MUSHROOMS AND ONION; SAUTÉ UNTIL TENDER. STIR IN BASIL, OREGANO AND GARLIC; COOK BRIEFLY. ADD WINE AND COOK UNTIL ALMOST ABSORBED. ADD SAUSAGE AND TOMATOES; SIMMER OVER MEDIUM HEAT UNTIL SAUCE IS THICKENED (ABOUT 25 MINUTES). STIR IN BUTTER, SALT AND PEPPER. TOSS COOKED PASTA WITH SAUCE. SPRINKLE WITH PARMESAN CHEESE.

# SPINACH FETTUCCINE ALFREDO WITH CHICKEN AND BROCCOLI

| | | |
|---|---|---|
| 12 OZ. | SPINACH FETTUCCINE | 340 G |
| 2 CUPS | BROCCOLI FLORETS | 500 ML |
| 2 TSP. | OLIVE OIL | 10 ML |
| 1 LB. | SKINLESS, BONELESS CHICKEN BREASTS, CUT INTO 1" (2.5 CM) PIECES | 500 G |
| 3 | GARLIC CLOVES, MINCED | 3 |
| 2 TBSP. | FLOUR | 30 ML |
| 1/2 TSP. | SALT | 2 ML |
| 1/4 TSP. | GROUND BLACK PEPPER | 1 ML |
| 1 1/2 CUPS | LOW-FAT MILK | 375 ML |
| 4 TBSP. | GRATED PARMESAN CHEESE | 60 ML |

COOK PASTA ACCORDING TO PACKAGE DIRECTIONS, ADDING BROCCOLI FOR THE LAST 30 SECONDS. DRAIN AND RETURN PASTA AND BROCCOLI TO POT. HEAT OIL IN A LARGE FRYING PAN OVER MEDIUM-HIGH HEAT. ADD CHICKEN AND GARLIC AND COOK FOR 3-5 MINUTES, UNTIL CHICKEN IS GOLDEN BROWN ON ALL SIDES. ADD FLOUR, SALT AND PEPPER; STIR TO COAT. ADD MILK AND 2 TBSP. (30 ML) CHEESE; BRING TO A BOIL, STIRRING CONSTANTLY. SIMMER FOR 1-2 MINUTES, UNTIL SAUCE THICKENS.

POUR SAUCE OVER FETTUCCINE AND BROCCOLI AND TOSS TO COMBINE. TOP WITH REMAINING PARMESAN WHEN SERVING. SERVES 4.

# PAD THAI

THAILAND'S MOST WELL-KNOWN NOODLE DISH – WITH EVERYTHING IN IT!

| | | |
|---|---|---|
| 8 OZ. | WIDE RICE STICK NOODLES | 250 G |
| 1/2 CUP | CHICKEN BROTH | 125 ML |
| 1/4 CUP | SUGAR | 60 ML |
| 1/4 CUP | FISH SAUCE | 60 ML |
| 3 TBSP. | LIME JUICE | 45 ML |
| 2 TBSP. | KETCHUP | 30 ML |
| 1/4 TSP. | HOT PEPPER FLAKES | 1 ML |
| 4 OZ. | BONELESS PORK OR CHICKEN BREASTS | 125 G |
| 6 OZ. | FIRM TOFU | 170 G |
| 1/4 CUP | VEGETABLE OIL | 60 ML |
| 1 | EGG, BEATEN | 1 |
| 3 | GARLIC CLOVES, MINCED | 3 |
| 8 OZ. | LARGE RAW SHRIMP, PEELED & DEVEINED | 250 G |
| 1 | RED PEPPER, DICED | 1 |
| 2 CUPS | BEAN SPROUTS | 500 ML |
| 1/2 CUP | COARSELY CHOPPED CILANTRO | 125 ML |
| 6 | GREEN ONIONS, THINLY SLICED | 6 |
| 1/4 CUP | PEANUTS, CHOPPED | 60 ML |

IN A LARGE BOWL, SOAK NOODLES IN WARM WATER FOR 15 MINUTES, DRAIN AND SET ASIDE. IN A SMALL BOWL, WHISK CHICKEN BROTH, SUGAR, FISH SAUCE, LIME JUICE, KETCHUP AND HOT PEPPER FLAKES; SET ASIDE. CUT PORK ACROSS GRAIN INTO 1/4" (6 MM) STRIPS. CUT TOFU INTO 1/2" (1.3 CM) CUBES; SET ASIDE. IN WOK OR LARGE FRYING PAN, HEAT 1 TSP. (5 ML) OIL OVER MEDIUM HEAT. COOK EGG, STIRRING OCCASIONALLY, UNTIL

# PAD THAI

CONTINUED FROM PAGE 134.

SCRAMBLED AND SET. TRANSFER TO A LARGE PLATE. WIPE WOK, ADD 1 TBSP. (15 ML) OIL, INCREASE HEAT TO MEDIUM-HIGH AND STIR-FRY GARLIC, SHRIMP AND PORK UNTIL SHRIMP ARE BRIGHT PINK. ADD TO EGG. HEAT REST OF OIL; STIR IN TOFU AND RED PEPPER. COOK, STIRRING OCCASIONALLY, UNTIL TOFU BEGINS TO BROWN. STIR IN NOODLES FOR 1 MINUTE, OR UNTIL THEY START TO SOFTEN. POUR IN SAUCE; STIR-FRY UNTIL NOODLES ARE TENDER. RETURN EGG MIXTURE TO PAN; ADD BEAN SPROUTS, CILANTRO AND HALF THE GREEN ONIONS. STIR UNTIL HEATED THROUGH. REMOVE TO WARM SERVING PLATTER. GARNISH WITH PEANUTS AND REMAINING GREEN ONIONS. SERVES 4. (PICTURED OPPOSITE PAGE 145.)

TAKE MY ADVICE – I'M NOT USING IT.

# ROASTED VEGETABLE MANICOTTI
## WITH CHEESE SAUCE

| | | |
|---|---|---|
| 1 | ONION | 1 |
| 2 CUPS | CHOPPED BROCCOLI | 500 ML |
| 2 CUPS | CHOPPED CAULIFLOWER | 500 ML |
| 2 CUPS | CHOPPED CARROT | 500 ML |
| 1 | RED PEPPER | 1 |
| 3 TBSP. | OLIVE OIL | 45 ML |
| 1 TBSP. | BALSAMIC VINEGAR | 15 ML |
| 2 | GARLIC CLOVES, MINCED | 2 |
| 3 CUPS | SPINACH | 750 ML |
| 1 CUP | FRESHLY GRATED PARMESAN CHEESE | 250 ML |
| 1 CUP | RICOTTA CHEESE | 250 ML |
| 1 | EGG, BEATEN | 1 |
| 2 | SLICES BREAD | 2 |
| 1/2 CUP | FRESH PARSLEY | 125 ML |
| 1/2 CUP | FRESH BASIL | 125 ML |
| | SALT & PEPPER TO TASTE | |
| 16 | MANICOTTI SHELLS | 16 |
| 2 | 14 OZ. (398 ML) CANS TOMATO SAUCE | 2 |
| | CHEESE SAUCE, PAGE 137 | |
| | ASIAGO CHEESE, GRATED | |

CHOP VEGETABLES INTO 1" (2.5 CM) PIECES. TOSS WITH
OIL, VINEGAR AND GARLIC. ROAST AT 350°F (180°C) FOR
40 MINUTES, STIRRING OCCASIONALLY.

MIX SPINACH WITH HOT VEGETABLES AND SET ASIDE
TO COOL. PULSE VEGETABLES IN FOOD PROCESSOR TO
A COARSE TEXTURE.

MIX TOGETHER PARMESAN, RICOTTA AND EGG. BLEND
WITH VEGETABLES. IN FOOD PROCESSOR, WHIRL BREAD,
HERBS AND SEASONINGS. ADD TO VEGETABLE MIXTURE.

# ROASTED VEGETABLE MANICOTTI

CONTINUED FROM PAGE 136.

COOK MANICOTTI ACCORDING TO PACKAGE DIRECTIONS. DRAIN WELL. FILL WITH VEGETABLE MIXTURE USING SPOON OR VERY SMALL KNIFE. POUR TOMATO SAUCE IN BOTTOM OF 2, 9 X 13" (23 X 33 CM) BAKING DISHES AND ARRANGE STUFFED MANICOTTI IN EACH BAKING DISH. MAKE CHEESE SAUCE, BELOW, AND POUR OVER MANICOTTI. SPRINKLE WITH GRATED ASIAGO. BAKE AT 350°F (180°C) FOR ABOUT 30 MINUTES. SERVES 8-10.

## CHEESE SAUCE

| | | |
|---|---|---|
| 3 TBSP. | BUTTER | 45 ML |
| 3 TBSP. | FLOUR | 45 ML |
| 3 CUPS | MILK | 750 ML |
| 2 CUPS | GRATED MOZZARELLA OR SWISS CHEESE | 500 ML |
| I TSP. | WORCESTERSHIRE SAUCE | 5 ML |
| | DASH HOT PEPPER SAUCE | |
| | SALT & PEPPER TO TASTE | |

MELT BUTTER OVER MEDIUM HEAT; BLEND IN FLOUR. COOK FOR I MINUTE, STIRRING UNTIL SMOOTH AND BUBBLY. REDUCE HEAT TO MEDIUM-LOW. GRADUALLY ADD MILK, STIRRING UNTIL THICKENED. ADD CHEESE, WORCESTERSHIRE AND PEPPER SAUCE. STIR UNTIL CHEESE MELTS. ADD SALT AND PEPPER.

# CRAB MANICOTTI
## WITH PARMESAN CHEESE SAUCE

A GREAT MAKE-AHEAD!

| | | |
|---|---|---|
| 14-16 | MANICOTTI SHELLS, COOKED | 14-16 |
| 1/2 LB. | FRESH OR FROZEN CRABMEAT, FLAKED (OR MOCK CRABMEAT) | 250 G |
| 1 LB. | FRESH SPINACH,* WILTED, DRAINED | 500 G |
| 1 1/2 CUPS | RICOTTA CHEESE | 375 ML |
| 1/2 CUP | FRESHLY GRATED PARMESAN CHEESE | 125 ML |
| 1/2 CUP | CHOPPED GREEN ONIONS | 125 ML |
| 1 | LARGE EGG, BEATEN | 1 |
| 1 TSP. | SALT | 5 ML |
| | PARMESAN CHEESE SAUCE, PAGE 139 | |
| 1/2 CUP | GRATED ASIAGO CHEESE | 125 ML |

PREHEAT OVEN TO 400°F (200°C). COOK MANICOTTI
SHELLS AS DIRECTED ON PACKAGE; SET ASIDE. SPRAY A
9 X 13" (23 X 33 CM) BAKING DISH. IN A MEDIUM BOWL,
COMBINE CRAB, SPINACH, CHEESES, ONIONS, EGG AND
SALT. MIX WELL. USING A SPOON OR YOUR FINGERS, (JULIA
CHILD SAYS IT'S OKAY) FILL SHELLS AND PLACE IN DISH.
COVER WITH PARMESAN CHEESE SAUCE. SPRINKLE WITH
ASIAGO CHEESE; BAKE, UNCOVERED, UNTIL BUBBLY, ABOUT
25 MINUTES. (PICTURED OPPOSITE PAGE 162.)

*TO WILT SPINACH, PLACE IN A SIEVE; POUR BOILING
WATER OVER, THEN POUR ICE-COLD WATER OVER. DRAIN
WELL ON PAPER TOWELS.

# PARMESAN CHEESE SAUCE

| ¼ CUP | BUTTER | 60 ML |
| ¼ CUP | FLOUR | 60 ML |
| 2½ CUPS | MILK | 625 ML |
| 1 CUP | FRESHLY GRATED PARMESAN CHEESE | 250 ML |
| ¼ TSP. | SALT | 1 ML |
| | PEPPER TO TASTE | |
| | TABASCO TO TASTE | |

IN A SAUCEPAN OVER MEDIUM HEAT, MELT BUTTER. ADD FLOUR AND STIR UNTIL BUBBLY. ADD MILK AND STIR UNTIL THICKENED. ADD CHEESE, SALT, PEPPER AND TABASCO. STIR UNTIL CHEESE MELTS.

RESEARCH HAS SHOWN THAT MEN USUALLY SLEEP ON THE RIGHT SIDE OF THE BED. EVEN IN THEIR SLEEP, THEY HAVE TO BE RIGHT.

# CREAMY RAVIOLI WITH SPINACH

| | | |
|---|---|---|
| 1 | GARLIC CLOVE, MINCED | 1 |
| 2 TSP. | OLIVE OIL | 10 ML |
| 1/2 CUP | CHICKEN BROTH | 125 ML |
| 2 CUPS | LIGHT CREAM | 500 ML |
| 1/4 CUP | FRESHLY GRATED PARMESAN CHEESE | 60 ML |
| 1 LB. | RICOTTA SPINACH RAVIOLI | 500 G |
| 2 CUPS | CHOPPED FRESH SPINACH | 500 ML |
| 8 OZ. | CRAB (OPTIONAL) | 250 G |
| 2 TBSP. | CHOPPED FRESH DILL | 30 ML |
| 2 | FRESH TOMATOES, CHOPPED | 2 |
| 1/4 CUP | FRESHLY GRATED PARMESAN CHEESE | 60 ML |

OVER MEDIUM HEAT, SAUTÉ GARLIC IN OIL, ADD BROTH AND SIMMER UNTIL REDUCED BY HALF. ADD CREAM AND PARMESAN, STIRRING UNTIL CHEESE HAS MELTED.

COOK RAVIOLI ACCORDING TO PACKAGE DIRECTIONS.

ADD RAVIOLI, SPINACH, CRAB AND DILL TO SAUCE AND HEAT THROUGH.

BLANCH TOMATOES IN BOILING WATER FOR 1 MINUTE, THEN PLUNGE INTO COLD WATER. PEEL OFF SKINS WITH A SHARP KNIFE. CUT IN HALF AND USE A SMALL SPOON TO REMOVE SEEDS. SPRINKLE WITH PARMESAN. SERVES 6.

# VEGETABLE LASAGNE

| 2 TBSP. | OLIVE OIL | 30 ML |
| I | MEDIUM ONION, CHOPPED | I |
| I | MEDIUM ZUCCHINI, GRATED | I |
| I | LARGE CARROT, GRATED | I |
| 4 CUPS | SLICED FRESH MUSHROOMS | I L |
| ½ TSP. | THYME | 2 ML |
| ½ TSP. | OREGANO | 2 ML |
| ½ TSP. | BASIL | 2 ML |
| 3 CUPS | SPAGHETTI SAUCE (HOT & SPICY IS GOOD) | 750 ML |
| 9 | LASAGNE NOODLES | 9 |
| 2 CUPS | RICOTTA CHEESE | 500 ML |
| 3-4 CUPS | FRESH SPINACH, CHOPPED | 750 ML-I L |
| 3 CUPS | GRATED MOZZARELLA CHEESE | 750 ML |

HEAT OIL IN FRYING PAN; SAUTÉ ONION, ZUCCHINI, CARROT AND MUSHROOMS UNTIL TENDER. ADD THYME, OREGANO AND BASIL. STIR IN SPAGHETTI SAUCE. SIMMER FOR 20 MINUTES. COOK LASAGNE NOODLES ACCORDING TO PACKAGE DIRECTIONS. GREASE A 9 X 13" (23 X 33 CM) CASSEROLE. LAYER WITH ½ OF THE SAUCE, 3 NOODLES, ½ OF THE RICOTTA CHEESE, COVER WITH ALL OF THE SPINACH, THEN ⅓ OF THE MOZZARELLA CHEESE. REPEAT LAYERS, ENDING WITH THE LAST 3 NOODLES AND MOZZARELLA. BAKE AT 350°F (180°C) FOR 40 MINUTES, OR UNTIL BUBBLY. LET SIT FOR AT LEAST 10 MINUTES BEFORE CUTTING. SERVES 8.

# BEST SEAFOOD LASAGNE

A TASTY VARIATION OF AN OLD FAVORITE.

| | | |
|---|---|---|
| 8 | LASAGNE NOODLES | 8 |
| 2 TBSP. | BUTTER | 30 ML |
| I CUP | CHOPPED ONION | 250 ML |
| 8 OZ. | PKG. CREAM CHEESE, SOFTENED | 250 G |
| I1/2 CUPS | RICOTTA CHEESE | 375 ML |
| I | EGG, BEATEN | I |
| 2 TSP. | BASIL | 10 ML |
| 1/2 TSP. | SALT | 2 ML |
| 1/8 TSP. | PEPPER | 0.5 ML |
| 2 | 10 OZ. (284 ML) CANS CREAM OF MUSHROOM SOUP | 2 |
| 1/3 CUP | DRY WHITE WINE OR DRY VERMOUTH | 75 ML |
| 5 OZ. | CRABMEAT | 140 ML |
| I LB. | SHRIMP, DEVEINED & COOKED | 500 G |
| 1/4 CUP | GRATED PARMESAN CHEESE | 60 ML |
| 1/2 CUP | SHREDDED, SHARP CHEDDAR CHEESE | 125 ML |

COOK NOODLES. PLACE 4 NOODLES IN A 9 X 13" (23 X 33 CM) BAKING DISH. COOK ONION IN BUTTER. ADD CHEESES, EGG, BASIL, SALT AND PEPPER. SPREAD HALF THE CHEESE MIXTURE OVER NOODLES. COMBINE SOUP AND WINE. STIR IN CRAB AND SHRIMP AND SPREAD HALF OVER CHEESE LAYER. REPEAT ALL LAYERS. SPRINKLE WITH PARMESAN AND CHEDDAR. BAKE, UNCOVERED, AT 350°F (180°C) FOR 45 MINUTES. LET STAND 15 MINUTES BEFORE SERVING. SERVES 8-10. FREEZES WELL.

# VEGGIES

Stir-Fried Sugar Snap Peas
Sesame Spinach
Cheese-Fried Zucchini
Dill and Parmesan Tomatoes
Veggie Stacks
Baked Corn Pudding with a Kick
Red Cabbage
Creamed Onions
Caramelized Onion and Potato Flan
Whipped Potato with Celery Root
Potatoes Rosti
Roasted Sweet Potato Wedges
Turnips 'n' Apples
Perfect Parsnips
Oven-Roasted Autumn Vegetables
Lemon Risotto
Mushroom Barley Risotto
Basmati Rice Pilaf
Oven-Baked Wild Rice

# STIR-FRIED SUGAR SNAP PEAS

FAST AND DELICIOUS. JUST REMEMBER NOT TO OVERCOOK THEM - THEY STILL NEED TO SNAP.

| | | |
|---|---|---|
| 1/2 LB. | FRESH SUGAR SNAP PEAS | 250 G |
| 2 TBSP. | VEGETABLE OIL | 30 ML |
| 1 TSP. | SESAME OIL | 5 ML |
| 3 TBSP. | PINE NUTS | 45 ML |
| 1 TBSP. | MINCED FRESH GINGER | 15 ML |
| 2 TBSP. | DRY SHERRY | 30 ML |
| 2 TBSP. | SOY SAUCE | 30 ML |

TO PREPARE PEAS, SNAP OFF STEMS AND PULL STRINGS OFF ALONG SEAMS. HEAT A WOK OR HEAVY FRYING PAN OVER HIGH HEAT. ADD VEGETABLE OIL AND, WHEN HOT, ADD SESAME OIL. STIR-FRY PINE NUTS AND GINGER UNTIL BROWN, BEING CAREFUL NOT TO BURN THEM. ADD SNAP PEAS AND STIR-FRY TO COAT WITH OIL. MIX IN SHERRY AND SOY SAUCE. COVER WOK AND LOWER HEAT TO MEDIUM. COOK FOR ABOUT 2 MINUTES.

I'VE DISCOVERED VICTORIA'S SECRET: NOBODY UNDER 30 CAN FIT INTO THEIR STUFF!

Garlicky Tortellini, Spinach and Tomato Soup, page 119

Pad Thai, page 134

# SESAME SPINACH

FINALLY, A SPINACH THAT STAYS BRIGHT GREEN.

| | | |
|---|---|---|
| 10 OZ. | PKG. FRESH SPINACH | 283 G |
| 2 TBSP. | DARK SESAME OIL | 30 ML |
| 1/4 TSP. | CRUSHED RED PEPPER FLAKES | 1 ML |
| 2 | GARLIC CLOVES, CHOPPED | 2 |
| 2 TSP. | SESAME SEEDS | 10 ML |
| PINCH | SALT | PINCH |

RINSE SPINACH WELL. PICK OVER AND DISCARD ANY TOUGH LEAVES AND STEMS. DRY LEAVES WELL.

IN FRYING PAN OVER MEDIUM HEAT, ADD SESAME OIL, CRUSHED RED PEPPER FLAKES, GARLIC AND SESAME SEEDS AND SAUTÉ UNTIL SLIGHTLY BROWNED. ADD SPINACH AND COOK, STIRRING FREQUENTLY. WATCH CAREFULLY AND REMOVE FROM HEAT WHEN JUST WILTED. DRAIN OFF ANY JUICES AND SEASON WITH SALT. (PICTURED OPPOSITE PAGE 180.)

EVER WONDER ABOUT THOSE PEOPLE WHO SPEND $2.95 ON THOSE LITTLE BOTTLES OF EVIAN WATER? TRY SPELLING IT BACKWARDS.

# CHEESE-FRIED ZUCCHINI

MAY ALSO BE SERVED AS AN APPETIZER.

| | | |
|---|---|---|
| 1/4 CUP | DRIED BREADCRUMBS | 60 ML |
| 2 TBSP. | GRATED PARMESAN CHEESE | 30 ML |
| 2 TBSP. | FLOUR | 30 ML |
| 1 TSP. | SALT (GARLIC SALT OR ONION SALT IF PREFERRED) | 5 ML |
| 2 | MEDIUM ZUCCHINI, SLICED LENGTHWISE IN STICKS | 2 |
| 1 | EGG, BEATEN | 1 |
| 2-4 TBSP. | OLIVE OIL | 30-60 ML |

COMBINE BREADCRUMBS, CHEESE, FLOUR AND SALT IN
A PLASTIC BAG. DIP ZUCCHINI IN EGG, THEN SHAKE IN
PLASTIC BAG. USING A LARGE SKILLET, HEAT OIL AND FRY
ZUCCHINI UNTIL GOLDEN BROWN AND CRISPY, TURNING
OCCASIONALLY. DRAIN ON PAPER TOWEL. SERVE
IMMEDIATELY. SERVES 4.

DUCT TAPE IS LIKE THE FORCE. IT HAS A LIGHT SIDE AND A
DARK SIDE, AND IT HOLDS THE UNIVERSE TOGETHER.

# DILL AND PARMESAN TOMATOES

QUICK AND DELICIOUS - VITAMINS AND COLOR FOR YOUR COMPANY!

| 3 | MEDIUM TOMATOES | 3 |
|---|---|---|
| 2 TBSP. | BUTTER | 30 ML |
| 1/2 CUP | BREAD CRUMBS | 125 ML |
| 1 TBSP. | FRESH CHOPPED DILL | 15 ML |
| | OR 1/2 TSP. (2 ML) DRIED DILL | |
| | SALT & PEPPER TO TASTE | |
| 1/2 CUP | GRATED PARMESAN CHEESE | 125 ML |

CUT EACH TOMATO INTO 4 SLICES AND PLACE ON A COOKIE SHEET. MELT BUTTER, ADD BREAD CRUMBS, DILL, SALT, PEPPER AND CHEESE. STIR TOGETHER AND SPOON CRUMB MIXTURE ONTO TOMATO SLICES. PLACE IN COLD OVEN UNDER BROILER (NOT TOO CLOSE) AND TURN ON BROILER. BROIL UNTIL CRUST TURNS GOLDEN - ABOUT 5 MINUTES. SERVES 6.

HARLEZ-VOUS FRANCAIS? CAN YOU DRIVE A FRENCH MOTORCYCLE?

# VEGGIE STACKS

GREAT WITH ROAST BEEF OR STEAK. ALLOW
1 STACK PER PERSON.

FOR ONE STACK

| | | |
|---|---|---|
| 1/4" | SLICE EGGPLANT OR PORTOBELLO MUSHROOM | 6 MM |
| 1/4" | SLICE RED ONION | 6 MM |
| 1/4" | SLICE BOCCONCINI CHEESE FRESH BASIL LEAVES | 6 MM |
| 1/4" | SLICE FRESH TOMATO GRATED ASIAGO CHEESE | 6 MM |

ASSEMBLE STACKS BY LAYERING 1 SLICE OF EGGPLANT, RED
ONION, BOCCONCINI, BASIL LEAVES AND TOMATO.
SPRINKLE WITH GRATED ASIAGO. PLACE STACKS ON A
COOKIE SHEET AND BAKE AT 375°F (190°C) FOR ABOUT
20 MINUTES, UNTIL CHEESE MELTS AND VEGGIES SOFTEN.

TEACHER: WHAT IS A FIBULA?

CHILD: A SMALL LIE.

# BAKED CORN PUDDING WITH A KICK

PARTNERS WELL WITH HAM OR ROAST PORK.

| | | |
|---|---|---|
| 4 TBSP. | BUTTER, DIVIDED | 60 ML |
| 2 CUPS | FROZEN KERNEL CORN, THAWED | 500 ML |
| I CUP | WHOLE MILK | 250 ML |
| 2 CUPS | FINELY CHOPPED ONION | 500 ML |
| 6 | GREEN ONIONS, CHOPPED | 6 |
| I TBSP. | DICED SERRANO CHILI PEPPER | 15 ML |
| 4 | LARGE EGGS | 4 |
| I TBSP. | FLOUR | 15 ML |
| 3/4 TSP. | SALT | 3 ML |
| 1/2 TSP. | PEPPER | 2 ML |
| 1 1/2 CUPS | GRATED PARMESAN CHEESE | 375 ML |

MELT 2 TBSP. (30 ML) BUTTER IN A LARGE FRYING PAN OVER
MEDIUM-HIGH HEAT. ADD CORN AND SAUTÉ 5 MINUTES.
ADD MILK; REDUCE HEAT TO MEDIUM. COVER AND SIMMER
5 MINUTES. TRANSFER TO A FOOD PROCESSOR; PURÉE
UNTIL A COARSE CONSISTENCY. MELT REMAINING BUTTER
IN THE SAME PAN. ADD ONIONS AND CHILI PEPPER; SAUTÉ
ABOUT 4 MINUTES. REMOVE FROM HEAT AND STIR IN CORN
PURÉE. COOL 15 MINUTES. PREHEAT OVEN TO 350°F (180°C).
IN A SMALL BOWL BEAT EGGS, FLOUR, SALT AND PEPPER.
STIR IN I CUP (250 ML) CHEESE. STIR EGG MIXTURE
INTO CORN MIXTURE. TRANSFER TO A GREASED 7 X 11"
(18 X 28 CM) GLASS BAKING DISH. SPRINKLE WITH
REMAINING CHEESE AND BAKE UNTIL GOLDEN, ABOUT
40 MINUTES. TO REHEAT, BAKE FOR 25 MINUTES.
SERVES 4-6.

# RED CABBAGE

## EXCELLENT WITH FOWL AND A MUST WITH WILD GAME!

| | | |
|---|---|---|
| 3 LB. | RED CABBAGE | 1.5 KG |
| 2 | GREEN APPLES, PEELED & CHOPPED | 2 |
| 1 | ONION, FINELY CHOPPED | 1 |
| 1/4 CUP | WHITE SUGAR | 60 ML |
| 1/4 CUP | VINEGAR | 60 ML |
| 2 TBSP. | BACON FAT | 30 ML |
| 1 TSP. | SALT | 5 ML |
| | FRESHLY GROUND PEPPER | |
| 1/2 CUP | BOILING WATER | 125 ML |

SHRED CABBAGE AND PLACE IN A LARGE SAUCEPAN WITH
REMAINING INGREDIENTS. BRING TO A BOIL; REDUCE HEAT;
COVER AND SIMMER FOR 1 HOUR. STIR OCCASIONALLY.
SERVES 6-8.

IF WILE E. COYOTE HAD ENOUGH MONEY TO BUY ALL THAT
ACME STUFF, WHY DIDN'T HE JUST BUY DINNER?

# CREAMED ONIONS

THE WAY YOUR GRANDMOTHER MADE THEM.

| 12 | BOILING ONIONS (SMALL) | 12 |
|---|---|---|

### CREAM SAUCE

| 3 TBSP. | BUTTER | 45 ML |
|---|---|---|
| 3 TBSP. | FLOUR | 45 ML |
| 2 CUPS | MILK | 500 ML |
| 1/2 TSP. | SALT | 2 ML |
| | PEPPER TO TASTE | |
| 1/4 TSP. | NUTMEG | 1 ML |
| 1/2 CUP | CRACKER CRUMBS OR BREAD CRUMBS | 125 ML |
| 2 TBSP. | BUTTER | 30 ML |
| | PARMESAN CHEESE | |

PEEL ONIONS AND PLACE IN A POT WITH A LARGE AMOUNT OF BOILING SALTED WATER. BOIL, UNCOVERED, FOR 20-30 MINUTES, UNTIL TENDER BUT NOT FALLING APART. DRAIN AND TRANSFER ONIONS TO A BUTTERED CASSEROLE.

TO PREPARE CREAM SAUCE: MELT BUTTER IN A MEDIUM SAUCEPAN AND STIR IN FLOUR. WHEN BLENDED, ADD MILK SLOWLY WHILE STIRRING. COOK ON LOW HEAT UNTIL SAUCE THICKENS. ADD SALT, PEPPER AND NUTMEG. POUR SAUCE OVER ONIONS. COMBINE CRACKER CRUMBS AND BUTTER AND SPRINKLE OVER ONIONS. TOP WITH PARMESAN CHEESE. BEFORE SERVING, PREHEAT OVEN TO 350°F (180°C) AND BAKE FOR 15-20 MINUTES, UNTIL LIGHTLY BROWNED. SERVES 4.

# CARAMELIZED ONION AND POTATO FLAN

EXCELLENT WITH HAM OR ROAST BEEF.

| 2 TBSP. | BUTTER | 30 ML |
|---|---|---|
| 2 | LARGE ONIONS, THINLY SLICED | 2 |
| 6-8 | MEDIUM BAKER POTATOES, PEELED & THINLY SLICED | 6-8 |
| | SALT & FRESHLY GROUND PEPPER TO TASTE | |
| 1/2-3/4 LB. | EMMENTHAL OR GRUYÈRE CHEESE, GRATED | 250-340 G |

IN A LARGE FRYING PAN OVER MEDIUM HEAT, SAUTÉ ONIONS IN BUTTER UNTIL DEEP GOLDEN BROWN, ABOUT 20 MINUTES. COOK SLOWLY TO CARAMELIZE. GREASE A 9 X 13" (23 X 33 CM) PAN OR LARGE ROUND BAKING DISH. LAYER HALF THE POTATO SLICES IN A SHINGLE FASHION AND SEASON. TOP WITH HALF THE ONIONS AND EMMENTHAL. REPEAT NEXT LAYER, ENDING WITH CHEESE. BAKE AT 350°F (180°C) FOR 50 MINUTES, OR UNTIL POTATOES ARE FORK-TENDER. CUT IN SQUARES OR WEDGES TO SERVE. SERVES 8.

DEAR GOD:
PLEASE SEND DENNIS CLARK TO A DIFFERENT CAMP THIS YEAR.

# WHIPPED POTATO
## WITH CELERY ROOT

CELERY ROOT DOES WONDERS FOR THE HUMBLE POTATO.

| | | |
|---|---|---|
| I | CELERY ROOT, PEELED & CHOPPED | I |
| 4-5 | BAKER POTATOES, PEELED & CUT INTO CHUNKS | 4-5 |
| 2 TBSP. | BUTTER | 30 ML |
| 3 TBSP. | SOUR CREAM | 45 ML |
| | GRATED ZEST OF I ORANGE | |
| | SALT & FRESHLY GROUND PEPPER TO TASTE | |

COOK CELERY ROOT IN SIMMERING SALTED WATER UNTIL TENDER. DRAIN AND PURÉE IN FOOD PROCESSOR. COOK POTATOES IN SALTED WATER UNTIL TENDER. DRAIN AND MASH, MIXING IN BUTTER AND SOUR CREAM. ADD ORANGE ZEST TO MASHED CELERY ROOT, THEN ADD TO MASHED POTATOES. SEASON WITH SALT AND PEPPER. SERVES 6.

WILL CARROTS HELP YOU SEE IN THE DARK?
YES - BUT THEY SURE ARE HARD TO LIGHT!

# POTATOES ROSTI

GREAT WITH STEAK, ROAST BEEF OR LAMB

|  |  |  |
|---|---|---|
|  | POTATOES, SCRUBBED, UNPEELED |  |
| 2 TBSP. | BUTTER | 30 ML |
| 2 TBSP. | VEGETABLE OIL | 30 ML |
|  | SEASONING SALT TO TASTE |  |

PREPARE POTATOES USING A MELON BALLER (ALLOW
8-10 BALLS PER PERSON). PREHEAT OVEN TO 350°F (180°C).
ADD BUTTER AND OIL TO ROASTING PAN AND HEAT FOR
10 MINUTES; ADD POTATOES AND BAKE FOR 45 MINUTES,
STIRRING OFTEN. DRAIN ON PAPER TOWEL. SPRINKLE
WITH SALT. THESE MAY ALSO BE COOKED IN A FRYING PAN.

## ANOTHER WAY:

USE SMALL NEW POTATOES, PLACE EACH ON A WOODEN
SPOON AND SLICE, BUT NOT ALL THE WAY THROUGH.
TOSS WITH MELTED BUTTER AND OIL. SPRINKLE WITH
SEASONING SALT. BAKE AT 350°F (180°C) FOR 30 MINUTES,
STIRRING OFTEN. THEY WILL FAN OUT WHILE COOKING -
VERY CLEVER!

GIVE ME AMBIGUITY OR GIVE ME SOMETHING ELSE.

# ROASTED SWEET POTATO WEDGES

SERVE WITH HAM OR PORK ROAST.

| 3 | SWEET POTATOES | 3 |
|---|---|---|
| 1 TBSP. | OLIVE OIL | 15 ML |
| 1 TBSP. | BROWN SUGAR | 15 ML |
| 1/2 TSP. | CHILI POWDER | 2 ML |
| 1/2 TSP. | SALT | 2 ML |
| 1/8-1/4 TSP. | CAYENNE PEPPER | 0.5-1 ML |

PREHEAT OVEN TO 400°F (200°C). PEEL POTATOES AND CUT INTO 1" (2.5 CM) WEDGES.

IN A LARGE BOWL, TOSS POTATOES WITH OIL. MIX SUGAR AND SEASONINGS TOGETHER. SPRINKLE ON POTATOES AND STIR UNTIL EVENLY COATED.

SPREAD ON A NON-STICK BAKING SHEET LARGE ENOUGH TO HOLD POTATOES WITHOUT OVERCROWDING.

ROAST POTATOES FOR 30 MINUTES, TURNING EVERY 10 MINUTES UNTIL TENDER AND BROWNED. SERVES 4.

THE ONLY TIME MY PRAYERS ARE NEVER ANSWERED IS ON THE GOLF COURSE. – BILLY GRAHAM

# TURNIPS 'N' APPLES

EVERYBODY WHO TRIES THIS WANTS THE RECIPE – YOU'VE GOT IT!

| | | |
|---|---|---|
| 1 | LARGE TURNIP, PEELED & DICED | 1 |
| 1 TBSP. | BUTTER | 15 ML |
| 2 | APPLES | 2 |
| 1/4 CUP | BROWN SUGAR | 60 ML |
| | PINCH OF CINNAMON | |

TOPPING

| | | |
|---|---|---|
| 1/3 CUP | FLOUR | 75 ML |
| 1/3 CUP | BROWN SUGAR | 75 ML |
| 2 TBSP. | BUTTER | 30 ML |

BRING A LARGE POT OF WATER TO A BOIL AND COOK TURNIP UNTIL TENDER. DRAIN AND MASH TURNIP WITH BUTTER. PEEL AND SLICE APPLES. TOSS WITH BROWN SUGAR AND CINNAMON. IN A GREASED CASSEROLE, ARRANGE TURNIPS AND APPLES IN ALTERNATE LAYERS, BEGINNING AND ENDING WITH TURNIPS. MIX TOPPING INGREDIENTS UNTIL CRUMBLY. PAT ON TOP OF TURNIPS AND BAKE AT 350°F (180°C) FOR 1 HOUR. SERVES 6-8.

IT'S GOOD SPORTSMANSHIP TO NOT PICK UP LOST GOLF BALLS WHILE THEY ARE STILL ROLLING. – MARK TWAIN

# PERFECT PARSNIPS

IF YOU ARE A DEVOTEE THESE ARE – PRESENTABLE, PALATABLE AND POSITIVELY A SNAP.

| | | |
|---|---|---|
| 3 | PARSNIPS, PEELED & SLICED IN MATCHSTICKS | 3 |
| 1 | CARROT, PEELED & SLICED IN MATCHSTICKS | 1 |
| 3 TBSP. | BUTTER | 45 ML |
| 1 TBSP. | FRESH LEMON JUICE | 15 ML |
| 1 TBSP. | FRESH DILL | 15 ML |
| | OR 1 TSP. (5 ML) DRIED DILL | |

MELT BUTTER IN A FRYING PAN AND STIR-FRY PARSNIPS AND CARROTS OVER MEDIUM-HIGH HEAT FOR 3-4 MINUTES, UNTIL TENDER-CRISP. REMOVE TO A SERVING DISH AND SPRINKLE WITH LEMON JUICE AND DILL. SERVES 4.

A GRENADE THROWN INTO A KITCHEN IN FRANCE WOULD RESULT IN LINOLEUM BLOWNAPART.

# OVEN-ROASTED AUTUMN VEGETABLES

FOR A DIFFERENT FLAVOR, ADD A SPRINKLING OF FRESH HERBS (ROSEMARY, THYME OR MARJORAM) BEFORE SERVING.

| | | |
|---|---|---|
| I | LARGE SWEET POTATO, PEELED & CUT INTO I" (2.5 CM) CUBES | I |
| I | FENNEL BULB (I LB./500 G), SCRUBBED, TRIMMED & CUT INTO WEDGES | I |
| 6 | SMALL RED POTATOES, SCRUBBED & QUARTERED | 6 |
| 3-4 | PARSNIPS, PEELED & CHOPPED | 3-4 |
| 4 | LARGE SHALLOTS, PEELED & CUT INTO QUARTERS | 4 |
| 2 TBSP. | OLIVE OIL | 30 ML |
| I TBSP. | BALSAMIC VINEGAR | 15 ML |
| I TSP. | COARSE SALT | 5 ML |
| I TBSP. | BALSAMIC VINEGAR | 15 ML |

PREHEAT OVEN TO 425°F (220°C). IN A LARGE ROASTING PAN, TOSS SWEET POTATO, FENNEL, RED POTATOES, PARSNIPS AND SHALLOTS WITH OIL AND I TBSP. (15 ML) VINEGAR AND SALT. ROAST, UNCOVERED, FOR 30-35 MINUTES, STIRRING AND TOSSING ONCE OR TWICE, UNTIL VEGETABLES ARE LIGHTLY BROWNED AND TENDER.

PLACE ROASTED VEGETABLES IN A LARGE SERVING BOWL. SPRINKLE WITH I TBSP. (15 ML) VINEGAR. SERVES 4-6.

# LEMON RISOTTO

WHEN YOU'RE WILLING TO FUSS . . .

| | | |
|---|---|---|
| I TBSP. | OLIVE OIL | 15 ML |
| 1½ CUPS | SLICED SHIITAKE MUSHROOMS | 375 ML |
| 2 | SHALLOTS OR GREEN ONIONS, THINLY SLICED | 2 |
| 2 | GARLIC CLOVES, MINCED | 2 |
| | DASH OF PEPPER | |
| I CUP | ARBORIO OR SHORT-GRAIN RICE | 250 ML |
| 2 CUPS | CHICKEN BROTH | 500 ML |
| ½ CUP | DRY WHITE WINE OR WATER | 125 ML |
| I | LARGE CARROT CUT INTO I" (2.5 CM) MATCHSTICKS | I |
| I | SMALL BUNCH ASPARAGUS SPEARS, CUT INTO I" (2.5 CM) PIECES | I |
| ¼ CUP | PARMESAN CHEESE | 60 ML |
| 2 TSP. | GRATED LEMON ZEST | 10 ML |
| | FRESH BASIL OR PARSLEY (OPTIONAL) | |

IN A LARGE SAUCEPAN, HEAT OIL AND COOK MUSHROOMS, SHALLOTS, GARLIC AND PEPPER UNTIL VEGETABLES ARE TENDER BUT NOT BROWN. ADD RICE AND COOK AND STIR 2 MINUTES MORE. STIR BROTH AND WINE INTO RICE MIXTURE AND BRING TO A BOIL. REDUCE HEAT; COVER AND SIMMER FOR 30 MINUTES (DO NOT LIFT COVER). REMOVE FROM HEAT. STIR IN CARROTS, ASPARAGUS, PARMESAN AND LEMON ZEST. COVER AND LET STAND FOR 5 MINUTES. ADD ADDITIONAL WATER, IF NECESSARY FOR THE DESIRED CONSISTENCY. GARNISH WITH BASIL OR PARSLEY. SERVES 8.

# MUSHROOM BARLEY RISOTTO

USE A MIXTURE OF MUSHROOMS SUCH AS SHIITAKE, CREMINI AND OYSTER TO GIVE A RICH FLAVOR.

| | | |
|---|---|---|
| 1/4 CUP | BUTTER, DIVIDED | 60 ML |
| 1/2 | ONION, DICED | 1/2 |
| | SALT & PEPPER TO TASTE | |
| I CUP | PEARL OR POT BARLEY | 250 ML |
| 3 CUPS | CHICKEN BROTH | 750 ML |
| 1 1/2 CUPS | WATER | 375 ML |
| 4 CUPS | CHOPPED MUSHROOMS | I L |
| | GRATED ZEST OF I LEMON | |
| I TBSP. | LEMON JUICE | 15 ML |
| 3 TBSP. | CHOPPED FRESH PARSLEY | 45 ML |
| 1/3 CUP | PINE NUTS, TOASTED | 75 ML |

IN A SAUCEPAN, MELT HALF OF THE BUTTER OVER MEDIUM HEAT. ADD ONION, SALT AND PEPPER; COOK AND STIR UNTIL ONION IS SOFTENED. STIR IN BARLEY AND COOK FOR I MINUTE. ADD BROTH AND WATER; BRING TO A BOIL. COVER, REDUCE HEAT AND SIMMER JUST UNTIL BARLEY IS TENDER AND LIQUID IS ABSORBED. REMOVE FROM HEAT; LET STAND FOR 5 MINUTES.

IN A FRYING PAN, MELT REMAINING BUTTER. ADD MUSHROOMS; COOK, STIRRING OCCASIONALLY, UNTIL NO LIQUID REMAINS.

PLACE MUSHROOMS OVER BARLEY AND SPRINKLE WITH LEMON ZEST AND JUICE. TOSS GENTLY WITH A FORK. SPRINKLE WITH PARSLEY AND PINE NUTS. A WONDERFUL ADDITION TO GRILLED MEAT OR FISH.

# BASMATI RICE PILAF

"THE ROAD TO MOROCCO."

| 2 TBSP. | BUTTER | 30 ML |
|---|---|---|
| I | MEDIUM ONION, CHOPPED | I |
| 1/3 CUP | SLIVERED ALMONDS | 75 ML |
| I CUP | UNCOOKED BASMATI RICE | 250 ML |
| 1/2 CUP | FINELY CHOPPED CARROTS | 125 ML |
| 1/3 CUP | CURRANTS | 75 ML |
| I TSP. | FINELY SHREDDED ORANGE PEEL | 5 ML |
| 1/4 TSP. | GROUND CINNAMON | I ML |
| 1/4 TSP. | GROUND BLACK PEPPER | I ML |
| 1/8-1/4 TSP. | RED PEPPER FLAKES | 0.5-1 ML |
| 1 3/4 CUPS | CHICKEN BROTH | 425 ML |
| 1/4 CUP | WATER | 60 ML |

IN A MEDIUM SAUCEPAN, MELT BUTTER AND SAUTÉ ONION AND ALMONDS OVER MEDIUM HEAT UNTIL ONION IS TENDER AND ALMONDS ARE GOLDEN. STIR IN RICE. COOK AND STIR FOR 4 MINUTES. STIR IN CARROT, CURRANTS, ORANGE PEEL, CINNAMON, BLACK PEPPER, AND RED PEPPER FLAKES. CAREFULLY STIR BROTH AND WATER INTO RICE MIXTURE IN SAUCEPAN. BRING TO A BOIL AND REDUCE HEAT. SIMMER, COVERED, UNTIL LIQUID IS ABSORBED AND RICE IS TENDER (ABOUT 20 MINUTES). TRANSFER TO SERVING BOWL. SERVES 6.

A CHICKEN CROSSING THE ROAD IS
POULTRY IN MOTION.

# OVEN BAKED WILD RICE

FABULOUS FLAVOR. MAKE IT IN THE MORNING AND BAKE IT WITH THE BEEF.

| | | |
|---|---|---|
| 1½ CUPS | WILD RICE | 375 ML |
| ½ CUP | BUTTER | 125 ML |
| 4 OZ. | CAN WATER CHESTNUTS | 115 ML |
| 2 CUPS | FRESH MUSHROOMS, SLICED | 500 ML |
| 3 | 10 OZ. (284 ML) CANS CONSOMMÉ, UNDILUTED | 3 |

SOAK RICE OVERNIGHT IN A GENEROUS AMOUNT OF WATER. DRAIN. MELT BUTTER IN A 2-QUART (2 L) CASSEROLE. ADD RICE, WATER CHESTNUTS AND MUSHROOMS AND STIR. POUR IN CONSOMMÉ. LET STAND UNTIL READY TO BAKE. BAKE AT 350°F (180°C) FOR 2-2½ HOURS. GREAT WITH BEEF. SERVES 8.

A THREE-LEGGED DOG WALKS INTO A SALOON IN THE OLD WEST. HE SLIDES UP TO THE BAR AND ANNOUNCES: "I'M LOOKING FOR THE MAN WHO SHOT MY PAW."

Crab Manicotti with Parmesan Cheese Sauce, page 138

Roasted Salmon Salad with Honey Mustard Vinaigrette, page 174

# FISH AND SEAFOOD

Crab Cakes with Roasted Red Pepper Aioli
Seared Scallops with Orzo Risotto
Mayan Grilled Shrimp
Ginger Shrimp Stir-Fry
with Sugar Snap Peas and Corn
Shrimp Stir-Fry
Shrimp with Artichokes
"The Ladies" Seafood Casserole
Quick Salmon Patties with
Lemon Caper Mayonnaise
Roasted Salmon Salad with
Honey Mustard Vinaigrette
Grilled Marinated Halibut
Wild West Salmon
Cedar Plank Salmon with Cucumber Dill Sauce
Layered Tuna Casserole

# CRAB CAKES WITH
# ROASTED RED PEPPER AIOLI

THESE CAN BE MADE ONE DAY AHEAD AND COOKED JUST BEFORE SERVING. SERVE WARM WITH ROASTED RED PEPPER AIOLI.

## BÉCHAMEL SAUCE

| | | |
|---|---|---|
| 2 TBSP. | BUTTER | 30 ML |
| 2 TBSP. | FLOUR | 30 ML |
| I CUP | HOT MILK | 250 ML |
| I | BAY LEAF | I |
| | | |
| I LB. | CRABMEAT OR MOCK CRAB | 500 G |
| ½ | RED PEPPER, FINELY DICED | ½ |
| 2 | GREEN ONIONS, DICED | 2 |
| ½ CUP | FRESH BREADCRUMBS | 125 ML |
| ½ TSP. | CAYENNE | 2 ML |
| I½ TSP. | LEMON JUICE | 7 ML |
| DASH | WORCESTERSHIRE SAUCE | DASH |
| | SALT & PEPPER TO TASTE | |
| I CUP | BREADCRUMBS | 250 ML |
| ¼ CUP | BUTTER | 60 ML |

## ROASTED RED PEPPER AIOLI

| | | |
|---|---|---|
| ½ CUP | ROASTED RED PEPPERS (FOUND IN YOUR DELI SECTION) | 125 ML |
| ½ CUP | MAYONNAISE | 125 ML |
| I | GARLIC CLOVE, MINCED | |
| I TSP. | LEMON JUICE | 5 ML |

MELT BUTTER IN A MEDIUM-SIZED SAUCEPAN AND ADD FLOUR. MIX THOROUGHLY AND COOK OVER MEDIUM HEAT FOR ABOUT 3 MINUTES. DO NOT BROWN. GRADUALLY STIR HOT MILK INTO FLOUR MIXTURE UNTIL IT FORMS

# CRAB CAKES WITH
## ROASTED RED PEPPER AIOLI

CONTINUED FROM PAGE 164.

A SMOOTH SAUCE. ADD BAY LEAF AND COOK FOR JUST A FEW MINUTES. CHILL. REMOVE BAY LEAF FROM SAUCE. SQUEEZE ANY LIQUID FROM CRABMEAT AND ADD CRAB TO BÉCHAMEL SAUCE. IF USING MOCK CRAB, CHOP IN FOOD PROCESSOR. ADD RED PEPPER, ONION, BREADCRUMBS, CAYENNE, LEMON JUICE, WORCESTERSHIRE, SALT AND PEPPER TO SAUCE. MIX THOROUGHLY. COVER AND CHILL FOR 30 MINUTES OR OVERNIGHT.

FORM CRAB MIXTURE INTO 2" (5 CM) BALLS FOR APPE-TIZER-SIZED CAKES (LARGER FOR MAIN COURSE). ROLL IN BREADCRUMBS AND FLATTEN. MELT BUTTER AND BROWN EACH SIDE.  MAKES 36 APPETIZERS.

TO MAKE AIOLI: PURÉE RED PEPPERS. ADD MAYONNAISE, GARLIC AND LEMON JUICE TO ROASTED RED PEPPER PURÉE. REFRIGERATE UNTIL SERVING.

IS IT MY IMAGINATION OR DO BUFFALO WINGS TASTE A LOT LIKE CHICKEN?

# SEARED SCALLOPS WITH ORZO RISOTTO

AWESOME WITH ASPARAGUS! AN ELEGANT DINNER FOR 4.

## ORZO RISOTTO

| | | |
|---|---|---|
| 1²/₃ CUPS | ORZO | 400 ML |
| 1 TBSP. | OLIVE OIL | 15 ML |
| 1 CUP | DICED MUSHROOMS | 250 ML |
| 1/3 CUP | DICED ONION | 75 ML |
| 1/3 CUP | DICED SUN-DRIED TOMATOES | 75 ML |
| 1/3 CUP | DICED RED PEPPER | 75 ML |
| 2 CUPS | CHICKEN BROTH | 500 ML |
| 1/2 CUP | FRESHLY GRATED PARMESAN CHEESE | 125 ML |
| 2 TBSP. | CHOPPED PARSLEY | 30 ML |
| 1/2 CUP | WHIPPING CREAM | 125 ML |

## SCALLOPS

| | | |
|---|---|---|
| 2 TBSP. | OLIVE OIL | 30 ML |
| 16 | LARGE (3/4 LB./340 G) NOVA SCOTIA SCALLOPS (LARGE SHRIMP ARE AN EXCELLENT SUBSTITUTE) | 16 |
| | SALT & FRESHLY GROUND PEPPER TO TASTE | |
| | FRESHLY GRATED PARMESAN CHEESE | |

TO MAKE RISOTTO: COOK ORZO ACCORDING TO PACKAGE DIRECTIONS AND SET ASIDE.

IN A LARGE HEAVY POT, HEAT OIL AND SAUTÉ MUSHROOMS, ONION, SUN-DRIED TOMATOES AND RED PEPPER UNTIL SOFT. ADD BROTH AND BRING TO A BOIL.

# SEARED SCALLOPS
## WITH ORZO RISOTTO

CONTINUED FROM PAGE 166.

STIR IN ORZO, PARMESAN AND PARSLEY. ADD CREAM AND SIMMER GENTLY, STIRRING FREQUENTLY, UNTIL MIXTURE IS CREAMY BUT NOT RUNNY, ABOUT 20 MINUTES.

HEAT OIL IN A VERY HOT PAN. SEASON SCALLOPS WITH SALT AND PEPPER AND SEAR UNTIL BROWN ON OUTSIDE BUT JUST OPAQUE IN THE MIDDLE.

SPRINKLE PARMESAN OVER RISOTTO AND TOP WITH SCALLOPS. SERVES 4.

MURPHY'S RULES OF GOLF:

SOMETIMES IT SEEMS THAT YOUR CUP MOVETH OVER.

THE REASON THAT YOUR REAL SWING IS NOT AS GOOD AS YOUR PRACTICE SWING IS THAT YOU ARE TERRIBLE.

GOLF BALLS ARE LIKE EGGS. THEY'RE WHITE, THEY'RE SOLD BY THE DOZEN, AND A WEEK LATER YOU HAVE TO BUY MORE.

# MAYAN GRILLED SHRIMP

EXCELLENT SERVED AS AN APPETIZER OR AN ENTRÉE.

|  | WOODEN SKEWERS |  |
|---|---|---|
| 2 LBS. | LARGE SHRIMP IN THE SHELL | 1 KG |

### TEQUILA LIME MARINADE

| 1/4 CUP | FRESH LIME JUICE | 60 ML |
|---|---|---|
| 1/4 CUP | TEQUILA | 60 ML |
| 2 | SHALLOTS, FINELY CHOPPED | 2 |
| 2 | GARLIC CLOVES, MINCED | 2 |
| 2 TSP. | GROUND CUMIN | 10 ML |
|  | SALT & GROUND PEPPER |  |
| 1/2 CUP | OLIVE OIL | 125 ML |

SOAK SKEWERS IN WATER FOR AT LEAST 30 MINUTES.

THREAD 4 SHRIMP ON EACH SKEWER. LAY IN A SINGLE LAYER IN A SHALLOW GLASS DISH.

TO MAKE MARINADE: WHISK TOGETHER LIME JUICE, TEQUILA, SHALLOTS, GARLIC, CUMIN, AND SALT AND PEPPER TO TASTE. SLOWLY ADD OIL, WHISKING UNTIL COMBINED. TASTE FOR SEASONING.

POUR MARINADE OVER SHRIMP AND LET MARINATE FOR AT LEAST 30 MINUTES, OR UP TO 4 HOURS IN THE REFRIGERATOR.

HEAT BARBECUE TO MEDIUM HEAT. GRILL SHRIMP ABOUT 2 MINUTES ON EACH SIDE, JUST UNTIL PINK. SERVES 8.

# GINGER SHRIMP STIR-FRY
## WITH SUGAR SNAP PEAS AND CORN

| | | |
|---|---|---|
| I LB. | UNCOOKED LARGE SHRIMP, PEELED & DEVEINED | 500 G |

### MARINADE

| | | |
|---|---|---|
| 2 TBSP. | CANOLA OIL | 30 ML |
| I TBSP. | PEELED MINCED FRESH GINGER | 15 ML |
| 2 | LARGE GARLIC CLOVES, MINCED | 2 |
| 1/2 TSP. | SALT | 2 ML |
| 1/4 TSP. | RED PEPPER FLAKES | I ML |
| I LB. | SUGAR SNAP PEAS | 500 G |
| I CUP | FRESH OR FROZEN CORN KERNELS | 250 ML |
| 1/2 CUP | DICED SWEET RED PEPPER | 125 ML |
| 3 | GREEN ONIONS, DIAGONALLY SLICED | 3 |
| 2 TSP. | TOASTED SESAME SEEDS | 10 ML |
| | BASMATI RICE, FRESH CILANTRO & SOY SAUCE | |

COMBINE SHRIMP, OIL, GINGER, GARLIC, SALT AND RED PEPPER FLAKES IN A MEDIUM BOWL. REFRIGERATE FOR I HOUR. HEAT LARGE NON-STICK FRYING PAN OVER HIGH HEAT. ADD SHRIMP MIXTURE, SAUTÉ UNTIL SHRIMP ARE JUST OPAQUE ABOUT 2 MINUTES. TRANSFER TO A BOWL. ADD A LITTLE OIL TO WOK; ADD PEAS, CORN, PEPPERS AND ONIONS. STIR-FRY UNTIL VEGGIES ARE TENDER-CRISP, ABOUT 3 MINUTES. RETURN SHRIMP AND JUICES TO WOK; STIR-FRY I MINUTE LONGER. SEASON WITH SALT AND PEPPER. SPRINKLE WITH SESAME SEEDS. SERVE OVER STEAMED RICE MIXED WITH CHOPPED FRESH CILANTRO. PASS THE SOY SAUCE. SERVES 4.

# SHRIMP STIR-FRY

GET OUT YOUR STOPWATCH!!

| | | |
|---|---|---|
| 2 TBSP. | SESAME OIL | 30 ML |
| 1 | GARLIC CLOVE, MINCED | 1 |
| 1/2 TSP. | MINCED FRESH GINGER | 2 ML |
| 24-36 | PEELED SHRIMP | 24-36 |
| | A HANDFUL OF SNOW PEAS | |
| 2 CUPS | BROCCOLI FLORETS | 500 ML |
| 2 | STALKS CELERY, SLICED DIAGONALLY | 2 |
| 1 | SMALL WHITE ONION, SLIVERED | 1 |
| 1 | RED BELL PEPPER, SLICED | 1 |
| 2 CUPS | FRESH BEAN SPROUTS | 500 ML |
| 1/2 CUP | OYSTER SAUCE | 125 ML |
| 1 TBSP. | SOY SAUCE | 15 ML |
| 1 TBSP. | LIQUID HONEY | 15 ML |
| 1/4 CUP | WHITE WINE | 60 ML |

HEAT SESAME OIL IN A WOK OR FRYING PAN OVER MEDIUM
HEAT. SAUTÉ GARLIC AND GINGER FOR 30 SECONDS. ADD
SHRIMP AND COOK FOR 30 SECONDS. ADD VEGGIES AND
STIR-FRY UNTIL TENDER-CRISP – ABOUT 3 MINUTES. STIR
IN OYSTER SAUCE, SOY SAUCE, HONEY AND WINE. TOSS
TOGETHER FOR 2 MINUTES. SERVE WITH RICE. SERVES 4.

HASTE CUISINE: FAST FRENCH FOOD.

# SHRIMP WITH ARTICHOKES

EXCELLENT CASSEROLE - GREAT SAUCE!

SAUCE

| | | |
|---|---|---|
| 2 TBSP. | BUTTER | 30 ML |
| 2 TBSP. | FLOUR | 30 ML |
| 1/2 TSP. | BLACK PEPPER | 2 ML |
| 1/4 TSP. | CAYENNE PEPPER | 1 ML |
| 2 CUPS | HALF & HALF CREAM | 500 ML |
| 1 TBSP. | KETCHUP | 15 ML |
| 1 TBSP. | WORCESTERSHIRE SAUCE | 15 ML |
| 3 TBSP. | LEMON JUICE | 45 ML |
| 3 TBSP. | SHERRY | 45 ML |
| 12 OZ. | JAR MARINATED ARTICHOKE HEARTS, DRAINED & COARSELY CHOPPED | 340 G |
| 2 LBS. | MEDIUM SHRIMP, PEELED, DEVEINED, TAIL OFF | 1 KG |
| 1 CUP | GRATED SHARP CHEDDAR CHEESE | 250 ML |

TO MAKE SAUCE: MELT BUTTER IN A SAUCEPAN; STIR IN FLOUR, PEPPER AND CAYENNE. ADD CREAM; COOK OVER LOW HEAT, STIRRING UNTIL THICKENED. STIR IN KETCHUP, WORCESTERSHIRE, LEMON JUICE AND SHERRY.

PREHEAT OVEN TO 400°F (200°C). IN A SHALLOW 9 X 13" (23 X 33 CM) BAKING DISH, LAYER ARTICHOKES AND SHRIMP. POUR SAUCE OVER AND SPRINKLE WITH CHEESE. (COVER AND REFRIGERATE IF MAKING AHEAD. UNCOVER AND BRING TO ROOM TEMPERATURE BEFORE BAKING.) BAKE FOR 20-30 MINUTES, OR UNTIL SHRIMP ARE PINK AND CHEESE IS MELTED. SERVE ON RICE WITH A GREEN SALAD. SERVES 8-10.

## "THE LADIES"
## SEAFOOD CASSEROLE

ASSEMBLE EARLY IN THE MORNING AND YOU'RE FREE TO ORGANIZE YOURSELF WITH LAST-MINUTE DETAILS. FRESH SEAFOOD IS BEST.

| | | |
|---|---|---|
| 1/3 CUP | BUTTER | 75 ML |
| 1/3 CUP | FLOUR | 75 ML |
| 2 TSP. | PREPARED MUSTARD | 10 ML |
| 1 TBSP. | GRATED ONION | 15 ML |
| 1 TBSP. | WORCESTERSHIRE SAUCE | 15 ML |
| 1/2 TSP. | PAPRIKA | 2 ML |
| 1/2 TSP. | SALT | 2 ML |
| 1/4 TSP. | TABASCO SAUCE | 1 ML |
| 3 CUPS | MILK | 750 ML |
| 6 OZ. | GRUYÈRE CHEESE, CUBED | 170 G |
| 2 CUPS | MEDIUM SHRIMP | 500 ML |
| 2 CUPS | CRABMEAT | 500 ML |
| 1/2 CUP | SLICED RIPE OLIVES | 125 ML |
| 1 TBSP. | LEMON JUICE | 15 ML |

IN A LARGE SAUCEPAN, MELT BUTTER OVER LOW HEAT. BLEND IN FLOUR, MUSTARD, ONION, WORCESTERSHIRE, PAPRIKA, SALT AND TABASCO. GRADUALLY ADD MILK, STIRRING CONSTANTLY UNTIL THICKENED. ADD CHEESE AND STIR UNTIL MELTED. REMOVE FROM HEAT AND BLEND IN SEAFOOD AND OLIVES. POUR INTO A LARGE CASSEROLE AND BRUSH WITH LEMON JUICE. MAY BE REFRIGERATED AT THIS POINT. BAKE AT 350°F (180°C) FOR 30 MINUTES, OR UNTIL BUBBLY. DELICIOUS SERVED OVER RICE WITH A GREEN SALAD AND WARM ROLLS.

# QUICK SALMON PATTIES WITH LEMON CAPER MAYONNAISE

THE LEMON CAPER MAYO IS MARVELOUS!

| | | |
|---|---|---|
| 2 | 7½ OZ. (213 G) CANS RED SALMON (LEFTOVER COOKED SALMON IS EVEN BETTER) | 2 |
| 1 TBSP. | CHOPPED FRESH PARSLEY | 15 ML |
| 2 | GREEN ONIONS, CHOPPED | 2 |
| 1 | STALK CELERY, FINELY DICED | 1 |
| 1 CUP | DRY BREADCRUMBS | 250 ML |
| 1 TSP. | LEMON PEPPER OR BLACK PEPPER | 5 ML |
| ½ TSP. | SALT | 2 ML |
| 2 | EGGS, BEATEN | 2 |
| 1 CUP | DRY BREADCRUMBS | 250 ML |
| 2 TSP. | VEGETABLE OIL | 10 ML |
| 2 TSP. | BUTTER | 10 ML |

## LEMON CAPER MAYONNAISE

| | | |
|---|---|---|
| ½ CUP | MAYONNAISE | 125 ML |
| 2 TBSP. | FRESH LEMON JUICE | 30 ML |
| 1 TBSP. | SMALL CAPERS | 15 ML |
| 1 TBSP. | CHOPPED FRESH DILL OR 1 TSP. (5 ML) DRIED DILL | 15 ML |
| PINCH | CAYENNE PEPPER | PINCH |

DRAIN SALMON; PLACE IN BOWL AND FLAKE WITH A FORK. ADD PARSLEY, ONION, CELERY, BREAD-CRUMBS, LEMON PEPPER, SALT AND EGGS; BLEND WELL. DIVIDE INTO 4 BALLS AND ROLL IN BREAD-CRUMBS; FLATTEN INTO PATTIES. IN A LARGE FRYING PAN, HEAT OIL AND BUTTER OVER MEDIUM HEAT. COOK PATTIES, TURNING ONCE, UNTIL CRISP AND GOLDEN.

TO MAKE LEMON CAPER MAYONNAISE: COMBINE INGREDIENTS; COVER; REFRIGERATE UNTIL SERVING.

# ROASTED SALMON SALAD
## WITH HONEY MUSTARD VINAIGRETTE

DELICIOUS AND HEALTHY TOO!

### HONEY MUSTARD VINAIGRETTE

| | | |
|---|---|---|
| 1/2 CUP | BALSAMIC VINEGAR | 125 ML |
| 1/2 CUP | WATER | 125 ML |
| 2 TBSP. | DRIED CRANBERRIES | 30 ML |
| 8 | DRIED APRICOTS, SLICED | 8 |
| 2 TSP. | DIJON MUSTARD | 10 ML |
| 2 TSP. | HONEY | 10 ML |
| 1 TBSP. | OLIVE OIL | 15 ML |

### SALAD

| | | |
|---|---|---|
| 1 LB. | SALMON FILLET, CUT INTO 4 EQUAL PORTIONS | 500 G |
| 1/2 TSP. | SALT | 2 ML |
| 1/4 TSP. | PEPPER | 1 ML |
| 8 CUPS | SPINACH LEAVES, STEMS REMOVED & WASHED | 2 L |
| 2 CUPS | SLICED YELLOW PEPPERS | 500 ML |
| 2 CUPS | SLICED RED PEPPERS | 500 ML |
| 3 TBSP. | CHOPPED TOASTED PECANS | 45 ML |

TO MAKE VINAIGRETTE: IN A SMALL SAUCEPAN, COMBINE BALSAMIC VINEGAR, WATER, CRANBERRIES AND APRICOTS. SET PAN OVER MEDIUM-HIGH HEAT AND BRING TO A BOIL. SIMMER FOR 5 MINUTES. STRAIN AND RESERVE LIQUID AND FRUITS. COMBINE LIQUID WITH MUSTARD, HONEY AND OIL. SET ASIDE.

## ROASTED SALMON SALAD
## WITH HONEY MUSTARD VINAIGRETTE

CONTINUED FROM PAGE 174.

PREHEAT OVEN TO 425°F (220°C). LIGHTLY COAT A BAKING SHEET WITH COOKING SPRAY. SEASON SALMON FILLETS WITH SALT AND PEPPER AND TRANSFER THEM TO BAKING SHEET. BAKE FOR 5-7 MINUTES, UNTIL FORK-TENDER.

DIVIDE SPINACH AMONG 4 PLATES. TOP WITH YELLOW AND RED PEPPERS. PLACE A COOKED SALMON FILLET ON TOP OF EACH SALAD AND SPRINKLE WITH TOASTED PECANS. DRIZZLE DRESSING OVER AND ADD SOME OF THE RESERVED FRUIT. (PICTURED OPPOSITE PAGE 163.)

AN OLDER WOMAN WILL NEVER WAKE YOU IN THE MIDDLE
OF THE NIGHT TO ASK WHAT YOU THINK.
THEY DON'T CARE WHAT YOU THINK.

# GRILLED MARINATED HALIBUT

## MARINADE

| | | |
|---|---|---|
| 1/4 TSP. | BLACK PEPPER | 1 ML |
| 1/4 TSP. | SALT | 1 ML |
| 1/4 TSP. | PAPRIKA | 1 ML |
| 1 TSP. | FENNEL SEED, CRUSHED | 5 ML |
| 2 TBSP. | TERIYAKI SAUCE | 30 ML |
| 2 TBSP. | OLIVE OIL | 30 ML |
| | JUICE OF 2 LIMES | |
| 4 | LIME WEDGES | 4 |
| | | |
| 4 | HALIBUT STEAKS, CUT 1" (2.5 CM) THICK | 4 |

TO MAKE MARINADE: COMBINE ALL INGREDIENTS. POUR MARINADE OVER HALIBUT IN A SHALLOW DISH. REFRIGERATE 1 HOUR.

GRILL OVER MEDIUM-HIGH HEAT (OR UNDER BROILER) 5 MINUTES EACH SIDE, OR UNTIL FISH IS JUST OPAQUE IN MIDDLE. SERVE WITH STEAMED BASMATI RICE, SESAME SPINACH, PAGE 145, AND DILL AND PARMESAN TOMATOES, PAGE 147. (PICTURED OPPOSITE PAGE 180.)

BORROW MONEY FROM PESSIMISTS - THEY DON'T EXPECT IT BACK.

# WILD WEST SALMON

## SCRUMPTIOUS COMPANY FARE FOR THE BARBECUE SEASON

| | | |
|---|---|---|
| I | WHOLE SALMON, BUTTERFLIED (SEE METHOD) | I |

### MARINADE

| | | |
|---|---|---|
| I TBSP. | BROWN SUGAR | 15 ML |
| ½ CUP | RYE WHISKEY | 125 ML |
| I TBSP. | MOLASSES | 15 ML |
| ½ CUP | VEGETABLE OIL | 125 ML |
| 2 TBSP. | SOY SAUCE | 30 ML |
| I TBSP. | EACH SALT & PEPPER | 15 ML |
| 2 | GARLIC CLOVES, MINCED | |

TO PREPARE SALMON: REMOVE HEAD, TAIL AND FINS FROM SALMON. RUN A SHARP KNIFE DOWN BACKBONE UNTIL SALMON OPENS FLAT. REMOVE BACKBONE. PLACE FLESH-SIDE DOWN IN A LARGE DISH.

COMBINE MARINADE INGREDIENTS; MIX WELL AND POUR OVER SALMON. COVER AND MARINATE OVERNIGHT IN REFRIGERATOR.

WHEN READY TO GRILL, REMOVE SALMON FROM MARINADE AND PLACE SKIN-SIDE DOWN ON HEAVY FOIL. BARBECUE UNTIL FLESH IS OPAQUE AND FLAKES EASILY, 20-30 MINUTES. SERVE WITH CRUSTY ROLLS.

# CEDAR PLANK SALMON
## WITH CUCUMBER DILL SAUCE

| | | |
|---|---|---|
| 1 | UNTREATED CEDAR PLANK | 1 |
| 2 | SHALLOTS, DICED | 2 |
| 10 | GARLIC CLOVES, MINCED | 10 |
| 3 TBSP. | SNIPPED FRESH DILL | 45 ML |
| 3 TBSP. | CHOPPED FRESH THYME | 45 ML |
| 2 TBSP. | CHOPPED FRESH CILANTRO | 30 ML |
| 2 TBSP. | GRATED LEMON ZEST | 30 ML |
| 3 TBSP. | FRESH LEMON JUICE | 45 ML |
| 2 | GREEN ONIONS, CHOPPED | 2 |
| 1 TSP. | OLIVE OIL | 5 ML |
| 3-4 LB. | SALMON FILLET | 1.5-2 KG |
| | SALT & FRESHLY GROUND PEPPER | |
| | TO TASTE | |

CUCUMBER DILL SAUCE

| | | |
|---|---|---|
| 1/4 | ENGLISH CUCUMBER, FINELY CHOPPED | 1/4 |
| 1/4 TSP. | SALT | 1 ML |
| 1 CUP | PLAIN YOGURT | 250 ML |
| 1/2 CUP | SOUR CREAM | 125 ML |
| 1 TSP. | LEMON JUICE | 5 ML |
| | PEPPER TO TASTE | |
| 3 | GREEN ONIONS, FINELY CHOPPED, | 3 |
| | WHITE PART ONLY | |
| 2 TSP. | CHOPPED FRESH DILL OR | 10 ML |
| | 1 TSP. (5 ML) DRIED DILL | |

SOAK CEDAR PLANK IN WATER FOR SEVERAL HOURS.

# CEDAR PLANK SALMON
## WITH CUCUMBER DILL SAUCE

CONTINUED FROM PAGE 178.

IN A SMALL GLASS BOWL, COMBINE SHALLOTS, GARLIC, DILL, THYME, CILANTRO, LEMON ZEST AND JUICE, GREEN ONIONS AND OIL. COVER AND PLACE IN REFRIGERATOR FOR AT LEAST 1 HOUR TO ALLOW FLAVORS TO GET ACQUAINTED.

PLACE SALMON ON CEDAR PLANK AND SPRINKLE WITH SALT AND PEPPER. COVER WITH HERB MIXTURE. SET PLANK ON BARBECUE AND CLOSE LID. BAKE FOR 30 MINUTES ON MEDIUM HEAT, UNTIL FISH FLAKES EASILY WITH A FORK.

TO PREPARE CUCUMBER DILL SAUCE: TOSS CUCUMBER WITH SALT AND LET STAND FOR 15 MINUTES.

COMBINE YOGURT, SOUR CREAM, LEMON JUICE, PEPPER, ONION AND DILL.

DRAIN WATER FROM CUCUMBER AND ADD TO YOGURT MIXTURE. SERVES 8.

THE PROBLEM WITH THE GENE POOL IS THAT THERE IS NO LIFEGUARD.

# LAYERED TUNA CASSEROLE

DOWN-HOME COOKIN'! A TASTY FAMILY CASSEROLE THAT TAKES ABOUT 20 MINUTES TO PREPARE, 30 MINUTES TO COOK AND HOW LONG IT TAKES TO EAT IS UP TO YOU!

| | | |
|---|---|---|
| 2 | 6½ OZ. (184 G) CANS CHUNK-STYLE TUNA, PACKED IN WATER | 2 |
| 3 CUPS | UNCOOKED EGG NOODLES | 750 ML |
| ½ CUP | CHOPPED CELERY | 125 ML |
| ⅓ CUP | FINELY CHOPPED GREEN ONIONS | 75 ML |
| ⅔ CUP | SOUR CREAM | 150 ML |
| 2 TSP. | DRY MUSTARD | 10 ML |
| ½ CUP | MAYONNAISE | 125 ML |
| ½ TSP. | THYME | 2 ML |
| ¼ TSP. | SALT | 1 ML |
| 1 | MEDIUM ZUCCHINI, SLICED | 1 |
| ½ CUP | GRATED MOZZARELLA CHEESE | 125 ML |
| ½ CUP | GRATED CHEDDAR CHEESE | 125 ML |
| 1 | TOMATO, CHOPPED (OPTIONAL) | 1 |

DRAIN AND FLAKE TUNA. SET ASIDE. COOK NOODLES ACCORDING TO PACKAGE DIRECTIONS. DRAIN; RINSE IN HOT WATER. COMBINE TUNA, NOODLES, CELERY AND ONIONS. BLEND TOGETHER SOUR CREAM, MUSTARD, MAYONNAISE, THYME AND SALT AND MIX INTO TUNA MIXTURE. SPOON HALF OF THIS MIXTURE INTO A GREASED 2 QUART (2 L) CASSEROLE. TOP WITH HALF THE ZUCCHINI. REPEAT LAYERS AND TOP WITH GRATED CHEESES. BAKE AT 350°F (180°C) FOR 30-40 MINUTES. TOP WITH CHOPPED TOMATO. SERVES 8.

Grilled Marinated Halibut, page 176
Sesame Spinach, page 145

Braised Lamb Shanks with Lentils, page 206

# CHICKEN

Skewers of Sticky Garlic Chicken
Thai Grilled Chicken
Chicken Burritos
Chicken Scallopini with Lemon-Caper Glaze
Spicy Orange Chicken Stir-Fry
Jerk Chicken with Pineapple-Rum Glaze
Chicken Curry
Sweet 'n' Speedy Chicken
Chicken, Artichoke and Wild Rice Casserole
Chicken Stew with Dumplings
Yummy Chicken
No-Fuss Moroccan Chicken
Roasted Thighs 'n' Peppers
Thigh Chicken
Pheasant Pie in Herb Pastry

# SKEWERS OF STICKY GARLIC CHICKEN

PREPARE THE NIGHT BEFORE AND COOK WHEN YOU WANT THEM. GREAT AS A MEAL OR APPETIZER.

| 12 | 10" (25 CM) WOODEN SKEWERS | 12 |

### GARLIC HONEY MARINADE

| 3 | GARLIC CLOVES, CRUSHED | 3 |
| 2 TBSP. | HONEY | 30 ML |
| 1/4 CUP | KETCHUP | 60 ML |
| 1/4 CUP | WORCESTERSHIRE SAUCE | 60 ML |
| 2 TSP. | DIJON MUSTARD | 10 ML |
| 2 TSP. | TABASCO | 10 ML |
| | SALT & PEPPER TO TASTE | |
| 3 | SKINLESS, BONELESS CHICKEN BREASTS, CUT IN THIN STRIPS | 3 |

SOAK SKEWERS IN WATER AT LEAST 30 MINUTES.

TO MAKE MARINADE: COMBINE ALL INGREDIENTS.

TOSS CHICKEN IN MARINADE AND STIR UNTIL WELL COATED. TRANSFER TO A NON-METALLIC DISH; COVER AND MARINATE OVERNIGHT.

PREHEAT BROILER TO HIGH. THREAD CHICKEN ONTO SKEWERS. ARRANGE ON A FOIL-LINED BAKING SHEET AND BROIL FOR 6-7 MINUTES, TURNING OCCASIONALLY, UNTIL WELL BROWNED AND COOKED THROUGH. THESE CAN ALSO BE GRILLED ON THE BARBECUE FOR 5-6 MINUTES.

# THAI GRILLED CHICKEN

SERVE WITH THAI NOODLE SALAD, PAGE 95.

MARINADE

| | | |
|---|---|---:|
| 1/3 CUP | FRESH BASIL | 75 ML |
| 1/3 CUP | FRESH MINT | 75 ML |
| 1/3 CUP | FRESH CILANTRO | 75 ML |
| 3 TBSP. | PEELED, CHOPPED GINGER | 45 ML |
| 2-3 | GARLIC CLOVES | 2-3 |
| 1 1/2 TBSP. | SOY SAUCE | 22 ML |
| 1 1/2 TBSP. | FISH SAUCE | 22 ML |
| 1 1/2 TBSP. | VEGETABLE OIL | 22 ML |
| 1 1/2 TBSP. | BROWN SUGAR | 22 ML |
| 1 | ANAHEIM PEPPER, CHOPPED | 1 |
| 6 | SKINLESS, BONELESS CHICKEN BREAST HALVES (2 LBS./1 KG) | 6 |

TO MAKE MARINADE: PROCESS ALL INGREDIENTS IN FOOD PROCESSOR OR BLENDER UNTIL FINELY CHOPPED.

ARRANGE CHICKEN IN A GLASS BAKING DISH. POUR MARINADE OVER. COVER AND REFRIGERATE SEVERAL HOURS OR OVERNIGHT. REMOVE CHICKEN FROM MARINADE AND GRILL UNTIL CHICKEN IS NO LONGER PINK IN THE MIDDLE.

EXPERIENCE IS SOMETHING YOU DON'T GET UNTIL JUST AFTER YOU NEED IT.

| | | |
|---|---|---|
| 4 | BONELESS CHICKEN BREASTS, SLICED IN THIN STRIPS | 4 |
| 1 TBSP. | OLIVE OIL | 15 ML |
| 2 CUPS | SOUR CREAM | 500 ML |
| 4 OZ. | CAN CHOPPED GREEN CHILIES | 115 G |
| 1 CUP | GRATED MONTEREY JACK CHEESE | 250 ML |
| 8 | MEDIUM FLOUR TORTILLAS | 8 |
| 1 CUP | GRATED SHARP CHEDDAR CHEESE | 250 ML |
| 1/2 | HEAD LETTUCE, SHREDDED | 1/2 |
| 2 | TOMATOES, DICED | 2 |
| 4 | GREEN ONIONS, CHOPPED | 4 |
| | RIPE OLIVES, SLICED | |

GUACAMOLE

| | | |
|---|---|---|
| 2 | AVOCADOS, PEELED & MASHED | 2 |
| | JUICE OF 1/2 LEMON | |
| 1 TBSP. | CHILI POWDER | 15 ML |
| 1/4 TSP. | CAYENNE PEPPER | 1 ML |
| 1 TBSP. | WORCESTERSHIRE SAUCE | 15 ML |
| 1 | GARLIC CLOVE, MINCED | 1 |
| 2 | DROPS TABASCO SAUCE | 2 |

SAUTÉ CHICKEN IN OIL UNTIL JUST DONE. REMOVE FROM HEAT. STIR IN 1 CUP (250 ML) SOUR CREAM, CHILIES AND JACK CHEESE. FILL TORTILLAS AND FOLD OVER BURRITO-STYLE. PLACE SIDE BY SIDE IN LIGHTLY GREASED CASSEROLE. SPRINKLE WITH CHEDDAR. BAKE AT 350°F (180°C) FOR 20 MINUTES, OR UNTIL CHEESE MELTS. REMOVE FROM OVEN; TOP WITH GUACAMOLE, REMAINING SOUR CREAM, LETTUCE, TOMATOES, ONIONS AND OLIVES.

TO MAKE GUACAMOLE: COMBINE ALL INGREDIENTS.

# CHICKEN SCALOPPINE WITH LEMON-CAPER GLAZE

| 4 | BONELESS, SKINLESS CHICKEN BREAST HALVES | 4 |
|---|---|---|
| 2 TBSP. | DIJON MUSTARD | 30 ML |
| 2 | EGGS | 2 |
| I CUP | DRY BREADCRUMBS | 250 ML |
| 1/2 TSP. | POULTRY SEASONING | 2 ML |
| 1/2 TSP. | GARLIC POWDER | 2 ML |
| 1/2 TSP. | SEASONING SALT | 2 ML |
| 2 TBSP. | OLIVE OIL | 30 ML |
| 1/4 CUP | CHICKEN BROTH | 60 ML |
| 2 TBSP. | FRESH LEMON JUICE | 30 ML |
| 4 TSP. | CAPERS | 20 ML |
| 1/4 TSP. | SALT | I ML |
| 4 | THIN LEMON SLICES | 4 |
|  | FRESH PARSLEY, CHOPPED |  |

PLACE CHICKEN BREASTS BETWEEN WAX PAPER; LIGHTLY POUND TO 1/3" (I CM) THICK. WHISK MUSTARD AND EGGS TOGETHER. SET ASIDE. COMBINE BREADCRUMBS, POULTRY SEASONING, GARLIC POWDER AND SEASONING SALT; SPREAD ON WAX PAPER. DIP CHICKEN IN EGG MIXTURE AND COAT WITH CRUMB MIXTURE. HEAT HALF THE OIL AND ADD HALF THE CHICKEN. SAUTÉ FOR 5 MINUTES EACH SIDE, OR UNTIL NO LONGER PINK INSIDE. REMOVE TO PLATE AND KEEP WARM. REPEAT WITH REMAINING CHICKEN. IN THE SAME PAN, ADD BROTH, LEMON JUICE, CAPERS AND SALT; BRING TO A BOIL, SCRAPING BROWN BITS FROM PAN. ADD LEMON SLICES AND PARSLEY. SPOON LEMON GLAZE OVER CHICKEN. SERVES 4.

# SPICY ORANGE CHICKEN STIR-FRY

WE LIKE THE SIMPLICITY OF THIS RECIPE – AND THE ORANGE FLAVOR!

## MARINADE

| | | |
|---|---|---|
| I TBSP. | SOY SAUCE | 15 ML |
| I TBSP. | DRY SHERRY | 15 ML |
| I TBSP. | OYSTER SAUCE | 15 ML |
| 2 TSP. | GRATED ORANGE ZEST | 10 ML |
| | | |
| 4 | BONELESS, SKINLESS CHICKEN BREAST HALVES, CUT INTO 1/2" (1.3 CM) CUBES | 4 |
| 2 | RED PEPPERS | 2 |
| I | SMALL ZUCCHINI | I |
| I | LARGE ONION | I |

## SPICY ORANGE SAUCE

| | | |
|---|---|---|
| | JUICE OF I ORANGE | |
| 1/4 CUP | DRY SHERRY | 60 ML |
| I TBSP. | OYSTER SAUCE | 15 ML |
| I TBSP. | SESAME OIL | 15 ML |
| 2-4 TSP. | ASIAN CHILI SAUCE | 10-20 ML |
| I TBSP. | CORNSTARCH | 15 ML |
| | | |
| 3 TBSP. | COOKING OIL | 45 ML |
| 4 | GARLIC CLOVES, MINCED | 4 |
| I" | PIECE FRESH GINGERROOT, PEELED & CHOPPED | 2.5 CM |

TO MAKE MARINADE: COMBINE ALL INGREDIENTS. ADD CHICKEN TO MARINADE AND MARINATE 15 MINUTES AT ROOM TEMPERATURE.

# SPICY ORANGE CHICKEN STIR-FRY

CONTINUED FROM PAGE 186.

SEED AND STEM PEPPERS. CUT INTO ½" (1.3 CM) CUBES. CUT ZUCCHINI LENGTHWISE (DON'T PEEL) INTO 4 STRIPS. CUT EACH STRIP CROSSWISE INTO ½" (1.3 CM) PIECES. PEEL ONION AND CUT INTO THIN WEDGES. CUT EACH WEDGE IN HALF. COMBINE VEGGIES IN BOWL.

YOU'RE PROBABLY WONDERING WHY YOU HAVE TO CUT EVERYTHING INTO UNIFORM SIZES! NOT ONLY DO THE INGREDIENTS COOK EVENLY, THEY LOOK CAREFULLY CONSIDERED. VERY ZEN!

TO MAKE SPICY ORANGE SAUCE: COMBINE ORANGE JUICE, SHERRY, OYSTER SAUCE, SESAME OIL, CHILI SAUCE AND CORNSTARCH IN A SMALL BOWL. SET ASIDE.

PLACE A WOK OR HEAVY FRYING PAN OVER HIGH HEAT. WHEN WOK BECOMES HOT, ADD 2 TBSP. (30 ML) OIL. WHEN OIL SMOKES, ADD CHICKEN AND STIR 2 MINUTES. REMOVE TO PLATE. ADD REMAINING 1 TBSP. (15 ML) OIL WITH GARLIC AND GINGER. STIR FOR 5 SECONDS. ADD VEGGIES AND STIR 2 MINUTES. ADD SPICY ORANGE SAUCE AND CHICKEN AND STIR UNTIL SAUCE THICKENS. SERVE IMMEDIATELY WITH STEAMED RICE. SERVES 4.

# JERK CHICKEN WITH PINEAPPLE-RUM GLAZE

GREAT FOR GRILLING - IN SHORTS OR A PARKA - IT'S THAT GOOD!

<u>RUB</u>

| | | |
|---|---|---|
| 1 TBSP. | DARK BROWN SUGAR | 15 ML |
| 1½ TSP. | COARSE SALT | 7 ML |
| 1 TSP. | CORIANDER | 5 ML |
| ½ TSP. | FRESHLY GROUND PEPPER | 2 ML |
| ½ TSP. | DRIED THYME | 2 ML |
| ½ TSP. | ONION POWDER | 2 ML |
| ½ TSP. | ALLSPICE | 2 ML |
| ½ TSP. | CINNAMON | 2 ML |
| ¼-½ TSP. | CAYENNE PEPPER | 1-2 ML |
| | | |
| 8-10 | CHICKEN LEGS, RINSED & PATTED DRY | 8-10 |
| 1½ TBSP. | VEGETABLE OIL | 22 ML |
| 2 | GARLIC CLOVES, MINCED | 2 |
| 2 | GREEN ONIONS, MINCED | 2 |

<u>PINEAPPLE-RUM GLAZE</u>

| | | |
|---|---|---|
| ¼ CUP | BUTTER | 60 ML |
| ¼ CUP | PACKED DARK BROWN SUGAR | 60 ML |
| ¼ CUP | DARK RUM | 60 ML |
| ¼ CUP | PINEAPPLE JUICE | 60 ML |

TO MAKE RUB: COMBINE SUGAR, SALT, CORIANDER, PEPPER, THYME, ONION POWDER, ALLSPICE, CINNAMON AND CAYENNE.

PLACE CHICKEN IN A 9 X 13" (23 X 33 CM) PAN AND DRIZZLE WITH OIL, RUBBING IT OVER THE CHICKEN ON ALL SIDES.

# JERK CHICKEN WITH PINEAPPLE-RUM GLAZE

CONTINUED FROM PAGE 188.

SPRINKLE THE RUB, GARLIC AND ONIONS ON THE CHICKEN, PATTING SEASONINGS INTO MEAT WITH YOUR FINGERS. REFRIGERATE AT LEAST I HOUR.

TO MAKE GLAZE: COMBINE BUTTER, SUGAR, RUM AND PINEAPPLE JUICE IN A HEAVY SAUCEPAN. SIMMER 7-10 MINUTES OVER MEDIUM-HIGH HEAT.

OIL THE GRILL AND HEAT BARBECUE TO HIGH. ARRANGE CHICKEN ON GRILL. BRUSH WITH GLAZE AND COOK, TURNING REGULARLY, UNTIL BROWN AND NO LONGER PINK INSIDE. SERVE DRIZZLED WITH ANY REMAINING GLAZE.

I LOVE MEN WHO CAN MAKE THINGS.
HOW MUCH DO YOU MAKE?

# CHICKEN CURRY

| | | |
|---|---|---:|
| 4 LBS. | BONELESS, SKINLESS CHICKEN BREASTS (APPROX. 8 BREASTS) CUT CROSSWISE IN 1/2" (1.3 CM) SLICES | 2 KG |
| 3 TBSP. | OIL | 45 ML |
| 3 CUPS | CHOPPED ONION | 750 ML |
| 1/4 CUP | MINCED FRESH GINGER | 60 ML |
| 3 | CLOVES GARLIC, MINCED | 3 |
| 3 TBSP. | CURRY POWDER (MORE IF YOU WANT IT HOTTER) | 45 ML |
| 1 TSP. | CUMIN | 5 ML |
| 1/4 TSP. | CINNAMON | 1 ML |
| 2 TBSP. | FLOUR | 30 ML |
| 1 CUP | PLAIN YOGURT | 250 ML |
| 3 TBSP. | TOMATO PASTE | 45 ML |
| 3 CUPS | CHICKEN BROTH | 750 ML |
| 1 CUP | APPLESAUCE | 250 ML |
| 12 OZ. | PKG. FROZEN PEAS | 340 G |
| 1/2 CUP | SOUR CREAM | 125 ML |
| 1/2 CUP | COCONUT MILK | 125 ML |

CONDIMENTS

MANGO CHUTNEY, DICED CUCUMBER, DICED BANANAS, CURRANTS, SHREDDED COCONUT & CHOPPED PEANUTS

IN A LARGE FRYING PAN, BROWN CHICKEN IN OIL; REMOVE AND SET ASIDE. ADD ONION AND SAUTÉ UNTIL GOLDEN. ADD GINGER AND GARLIC AND SAUTÉ ABOUT 1 MINUTE. ADD CURRY, CUMIN AND CINNAMON AND MIX WELL. COOK FOR 1 MINUTE. ADD FLOUR, YOGURT AND TOMATO PASTE, WHISKING UNTIL SAUCE IS SMOOTH.

## CHICKEN CURRY

CONTINUED FROM PAGE 190.

POUR IN BROTH AND APPLESAUCE AND SIMMER, UNCOVERED, UNTIL MIXTURE THICKENS (APPROXIMATELY 30 MINUTES). ADD BROWNED CHICKEN (AND ANY JUICE), FROZEN PEAS, SOUR CREAM AND COCONUT MILK. SIMMER ANOTHER 15 MINUTES. SERVE OVER BASMATI RICE WITH A VARIETY OF CONDIMENTS. SERVES 6-8.

## SWEET 'N' SPEEDY CHICKEN

FAST AND TASTY! SERVES 4 DEPENDING ON THE SIZE OF YOUR THIGHS!

| | | |
|---|---|---|
| 6 | CHICKEN THIGHS, BONELESS, SKIN ON OR OFF | 6 |
| | SALT & PEPPER TO TASTE | |
| 1/4 CUP | JALAPEÑO PEPPER JELLY | 60 ML |
| 2 TSP. | LIQUID HONEY | 10 ML |
| 1 TSP. | DIJON MUSTARD | 5 ML |

PREHEAT OVEN TO 425°F (220°C). LINE A 9 X 13" (23 X 33 CM) BAKING DISH WITH FOIL. SALT AND PEPPER CHICKEN AND PLACE IN A DISH. COMBINE JELLY, HONEY AND MUSTARD AND SPREAD OVER CHICKEN. BAKE FOR 30 MINUTES, UNCOVERED. BASTE AT LEAST ONCE DURING COOKING. SERVE OVER RICE. SERVES 4.

# CHICKEN, ARTICHOKE AND WILD RICE CASSEROLE

AN "ENTERTAINING" CASSEROLE.

| | | |
|---|---|---|
| 3 CUPS | WATER | 750 ML |
| I CUP | WILD RICE | 250 ML |
| 1/2 TSP. | SALT | 2 ML |
| I TBSP. | BUTTER | 15 ML |
| I CUP | CHOPPED ONION | 250 ML |
| I CUP | THINLY SLICED CELERY | 250 ML |
| I CUP | SHREDDED CARROT | 250 ML |
| 1 3/4 CUPS | CHICKEN BROTH | 425 ML |
| 2 CUPS | LIGHT CREAM | 500 ML |
| 1/4 CUP | FLOUR | 60 ML |
| 3/4 TSP. | SALT | 3 ML |
| 2 TBSP. | SHERRY | 30 ML |
| | FRESHLY GROUND PEPPER | |
| 3 CUPS | COOKED CUBED CHICKEN | 750 ML |
| 14 OZ. | CAN ARTICHOKES, DRAINED & CHOPPED | 398 ML |
| 1/3 CUP | TOASTED SLICED ALMONDS | 75 ML |

IN A MEDIUM-SIZED SAUCEPAN, BRING WATER TO A BOIL. STIR IN RICE AND SALT. COVER AND SIMMER 45-55 MINUTES, OR UNTIL RICE IS TENDER BUT STILL CHEWY. DRAIN RICE IN A COLANDER. MELT BUTTER IN A LARGE FRYING PAN OVER MEDIUM HEAT. ADD ONION, CELERY AND CARROT; COOK 10 MINUTES, STIRRING OCCASIONALLY, UNTIL SOFTENED. ADD BROTH TO VEGGIES IN FRYING PAN AND BRING TO A BOIL.

# CHICKEN, ARTICHOKE AND
# WILD RICE CASSEROLE

CONTINUED FROM PAGE 192.

IN A BOWL, WHISK CREAM AND FLOUR UNTIL SMOOTH. GRADUALLY WHISK INTO BOILING BROTH. ADD SALT, SHERRY AND PEPPER. BRING TO A BOIL. REDUCE HEAT AND SIMMER 5 MINUTES, STIRRING OCCASIONALLY. ADD RICE TO SAUCE. ADD CHICKEN AND ARTICHOKES TO SAUCE AND MIX WELL. POUR MIXTURE INTO A SHALLOW $2\frac{1}{2}$-3 QUART (2-3 L) BAKING DISH. COVER AND BAKE AT 350°F (180°C) FOR 35-40 MINUTES, OR UNTIL HOT AND BUBBLY. SPRINKLE WITH ALMONDS. SERVES 8-10.

IF YOU THINK IT'S HARD TO MEET NEW PEOPLE, TRY PICKING UP THE WRONG GOLF BALL. - JACK LEMMON.

# CHICKEN STEW WITH DUMPLINGS

HERE IT IS - THAT OLD STANDARD - AND IT'S EXACTLY WHAT YOU'D EXPECT - COMFORT FOOD!

## THE STEW

| | | |
|---|---|---|
| 5 CUPS | CHICKEN BROTH | 1.25 L |
| 14 | CHICKEN THIGHS, SKINNED | 2 KG |
| 7 | MEDIUM CARROTS, PEELED & CUT IN CHUNKS | 7 |
| 4 | POTATOES, PEELED & CUT IN 1" (2.5 CM) CUBES | 4 |
| 8 | BOILING ONIONS, PEELED | 8 |
| 3 TBSP. | BUTTER | 45 ML |
| 3 | STALKS CELERY, CHOPPED | 3 |
| 1 | ONION, CHOPPED | 1 |
| 8 OZ. | SMALL BUTTON MUSHROOMS | 250 G |
| 1/3 CUP | FLOUR | 75 ML |
| 1/2-1 TSP. | DRIED THYME OR TARRAGON | 2-5 ML |
| | SALT & PEPPER TO TASTE | |
| 1/2 CUP | FROZEN PEAS | 125 ML |
| 1/4 CUP | WHIPPING CREAM | 60 ML |

## THE DUMPLINGS

| | | |
|---|---|---|
| 1 1/2 CUPS | FLOUR | 375 ML |
| 2 TSP. | BAKING POWDER | 10 ML |
| 1/2 TSP. | SALT | 2 ML |
| 2/3 CUP | MILK | 150 ML |
| 2 TBSP. | OIL | 30 ML |
| 1 | EGG, SLIGHTLY BEATEN | 1 |
| 1 TBSP. | CHOPPED PARSLEY (OPTIONAL) | 15 ML |

TO MAKE STEW: IN A LARGE DUTCH OVEN, BRING BROTH TO A BOIL. ADD CHICKEN, COVER AND SIMMER OVER MEDIUM-LOW HEAT FOR 30 MINUTES. TRANSFER TO A PLATE AND LET COOL.

# CHICKEN STEW WITH DUMPLINGS

CONTINUED FROM PAGE 194.

CUT MEAT INTO BITE-SIZE PIECES. ADD CARROTS AND POTATOES TO BROTH; COVER AND COOK FOR 10 MINUTES. ADD ONIONS AND SIMMER, COVERED, UNTIL ONIONS ARE TENDER, ABOUT 5 MINUTES. TRANSFER VEGETABLES TO A PLATE. POUR BROTH INTO A LARGE MEASURING CUP, ADDING MORE BROTH IF NECESSARY TO MAKE 5 CUPS (1.25 L). USING THE SAME POT, MELT BUTTER AND COOK CELERY, ONION AND MUSHROOMS, STIRRING OFTEN, UNTIL SOFTENED. ADD FLOUR, THYME, SALT AND PEPPER. COOK AND STIR FOR 1 MINUTE. GRADUALLY WHISK IN BROTH AND BRING TO A BOIL, STIRRING. REDUCE HEAT TO MEDIUM-LOW; SIMMER, STIRRING OFTEN, FOR ABOUT 5 MINUTES. RETURN CHICKEN AND JUICES TO POT. STIR IN VEGETABLE MIXTURE, PEAS AND CREAM.

TO MAKE DUMPLINGS: IN A MEDIUM BOWL, COMBINE FLOUR, BAKING POWDER AND SALT. MIX MILK, OIL AND EGG TOGETHER AND ADD TO FLOUR MIXTURE. STIR UNTIL DRY INGREDIENTS ARE JUST MOISTENED. DROP DUMPLING DOUGH BY ROUNDED TABLESPOONFULS ONTO BOILING STEW, LEAVING SPACE AROUND EACH. REDUCE HEAT, COVER TIGHTLY (DON'T PEEK!) AND SIMMER 15 MINUTES, OR UNTIL DUMPLINGS ARE FLUFFY AND NO LONGER DOUGHY ON BOTTOM. SERVES 8.

# YUMMY CHICKEN

THE NAME SAYS IT ALL!

| | | |
|---|---|---:|
| ¼ CUP | FLOUR | 50 ML |
| 2 TSP. | SALT | 10 ML |
| ¼ TSP. | PEPPER | 1 ML |
| | DASH OF THYME | |
| ¼ CUP | MELTED BUTTER | 60 ML |
| 3-4 LBS. | CUT-UP CHICKEN | 1.5-2 KG |
| 4 | GREEN ONIONS, CHOPPED | 4 |
| ½ CUP | SLICED MUSHROOMS | 125 ML |
| 2 TBSP. | LEMON JUICE | 30 ML |
| 1 TSP. | SUGAR | 5 ML |
| 1 TSP. | SALT | 5 ML |
| ⅓ CUP | APPLE JUICE | 75 ML |

MIX FLOUR, SALT, PEPPER AND THYME IN A PLASTIC BAG. SHAKE CHICKEN IN FLOUR MIXTURE TO COAT WELL. MELT BUTTER IN A LARGE FRYING PAN AND BROWN CHICKEN. REMOVE CHICKEN TO A CASSEROLE. ADD GREEN ONIONS AND MUSHROOMS TO FRYING PAN. COVER AND SIMMER FOR 3 MINUTES. ADD TO CASSEROLE. COMBINE LEMON JUICE, SUGAR, SALT AND APPLE JUICE. POUR OVER CHICKEN AND BAKE AT 325°F (160°C) FOR 1 HOUR. SERVES 6.

MY MIND WORKS LIKE LIGHTNING: ONE BRILLIANT FLASH AND IT'S GONE.

# — NO-FUSS MOROCCAN CHICKEN —

SERVE WITH RICE OR COUSCOUS.

| 2 TBSP. | VEGETABLE OIL | 30 ML |
| 1½ LBS. | BONELESS, SKINLESS CHICKEN BREAST HALVES | 750 G |
| ½ CUP | CHOPPED ONION | 125 ML |
| 1 | GARLIC CLOVE, MINCED | 1 |
| 2 CUPS | SALSA | 500 ML |
| ½ CUP | WATER | 125 ML |
| ¼ CUP | CURRANTS | 60 ML |
| 2 TBSP. | LIQUID HONEY | 30 ML |
| 1½ TSP. | CUMIN | 7 ML |
| 1 TSP. | CINNAMON | 5 ML |
| ½ CUP | TOASTED SLIVERED ALMONDS | 125 ML |

PREHEAT OVEN TO 325°F (160°C). HEAT OIL IN A LARGE FRYING PAN AND BROWN CHICKEN. PLACE CHICKEN IN A BAKING DISH. LIGHTLY SAUTÉ ONION AND GARLIC. SPOON OVER CHICKEN. COMBINE SALSA, WATER, CURRANTS, HONEY, CUMIN AND CINNAMON. POUR OVER CHICKEN. COVER AND BAKE FOR 1 HOUR. SPRINKLE WITH ALMONDS. SERVES 4.

I CHILD-PROOFED MY HOME BUT THEY STILL GET IN.

# ROASTED THIGHS 'N' PEPPERS

THIS RECIPE GOES TOGETHER IN MINUTES.

| | | |
|---|---|---|
| 8 | CHICKEN THIGHS (ABOUT 1½ LBS.) | 750 G |
| 4-6 | GARLIC CLOVES, HALVED | 4-6 |
| 3-4 | NEW POTATOES, QUARTERED | 3-4 |
| 1 | RED PEPPER, SEEDED, CUT LENGTHWISE INTO ½" (1.3 CM) STRIPS | 1 |
| 1 | GREEN PEPPER, SEEDED, CUT LENGTHWISE INTO ½" (1.3 CM) STRIPS | 1 |
| 1 | ONION, CUT INTO WEDGES | 1 |
| ½ TSP. | DRIED THYME | 2 ML |
| | SALT & FRESHLY GROUND PEPPER TO TASTE | |
| 1-2 TBSP. | OLIVE OIL | 15-30 ML |

PREHEAT OVEN TO 425°F (220°C). IN A 9 X 13" (23 X 33 CM) BAKING DISH, LIGHTLY COATED WITH COOKING SPRAY, TOSS ALL INGREDIENTS WITH OIL AND SPREAD IN A SINGLE LAYER. ROAST, UNCOVERED, UNTIL VEGETABLES ARE TENDER-CRISP, ABOUT 30 MINUTES. TURN CHICKEN AND VEGETABLES AND COOK UNTIL CHICKEN IS NO LONGER PINK IN THE CENTER, 15-20 MINUTES LONGER. ARRANGE ON A HEATED PLATTER AND SERVE IMMEDIATELY.

IF ALL IS LOST, WHERE IS IT?

sland Pork Tenderloin Salad, page 210

Chocolate Raspberry Truffle Squares, page 252

# THIGH CHICKEN

A MILD-FLAVORED CASSEROLE, BUT IF YOU REALLY WANT TO "THAI" ONE ON – ADD MORE HOT CHILI SAUCE.

| | | |
|---|---|---|
| 2 TBSP. | VEGETABLE OIL | 30 ML |
| 2 LBS. | CHICKEN THIGHS, SKIN REMOVED | 1 KG |
| 1 | MEDIUM ONION, CHOPPED | 1 |
| 1 | GARLIC CLOVE, MINCED | 1 |
| 1 TSP. | CORIANDER | 5 ML |
| 1 TSP. | CUMIN | 5 ML |
| 1 TSP. | SALT | 5 ML |
| 2 TSP. | GRATED FRESH GINGER | 10 ML |
| 2-3 TSP. | SWEET HOT ORIENTAL CHILI SAUCE | 10-15 ML |
| 2 TBSP. | SOY SAUCE | 30 ML |
| 2 TBSP. | PEANUT BUTTER | 30 ML |
| 14 OZ. | CAN COCONUT MILK | 398 ML |
| 1 TSP. | GRATED LIME ZEST | 5 ML |
| | JUICE OF 1 LIME | |

IN A DUTCH OVEN, HEAT OIL AND BROWN CHICKEN, ABOUT 15 MINUTES. SET ASIDE IN A LARGE CASSEROLE. SAUTÉ ONION AND GARLIC AND COOK UNTIL TENDER. STIR IN CORIANDER, CUMIN, SALT, GINGER, CHILI SAUCE, SOY SAUCE AND PEANUT BUTTER. ADD COCONUT MILK AND STIR TO BLEND. POUR SAUCE OVER CHICKEN; COVER AND COOK FOR 1 HOUR AT 325°F (160°C). JUST BEFORE SERVING, STIR IN LIME ZEST AND JUICE. SERVE OVER RICE.

# PHEASANT PIE IN HERB PASTRY

AN OLD FAVORITE WITH OUR NEW HERB PASTRY OR FROZEN PUFF PASTRY.

## THE BROTH

| | | |
|---|---|---|
| 2 | PHEASANTS | 2 |
| 6 CUPS | WATER | 1.5 L |
| 1 TSP. | SALT | 5 ML |
| 1 | MEDIUM ONION, PEELED & CUT IN HALF | 1 |
| 4 | WHOLE CLOVES | 4 |
| 2 | BAY LEAVES | 2 |
| 10 | PEPPERCORNS | 10 |

## THE SAUCE

| | | |
|---|---|---|
| 3 TBSP. | BUTTER | 45 ML |
| 1/4 CUP | FLOUR | 60 ML |
| 2 CUPS | PHEASANT BROTH | 500 ML |
| 1/2 CUP | WHIPPING CREAM | 125 ML |
| 3 | MEDIUM CARROTS, SLICED | 3 |
| 8 OZ. | MUSHROOMS, QUARTERED | 250 G |
| | SALT & PEPPER TO TASTE | |
| 1 CUP | PEAS, FRESH OR FROZEN | 250 ML |
| | HERB PASTRY (PAGE 202) | |
| | OR 7 OZ. (200 G) PKG. FROZEN PUFF PASTRY, ROOM TEMPERATURE | |

TO MAKE BROTH: CUT PHEASANTS INTO QUARTERS, WASH AND PLACE IN A LARGE POT (DON'T FORGET THE NECKS!). ADD WATER AND SALT AND BRING TO A BOIL. ADD ONION, CLOVES, BAY LEAVES AND PEPPERCORNS. SIMMER 1 HOUR, OR UNTIL MEAT IS TENDER. REMOVE MEAT, SET ASIDE AND LET COOL. STRAIN AND RESERVE BROTH.

# PHEASANT PIE IN HERB PASTRY

CONTINUED FROM PAGE 200.

TO MAKE SAUCE: MELT BUTTER IN A SAUCEPAN OVER MEDIUM HEAT. ADD FLOUR AND COOK FOR A FEW MINUTES, STIRRING CONSTANTLY. WHISK IN BROTH AND BRING TO BOIL. ADD CREAM, CARROTS AND MUSHROOMS AND SIMMER FOR 15 MINUTES. SPRINKLE WITH SALT AND PEPPER. ADD PEAS AND REMOVE FROM HEAT.

PREHEAT OVEN TO 400°F (200°C). REMOVE PHEASANT MEAT FROM BONES AND DISCARD SKIN. CUT MEAT INTO PIECES AND PLACE IN A 4-QUART (4 L) CASSEROLE. POUR SAUCE OVER PHEASANT. ROLL OUT HERB PASTRY (PAGE 202) TO 1/8" (3 MM) THICKNESS. COVER CASSEROLE WITH PASTRY AND MAKE SEVERAL SLASHES ON TOP. PLACE IN OVEN FOR 30 MINUTES, OR UNTIL PASTRY IS GOLDEN BROWN. SERVE WITH WILD RICE OR BOILED NEW POTATOES. SERVES 6.

I STARTED WITH NOTHING AND I HAVE MOST OF IT LEFT.

# HERB PASTRY

GREAT FOR CHICKEN PIE TOO!

| | | |
|---|---|---|
| 2½ CUPS | FLOUR | 625 ML |
| 2 TBSP. | CHOPPED FRESH PARSLEY | 30 ML |
| I TBSP. | CHOPPED FRESH THYME | 15 ML |
| I TSP. | SALT | 5 ML |
| I TSP. | SUGAR | 5 ML |
| ½ CUP | CHILLED UNSALTED BUTTER, CUT INTO ½" (1.3 CM) PIECES | 125 ML |
| ½ CUP | CHILLED SOLID VEGETABLE SHORTENING, CUT INTO ½" (1.3 CM) PIECES | 125 ML |
| 6½ TBSP. | (ABOUT) ICE WATER | 97 ML |

BLEND FLOUR, PARSLEY, THYME, SALT AND SUGAR IN FOOD PROCESSOR UNTIL HERBS ARE VERY FINELY CHOPPED. ADD BUTTER AND SHORTENING. BLEND UNTIL MIXTURE RESEMBLES COARSE MEAL. TRANSFER MIXTURE TO LARGE BOWL. USING A FORK, MIX ENOUGH ICE WATER INTO FLOUR MIXTURE TO FORM MOIST CLUMPS. GATHER DOUGH INTO A BALL; FLATTEN INTO A RECTANGLE. COVER AND CHILL 30 MINUTES (THIS CAN BE MADE UP TO 2 DAYS AHEAD. KEEP CHILLED BUT LET DOUGH SOFTEN SLIGHTLY BEFORE ROLLING OUT.) ROLL PASTRY TO REQUIRED THICKNESS. THIS MAKES 2 CRUSTS.

# LAMB

Rack of Lamb with Herb and Mustard Crust
Leg of Lamb with Red Currant Sauce
Braised Lamb Shanks with Lentils

# PORK

Balsamic Honey Tenderloin
Roast Pork Loin with Apple Topping
Island Pork Tenderloin Salad
Adobo Stew
Tourtière with Mushroom Sauce
Chop Suey
Patio Ribs
Sweet 'n' Sour Chili Ribs
Baked Ham with Maple Glaze
Ham Baked in Beer
Ham Casserole

# BEEF

Châteaubriand with Cognac Sauce
Beef Bourguignon
Cowboy Pot Roast with Yams
and Jalapeño Ketchup
Ginger's Beef Stroganoff
Tex-Mex Fajitas
The Best Darn Chili Around
Saturday Night Special
Playoff Casserole
Braised Short Ribs

# RACK OF LAMB
## WITH HERB AND MUSTARD CRUST

| | | |
|---|---|---:|
| 2 | SLICES BREAD, TORN INTO PIECES | 2 |
| 2 TBSP. | CHOPPED FRESH PARSLEY | 30 ML |
| I TBSP. | CHOPPED FRESH ROSEMARY | 15 ML |
| 2 TBSP. | CHOPPED FRESH BASIL | 30 ML |
| I | GARLIC CLOVE, MINCED | I |
| | OLIVE OIL | |
| 2 | RACKS OF 8 LAMB CHOPS | 2 |
| 3 TBSP. | DIJON MUSTARD | 45 ML |

### FRESH MINT PESTO

| | | |
|---|---|---:|
| 2 CUPS | FRESH MINT | 500 ML |
| ¼ CUP | CHOPPED ONION | 60 ML |
| ¼ CUP | LIME JUICE | 60 ML |
| 2 TBSP. | WHITE WINE VINEGAR | 30 ML |
| 2 TBSP. | SUGAR | 30 ML |
| ¼ CUP | CHOPPED PARSLEY | 60 ML |

PLACE BREAD, PARSLEY, ROSEMARY, BASIL AND GARLIC IN FOOD PROCESSOR. PULSE TO MAKE FINE CRUMBS. HEAT OIL IN A HEAVY FRYING PAN; SEAR LAMB ON ALL SIDES. BRUSH MUSTARD OVER LAMB, PRESS INTO CRUMBS. THIS CAN BE DONE AHEAD OF TIME. PREHEAT OVEN TO 400°F (200°C). ROAST FOR 20-30 MINUTES FOR MEDIUM-RARE. REMOVE FROM OVEN AND REST LAMB FOR 5 MINUTES BEFORE CARVING INTO CHOPS. ALLOW 4 CHOPS PER PERSON. SERVES 4.

TO MAKE MINT PESTO: COMBINE INGREDIENTS IN BLENDER AND PURÉE. CHILL AND SERVE WITH LAMB.

# LEG OF LAMB
## WITH RED CURRANT SAUCE

| 4-5 LB. | LEG OF LAMB | 2-2.5 KG |
|---|---|---|
| 1 TBSP. | GIN | 15 ML |
| 2 TSP. | SALT | 10 ML |
| 1/2 TSP. | DRY MUSTARD | 2 ML |
| 1/4 TSP. | PEPPER | 1 ML |

RED CURRANT SAUCE

| 1/2 CUP | RED CURRANT JELLY | 125 ML |
|---|---|---|
| 1 CUP | WATER | 250 ML |
| 1/4 TSP. | SALT | 1 ML |
| 1/4 CUP | GIN | 60 ML |
| 3 TBSP. | FLOUR | 45 ML |
| 1/4 CUP | WATER | 60 ML |

PLACE LAMB ON A RACK IN ROASTING PAN, FAT SIDE UP.
COMBINE GIN, SALT, MUSTARD AND PEPPER TO MAKE A
PASTE; SPREAD OVER LAMB. ROAST AT 350°F (180°C) FOR
2 1/2 HOURS, OR UNTIL MEAT THERMOMETER READS
180°F (90°C). SET ON A PLATTER AND COVER WITH FOIL.

TO MAKE SAUCE: REMOVE EXCESS FAT FROM ROASTING
PAN. BLEND JELLY INTO PAN JUICES. ADD WATER AND HEAT
OVER MEDIUM-LOW HEAT UNTIL JELLY MELTS. STIR IN SALT
AND GIN. BLEND FLOUR IN WATER AND STIR INTO SAUCE.
STIR UNTIL SAUCE BOILS AND THICKENS. POUR INTO
GRAVY BOAT AND SERVE WITH LAMB. SERVE WITH WHIPPED
POTATO WITH CELERY ROOT, PAGE 153, AND STIR-FRIED
SUGAR SNAP PEAS, PAGE 144.

# BRAISED LAMB SHANKS WITH LENTILS

A HEARTY MID-WINTER MEAL OF TENDER LAMB AND RICH FLAVORFUL JUICES. THIS RECIPE IS FROM NATIONALLY RENOWNED FOOD WRITER AND COOKBOOK AUTHOR JULIA AITKEN.

| | | |
|---|---|---|
| 6 | LAMB SHANKS (ABOUT 4½ LBS.) | 2.25 KG |
| 1 TSP. | SALT | 5 ML |
| 1 TSP. | PEPPER | 5 ML |
| 2 TBSP. | OLIVE OIL | 30 ML |
| 1 | LARGE ONION, THINLY SLICED | 1 |
| 2¼ CUPS | BEEF BROTH | 550 ML |
| 2 CUPS | RED WINE | 500 ML |
| ¼ CUP | TOMATO PASTE | 60 ML |
| 3 | GARLIC CLOVES, MINCED | 3 |
| 2 TBSP. | MINCED FRESH ROSEMARY LEAVES | 30 ML |
| 2 TBSP. | PACKED BROWN SUGAR | 30 ML |
| 2 TBSP. | WORCESTERSHIRE SAUCE | 30 ML |
| 2 TBSP. | RED WINE VINEGAR | 30 ML |
| 1½ CUPS | LENTILS, RINSED & DRAINED | 375 ML |
| | FRESH ROSEMARY SPRIGS | |

PREHEAT OVEN TO 350°F (180°C). PAT LAMB SHANKS DRY WITH PAPER TOWELS, THEN SPRINKLE BOTH SIDES WITH HALF OF THE SALT AND PEPPER. HEAT OIL IN A LARGE FRYING PAN OVER MEDIUM-HIGH HEAT. COOK LAMB SHANKS, A FEW AT A TIME, FOR 3-5 MINUTES, TURNING OFTEN, UNTIL BROWNED ON ALL SIDES. REMOVE TO A ROASTING PAN AND ARRANGE IN A SINGLE LAYER AFTER BROWNING EACH BATCH.

# BRAISED LAMB SHANKS
## WITH LENTILS

CONTINUED FROM PAGE 206.

REDUCE HEAT TO MEDIUM AND ADD ONION TO OIL REMAINING IN FRYING PAN. COOK, STIRRING OFTEN, FOR 4-6 MINUTES, UNTIL ONION IS GOLDEN BROWN. STIR IN 2 CUPS (500 ML) BROTH, WINE, TOMATO PASTE, GARLIC, ROSEMARY, SUGAR, WORCESTER-SHIRE, VINEGAR AND REMAINING SALT AND PEPPER. BRING TO A BOIL OVER HIGH HEAT, STIRRING TO SCRAPE UP ANY BROWN BITS FROM BOTTOM OF FRYING PAN. POUR CONTENTS OVER LAMB SHANKS AND COVER ROASTING PAN TIGHTLY WITH FOIL. TRANSFER TO OVEN AND COOK FOR 30 MINUTES.

TURN SHANKS OVER AND STIR LENTILS INTO COOKING JUICES. RE-COVER WITH FOIL AND COOK AT LEAST I HOUR, OR UNTIL LAMB SHANKS AND LENTILS ARE VERY TENDER. IF LENTIL MIXTURE SEEMS TOO THICK, ADD A LITTLE OF THE REMAINING BEEF BROTH, HEATING IT BEFORE ADDING TO ROASTING PAN. TASTE AND ADJUST SEASONING IF NECESSARY. SPOON ALL INTO A SHALLOW SERVING DISH AND GARNISH WITH FRESH ROSEMARY. SERVES 6. (PICTURED OPPOSITE PAGE 181.)

# BALSAMIC HONEY TENDERLOIN

MARINATED AND SEARED, THIS PORK IS JUICY AND DELICIOUS. MY HUSBAND SAYS, "IS THIS ALL YOU KNOW HOW TO MAKE?"

## MARINADE

| | | |
|---|---|---:|
| 2 TBSP. | LIQUID HONEY | 30 ML |
| 2 TBSP. | GRAINY MUSTARD | 30 ML |
| 2 TBSP. | BALSAMIC VINEGAR | 30 ML |
| 1 TBSP. | OLIVE OIL | 15 ML |
| 1 | GARLIC CLOVE, MINCED | 1 |
| | SALT & PEPPER TO TASTE | |
| | | |
| 2 | PORK TENDERLOINS | |

TO MAKE MARINADE: IN A LARGE BOWL, COMBINE INGREDIENTS.

ADD PORK TO MARINADE AND TURN TO COAT. MARINATE IN REFRIGERATOR FOR UP TO 24 HOURS.

REMOVE PORK FROM MARINADE AND RESERVE LIQUID. PLACE PORK ON GREASED GRILL OVER MEDIUM-HIGH HEAT. BRUSH WITH MARINADE. CLOSE LID AND COOK, TURNING AND BASTING OCCASIONALLY, FOR ABOUT 18 MINUTES, OR UNTIL INSIDE HAS JUST A HINT OF PINK. TRANSFER PORK TO CUTTING BOARD AND LET SIT FOR 5 MINUTES. CUT INTO 1/3" (1 CM) THICK SLICES. SERVE WITH NEW POTATOES, FRESH GREEN BEANS, AND SPINACH SALAD WITH PEARS, BRIE AND RASPBERRIES, PAGE 87. SERVES 4-6.

# ROAST PORK LOIN
## WITH APPLE TOPPING

### MUSTARD CARAWAY RUB

| | | |
|---|---|---|
| 1/2 TSP. | SUGAR | 2 ML |
| 2 TBSP. | FLOUR | 30 ML |
| 1 1/2 TSP. | SALT | 7 ML |
| 1 TSP. | DRY MUSTARD | 5 ML |
| 1 TSP. | CARAWAY SEEDS | 5 ML |
| 1/4 TSP. | BLACK PEPPER | 1 ML |
| 1/4 TSP. | GROUND SAGE | 1 ML |
| | | |
| 4-5 LB. | PORK LOIN ROAST | 2-2.2 KG |

### TOPPING

| | | |
|---|---|---|
| 1 1/2 CUPS | APPLESAUCE (OR MINCED APPLE) | 375 ML |
| 1/2 CUP | BROWN SUGAR | 125 ML |
| 1/4 TSP. | CINNAMON | 1 ML |
| 1/4 TSP. | MACE | 1 ML |
| 1/4 TSP. | SALT | 1 ML |
| | SMALL AMOUNT OF WATER FOR GRAVY | |

TO MAKE RUB: COMBINE INGREDIENTS AND RUB INTO PORK.
PLACE FAT SIDE UP IN A ROASTING PAN AND BAKE AT 325°F
(160°C) FOR 1 1/2 HOURS.

TO PREPARE TOPPING: COMBINE INGREDIENTS AND SPREAD
OVER ROAST. BAKE 1 HOUR LONGER, ADDING A LITTLE
WATER TO PAN TO MAKE EXCELLENT GRAVY.

# ISLAND PORK TENDERLOIN SALAD

THE SUPERB FLAVOR OF JERK PORK – THE PERFECT DINNER FOR A SUMMER'S DAY. THIS RECIPE LOOKS INVOLVED BUT IT'S NOT.

### PORK

| | | |
|---|---|---|
| 2 TSP. | SALT | 10 ML |
| 1/2 TSP. | BLACK PEPPER | 2 ML |
| 1 TSP. | GROUND CUMIN | 5 ML |
| 1 TSP. | CHILI POWDER | 5 ML |
| 1 TSP. | CINNAMON | 5 ML |
| 2-3 | PORK TENDERLOINS (2 1/2-3 LBS. TOTAL) | 1-1.5 KG |
| 2 TBSP. | OLIVE OIL | 30 ML |

### GLAZE

| | | |
|---|---|---|
| 1 CUP | PACKED DARK BROWN SUGAR | 250 ML |
| 2 TBSP. | FINELY CHOPPED GARLIC | 30 ML |
| 1 TBSP. | TABASCO | 15 ML |

### VINAIGRETTE

| | | |
|---|---|---|
| 3 TBSP. | FRESH LIME JUICE | 45 ML |
| 1 TBSP. | FRESH ORANGE JUICE | 15 ML |
| 1 TBSP. | DIJON MUSTARD | 15 ML |
| 1 TSP. | CURRY POWDER | 5 ML |
| 1/4 TSP. | BLACK PEPPER | 1 ML |
| 1/2 CUP | OLIVE OIL | 125 ML |

### SALAD

| | | |
|---|---|---|
| 3 | NAVEL ORANGES, PEELED, WHITE PITH REMOVED | 3 |
| 6 CUPS | BABY SPINACH, TRIMMED | 1.5 L |
| 4 CUPS | THINLY SLICED NAPA CABBAGE | 1 L |
| 1 | RED PEPPER, IN THIN STRIPS | 1 |
| 1/2 CUP | GOLDEN RAISINS | 125 ML |
| 2 | FIRM-RIPE AVOCADOS, PEELED & CUT DIAGONALLY INTO THIN SLICES | 2 |

# ISLAND PORK TENDERLOIN SALAD

CONTINUED FROM PAGE 210.

TO PREPARE PORK: PREHEAT OVEN TO 350°F (180°C). COMBINE SALT, PEPPER, CUMIN, CHILI POWDER AND CINNAMON. COAT PORK WITH SPICES. HEAT OIL IN OVENPROOF FRYING PAN OVER MODERATELY HIGH HEAT; BROWN PORK, TURNING OFTEN. LEAVE IN PAN.

TO MAKE GLAZE: COMBINE INGREDIENTS AND PAT ONTO TOPS OF TENDERLOINS. ROAST IN MIDDLE OF OVEN FOR ABOUT 20 MINUTES. LET STAND AT ROOM TEMPERATURE FOR 10 MINUTES.

TO MAKE VINAIGRETTE: WHISK TOGETHER JUICES, MUSTARD, CURRY POWDER AND PEPPER. ADD OIL IN A STREAM, WHISKING THOROUGHLY.

FOR THE SALAD: CUT ORANGES CROSSWISE INTO THIN SLICES. TOSS SPINACH, CABBAGE, PEPPERS AND RAISINS IN A LARGE BOWL WITH ½ CUP (125 ML) VINAIGRETTE.

TO ASSEMBLE SALAD: CUT PORK AT A 45° ANGLE INTO ½" (1.3 CM) SLICES. LINE A LARGE PLATTER WITH DRESSED SALAD. ARRANGE SLICED PORK, ORANGES AND AVOCADO IN ROWS ON TOP. DRIZZLE SOME VINAIGRETTE OVER AVOCADO AND ORANGES. POUR JUICES FROM FRYING PAN OVER PORK. (PICTURED OPPOSITE PAGE 198.)

# ADOBO STEW

A PHILIPPINE STEW FOR COMPANY – THE SWEET AND SOUR FLAVOR APPEALS TO EVERYONE. SERVE OVER RICE. GOOD CROCKPOT RECIPE. THIS STEW FREEZES WELL.

| | | |
|---|---|---|
| 2 CUPS | PEARL ONIONS | 500 ML |
| 3 LBS. | LEAN BONELESS PORK SHOULDER BUTT | 1.5 KG |
| 1 TBSP. | VEGETABLE OIL | 15 ML |
| 2 | MEDIUM ONIONS, CHOPPED | 2 |
| 6 | CARROTS, CUT IN THICK CHUNKS | 6 |
| 4 | GARLIC CLOVES, MINCED | 4 |
| 1 TSP. | FINELY CHOPPED GINGER ROOT | 5 ML |
| 3 | BAY LEAVES | 3 |
| 3 | WHOLE CLOVES | 3 |
| 1 | CINNAMON STICK | 1 |
| | FRESHLY GROUND PEPPER TO TASTE | |
| 2 CUPS | WATER | 500 ML |
| 1/2 CUP | RICE OR CIDER VINEGAR | 125 ML |
| 1/2 CUP | SOY SAUCE | 125 ML |
| 4 TSP. | CORNSTARCH MIXED WITH 2 TBSP. (30 ML) WATER | 20 ML |
| 2 | CELERY STALKS, SLICED INTO THIN 1" (2.5 CM) STRIPS | 2 |

PARBOIL PEARL ONIONS FOR 3 MINUTES. PLUNGE INTO COLD WATER, CUT OFF ENDS AND POP ONIONS OUT OF THEIR SKINS. SET ASIDE.

TRIM FAT FROM PORK AND CUT INTO BITE-SIZED CUBES. IN A DUTCH OVEN, HEAT OIL OVER MEDIUM-HIGH HEAT AND BROWN PORK IN 3 BATCHES. TRANSFER TO A BOWL.

# ADOBO STEW

CONTINUED FROM PAGE 212.

REDUCE HEAT TO MEDIUM AND SAUTÉ CHOPPED ONIONS, CARROTS, GARLIC, GINGER, BAY LEAVES, CLOVES, CINNAMON AND PEPPER, STIRRING UNTIL ONIONS ARE GOLDEN, ABOUT 6 MINUTES.

STIR IN WATER, VINEGAR AND SOY SAUCE; BRING TO A BOIL AND STIR TO SCRAPE UP BROWN BITS.

RETURN PORK AND ANY ACCUMULATED JUICES TO POT. COVER AND BAKE AT 325°F (160°C) FOR 2 HOURS. CHECK AFTER 1 HOUR AND ADD WATER IF NEEDED. DISCARD BAY LEAVES AND CINNAMON STICK. ADD CORNSTARCH MIXTURE, CELERY AND RESERVED PEARL ONIONS AND STIR GENTLY – YOU TOOK SO MUCH TROUBLE TO PEEL THE ONIONS, YOU DON'T WANT THEM TO FALL APART! RETURN TO OVEN FOR 15 MINUTES. DINNER'S READY! SERVES 6.

RETIREMENT: TWICE AS MUCH HUSBAND AND HALF AS MUCH MONEY.

# TOURTIÈRE WITH MUSHROOM SAUCE

A CHRISTMAS EVE TRADITION AND A PERFECT GIFT.
SAVE TIME AND YOUR SANITY – MAKE AHEAD AND FREEZE.

|  | ENOUGH PASTRY FOR 3, 2-CRUST PIES | |
|---|---|---|
| 1½ LBS. | LEAN GROUND PORK | 750 G |
| 1½ LBS. | LEAN GROUND BEEF | 750 G |
| 1½ CUPS | FINELY CHOPPED ONION | 375 ML |
| 1 TSP. | THYME | 5 ML |
| 1 TSP. | SAGE | 5 ML |
| 1 TSP. | DRY MUSTARD | 5 ML |
| 2 TSP. | SALT | 10 ML |
| ½ CUP | CHOPPED FRESH PARSLEY | 125 ML |
| 2 | GARLIC CLOVES, MINCED | 2 |
|  | PEPPER TO TASTE | |
| 1 CUP | WATER | 250 ML |
| 1 CUP | BREAD CRUMBS OR 2 CUPS | 250 ML |
|  | (500 ML) MASHED POTATOES | |

## MUSHROOM SAUCE

| 2 TBSP. | BUTTER | 30 ML |
|---|---|---|
| 3 CUPS | SLICED MUSHROOMS | 750 ML |
| ½ CUP | SLICED ONIONS | 125 ML |
| 2 TBSP. | BUTTER | 30 ML |
| 2 TSP. | FLOUR | 10 ML |
| 1 CUP | BEEF BROTH | 250 ML |
| ½ CUP | DRY RED WINE | 125 ML |

TO MAKE PIES: IN A FRYING PAN, LIGHTLY BROWN MEAT.
DRAIN OFF FAT. ADD ONION AND STIR IN SEASONINGS.
ADD WATER, COVER AND SIMMER FOR 15 MINUTES, OR
UNTIL MOST OF LIQUID IS ABSORBED BUT MIXTURE
IS STILL MOIST.

## CONTINUED FROM PAGE 214.

ADD BREAD CRUMBS. LET COOL. SPOON FILLING INTO PASTRY-LINED 9" (23 CM) PIE PLATES. COVER WITH TOP CRUSTS, SEAL AND FLUTE EDGES. MAY BE FROZEN AT THIS POINT. CUT SLASHES ON TOP TO RELEASE STEAM. BAKE AT 425°F (220°C) FOR 15 MINUTES, REDUCE HEAT TO 350°F (180°C) AND BAKE FOR 30 MINUTES, OR UNTIL WELL BROWNED. THIS RECIPE CAN ALSO BE MADE AS AN APPETIZER USING TART SHELLS.

TO MAKE MUSHROOM SAUCE: MELT BUTTER IN A LARGE FRYING PAN AND SAUTÉ MUSHROOMS AND ONIONS FOR 10 MINUTES. REMOVE TO A PLATE. MELT BUTTER AND BLEND FLOUR AND A FEW TABLESPOONS OF BROTH INTO PAN JUICES. STIR IN REMAINING BROTH AND WINE. BRING TO A BOIL UNTIL SAUCE THICKENS. ADD MUSHROOMS AND ONIONS TO SAUCE. SERVE WARM WITH TOURTIÈRE.

MY WIFE COMES WITH INSTRUCTIONS – LOTS OF INSTRUCTIONS.

# CHOP SUEY

A YUMMY WAY TO USE UP LEFTOVERS.

| | | |
|---|---|---:|
| 3 TBSP. | SOY SAUCE | 45 ML |
| I TBSP. | BROWN SUGAR | 15 ML |
| 2 CUPS | SLICED LEFTOVER ROAST PORK, BEEF OR CHICKEN | 500 ML |
| 2 TBSP. | CORNSTARCH | 30 ML |
| I CUP | WATER | 250 ML |
| ¼ CUP | VEGETABLE OIL | 60 ML |
| I | MEDIUM ONION, SLICED | I |
| 2 | GARLIC CLOVES, MINCED | 2 |
| I | GREEN OR RED PEPPER, SLICED | I |
| 3 | CELERY STALKS, SLICED | 3 |
| 2 CUPS | MUSHROOMS, SLICED | 500 ML |
| | SALT & PEPPER TO TASTE | |
| 2 CUPS | FRESH BEAN SPROUTS | 500 ML |

COMBINE SOY SAUCE, BROWN SUGAR AND MIX WITH MEAT. LET STAND FOR 15 MINUTES. MIX CORNSTARCH WITH WATER AND SET ASIDE. NOW, YOU'RE READY TO START COOKING.

IN A WOK OR FRYING PAN OVER HIGH HEAT, HEAT OIL; ADD ONION; STIR FOR 2 MINUTES. ADD GARLIC AND SLICED VEGETABLES; STIR FOR 2 MINUTES. ADD MEAT MIXTURE; STIR FOR 2 MINUTES. ADD CORNSTARCH MIXTURE; STIR FOR 2 MINUTES. ADD BEAN SPROUTS; STIR FOR 2 MINUTES. NOW YOU'RE STIR CRAZY BUT DINNER'S READY! SERVE OVER RICE AND PASS THE SOY SAUCE. SERVES 6-8.

# PATIO RIBS

STICKY RIBS – "DEE-RISHUS GRAMMA!" ALSO GREAT AS AN APPETIZER.

| 4 LBS. | (3-4 RACKS) PORK BACK SPARERIBS | 2 KG |
|---|---|---|

### SAUCE

| ½ CUP | HOISIN SAUCE | 125 ML |
|---|---|---|
| ½ CUP | OYSTER SAUCE | 125 ML |
| 3 TBSP. | HOT CHILI SAUCE | 45 ML |
| 2 TBSP. | LIQUID HONEY | 30 ML |

REMOVE SKIN FROM UNDERSIDE OF RIBS. TO TENDERIZE RIBS, SLICE EACH RACK IN HALF AND ADD TO A LARGE POT OF BOILING WATER. BOIL GENTLY UNTIL RIBS ARE FORK-TENDER, ABOUT 45 MINUTES. DRAIN.

TO MAKE SAUCE: STIR HOISIN, OYSTER, HOT CHILI SAUCE AND HONEY TOGETHER.

GENEROUSLY COAT RIBS WITH SAUCE ON BOTH SIDES. WHEN READY TO BARBECUE, SPRAY GRILL WITH OIL AND COOK RIBS OVER MEDIUM HEAT, BASTING WITH SAUCE AND TURNING OFTEN UNTIL WELL GLAZED, ABOUT 15 MINUTES. SERVES 4.

I CAN'T BE OVERDRAWN – I STILL HAVE SOME CHECKS!

# SWEET 'N' SOUR CHILI RIBS

THE AROMA OF THESE RIBS WILL BRING YOUR FAMILY RUNNING.

| 4 LBS. | PORK RIBS | 2 KG |
|--------|-----------|------|

SAUCE

| 3/4 CUP | BROWN SUGAR | 175 ML |
|---------|-------------|--------|
| 1/2 CUP | KETCHUP | 125 ML |
| 1/2 CUP | WHITE VINEGAR | 125 ML |
| 2 TBSP. | WORCESTERSHIRE SAUCE | 30 ML |
| 1 TSP. | CHILI POWDER | 5 ML |
| 3/4 CUP | WATER | 175 ML |
| 1 | ONION, DICED | 1 |

PARBOIL RIBS IN A LARGE POT FOR 30-45 MINUTES. PLACE RIBS IN A LARGE SHALLOW BAKING PAN.

TO MAKE SAUCE: IN A MEDIUM BOWL, COMBINE INGREDIENTS.

POUR SAUCE OVER RIBS. BAKE, UNCOVERED, AT 250°F (120°C) FOR 3 HOURS. SERVES 4-6.

I CAME FROM A FAMILY OF 8 KIDS – I WAS 18 BEFORE I FOUND OUT MACARONI WASN'T MEAT.

# BAKED HAM WITH MAPLE GLAZE

SERVE WITH BAKED CORN PUDDING WITH A KICK, PAGE 149, AND PATRICK'S SALAD, PAGE 93.

| 5-6 LB. | HAM, BONE-IN | 2.5-3 KG |
| | WHOLE CLOVES | |

## MAPLE GLAZE

| 2 CUPS | ORANGE JUICE | 500 ML |
| 1/2 CUP | MAPLE SYRUP | 125 ML |
| 1/4 CUP | MARMALADE | 60 ML |
| 2 TBSP. | DIJON MUSTARD | 30 ML |

PREHEAT OVEN TO 325°F (160°C). USING A SHARP KNIFE, REMOVE SKIN FROM HAM. SCORE FAT DIAGONALLY IN DIAMOND DESIGN. STUD TOP OF HAM WITH CLOVES. PLACE HAM ON A WIRE RACK IN A ROASTING PAN LINED WITH FOIL.

TO MAKE GLAZE: COMBINE INGREDIENTS IN A MEDIUM SAUCEPAN. BRING TO A BOIL AND SIMMER FOR 5 MINUTES, UNTIL WELL BLENDED.

BAKE HAM FOR 2-3 HOURS. POUR 1/4 CUP (60 ML) OF GLAZE OVER HAM EVERY HALF-HOUR OR SO.

GOLF IS A GAME INVENTED BY THE SAME PEOPLE WHO THINK MUSIC COMES OUT OF A BAGPIPE.

# HAM BAKED IN BEER

YOUR FAMILY WILL WONDER WHERE THE COMPANY IS!

| | | |
|---|---|---|
| 5 LB. | HAM, BONE-IN | 2.5 KG |
| 1 | CAN GINGER ALE | 355 ML |
| | WHOLE CLOVES | |

BEER MARINADE

| | | |
|---|---|---|
| 1 CUP | MOLASSES | 250 ML |
| 2 TSP. | DRY MUSTARD | 10 ML |
| 1 TSP. | PEPPER | 5 ML |
| 1 CUP | BEER | 250 ML |

PREHEAT OVEN TO 325°F (160°C). USING A SHARP KNIFE, REMOVE SKIN FROM HAM. SCORE FAT DIAGONALLY IN DIAMOND DESIGN. SOAK HAM IN GINGER ALE FOR AT LEAST 2 HOURS TO REMOVE EXCESS SALT. DRAIN. STUD TOP OF HAM WITH CLOVES. PLACE HAM IN MIDDLE OF A LARGE PIECE OF FOIL IN A SHALLOW ROASTING PAN.

TO MAKE MARINADE: COMBINE INGREDIENTS.

POUR MARINADE OVER HAM, THEN COVER COMPLETELY WITH FOIL SO JUICES DON'T ESCAPE. BAKE FOR 20 MINUTES PER POUND. SERVE WITH CARMELIZED ONION AND POTATO FLAN ON PAGE 152.

# HAM CASSEROLE

THAT'S IT FOR THE LEFTOVER HAM!

| | | |
|---|---|---|
| 2 TBSP. | BUTTER | 30 ML |
| 1/2 CUP | CHOPPED ONION | 125 ML |
| 3 TBSP. | FLOUR | 45 ML |
| | SALT & PEPPER TO TASTE | |
| 1 1/4 CUPS | MILK | 300 ML |
| 1/2 CUP | SHREDDED SWISS CHEESE | 125 ML |
| 2 CUPS | CUBED COOKED HAM | 500 ML |
| | (OR MORE) | |
| 1 CUP | CUBED COOKED POTATOES | 250 ML |
| 1 1/2 CUPS | SOFT BREADCRUMBS | 375 ML |
| 2 TBSP. | BUTTER | 30 ML |

IN A FRYING PAN, MELT BUTTER AND SAUTÉ ONION. BLEND IN FLOUR, SALT AND PEPPER. SLOWLY ADD MILK; STIR CONSTANTLY AND COOK UNTIL THICKENED. ADD CHEESE AND STIR UNTIL MELTED. ADD HAM AND POTATOES AND MIX GENTLY. POUR INTO A CASSEROLE. SPRINKLE WITH BREADCRUMBS AND DOT WITH BUTTER. PREHEAT OVEN TO 400°F (200°C) AND BAKE FOR 30 MINUTES. SERVES 6.

THERE'S A SPECIAL TRICK I DO WITH FAT-FREE FOOD. I THROW IT AWAY.

# CHÂTEAUBRIAND WITH COGNAC SAUCE

IF YOU'RE GOING ALL OUT BUT WANT TO STAY IN . . .

| 2 | 2½ LBS. (1.25 KG) EACH BEEF TENDERLOINS | 2 |
| 5 | MEDIUM GARLIC CLOVES, FINELY SLIVERED | 5 |
| 2½ TBSP. | OLIVE OIL | 37 ML |

## COGNAC MUSTARD SAUCE

| 1½ TBSP. | BUTTER | 22 ML |
| 4 | MEDIUM SHALLOTS, MINCED | 4 |
| 2 CUPS | BEEF STOCK | 500 ML |
| 2 TBSP. | COGNAC OR BRANDY | 30 ML |
| 2 TBSP. | DIJON MUSTARD | 30 ML |
| ½ CUP | BUTTER, CUT INTO 8 PIECES | 125 ML |
| 3 TBSP. | CHOPPED, FRESH PARSLEY | 45 ML |
| | SALT & FRESHLY GROUND PEPPER TO TASTE | |

CUT ¾" (2 CM) DEEP SLITS IN MEAT. INSERT GARLIC SLIVERS INTO SLITS. PREHEAT OVEN TO 450°F (230°C). IN LARGE FRYING PAN, HEAT OIL; BROWN MEAT ON ALL SIDES. PLACE MEAT ON A RACK IN ROASTING PAN. SET FRYING PAN ASIDE. ROAST MEAT TO DESIRED DONENESS, ABOUT 40 MINUTES FOR MEDIUM-RARE. LET STAND FOR 10 MINUTES.

# CHÂTEAUBRIAND WITH COGNAC SAUCE

CONTINUED FROM PAGE 222.

TO MAKE SAUCE: MELT 1½ TBSP. (22 ML) BUTTER IN FRYING PAN. ADD SHALLOTS AND SAUTÉ UNTIL SOFTENED. STIR IN STOCK, SCRAPING UP BROWN BITS. BRING TO A BOIL AND COOK UNTIL REDUCED BY HALF. ADD COGNAC AND BOIL 1 MINUTE. REDUCE HEAT TO LOW. WHISK IN MUSTARD THEN BUTTER, 1 PIECE AT A TIME. STIR IN PARSLEY. SEASON WITH SALT AND PEPPER.

CARVE MEAT IN ½" (1.3 CM) SLICES. SPOON SAUCE OVER AND SERVE IMMEDIATELY WITH A VARIETY OF FRESH GARDEN VEGETABLES AND YOUR BEST BEAUJOLAIS. SERVES 12.

THERE ARE TWO THEORIES ABOUT ARGUING WITH WOMEN. NEITHER ONE WORKS.

# BEEF BOURGUIGNON

AN ELEGANT FRENCH STEW FOR 8 GOOD FRIENDS.
SERVE WITH BEAUCOUP BAGUETTES ... C'EST SI BON!

| | | |
|---|---|---|
| ½ LB. | THICK-SLICED BACON | 250 G |
| 12–15 | SMALL WHOLE ONIONS, PEELED, OR 4 HANDFULS PEARL ONIONS, SKINS REMOVED | 12–15 |
| 3 LBS. | LEAN BEEF CHUCK, CUT INTO 1" (2.5 CM) PIECES | 1.5 KG |
| | OLIVE OIL | |
| 2 | CLOVES GARLIC, MINCED | 2 |
| 3 TBSP. | FLOUR | 45 ML |
| | SALT AND PEPPER TO TASTE | |
| 3 CUPS | DRY RED WINE | 750 ML |
| 2 CUPS | BEEF BROTH | 500 ML |
| | BAY LEAF | |
| ½ TSP. | DRIED THYME | 2 ML |
| 2 CUPS | SLICED MUSHROOMS | 500 ML |
| 4–6 | LARGE CARROTS, PEELED AND CUT IN BITE-SIZED PIECES | 4–6 |
| 2 TBSP. | BUTTER | 30 ML |
| | CHOPPED FRESH PARSLEY FOR GARNISH | |

PREHEAT OVEN TO 300°F (150°C). IN A DUTCH OVEN,
SAUTÉ BACON UNTIL CRISP. REMOVE, COOL AND COARSELY
CHOP. RESERVE 1-2 TBSP. (15-30 ML) BACON DRIPPINGS.
ADD ONIONS AND SAUTÉ LIGHTLY; REMOVE TO ANOTHER
DISH. ADD BEEF TO POT (AND SOME OIL IF NECESSARY)
AND BROWN OVER MEDIUM-HIGH HEAT FOR 5 MINUTES;
ADD GARLIC FOR THE LAST MINUTE (BE CAREFUL NOT
TO BURN). SPRINKLE WITH FLOUR, SALT AND PEPPER;

# BEEF BOURGUIGNON

CONTINUED FROM PAGE 224.

STIR UNTIL FLOUR BEGINS TO BROWN. ADD WINE, BEEF BROTH, BAY LEAF AND THYME. STIR TO LOOSEN BROWNED BITS ON BOTTOM OF POT, ADD ONIONS, COVER AND PLACE IN OVEN FOR AT LEAST 2 HOURS.

MEANWHILE, LIGHTLY SAUTÉ MUSHROOMS AND CARROTS IN BUTTER AND SET ASIDE. REMOVE POT FROM OVEN, ADD SAUTÉED VEGGIES AND RETURN TO OVEN FOR ANOTHER $1/2$ HOUR. IF MORE LIQUID IS NEEDED, ADD BEEF BROTH. GARNISH WITH PARSLEY.

WITH HER MARRIAGE, SHE GOT A NEW NAME AND – A DRESS.

# COWBOY POT ROAST
## WITH YAMS AND JALAPEÑO KETCHUP

SERVE WITH HOMEMADE BISCUITS. THE BEST POT ROAST WE'VE TASTED IN YEARS. YAHOO!

### JALAPEÑO KETCHUP

| | | |
|---|---|---|
| 3 | JALAPEÑO PEPPERS, STEMMED, SEEDED & DICED | 3 |
| 1/4 CUP | MINCED ONION | 60 ML |
| 2 | GARLIC CLOVES, MINCED | 2 |
| 1 1/2 CUPS | WATER | 375 ML |
| 2 TBSP. | BROWN SUGAR | 30 ML |
| 1 1/2 TSP. | CUMIN | 7 ML |
| 4 1/2 OZ. | TOMATO PASTE | 123 G |
| | SALT & FRESHLY GROUND PEPPER | |

### POT ROAST

| | | |
|---|---|---|
| 1/2 CUP | FLOUR | 125 ML |
| 1 TSP. | SALT | 5 ML |
| 1 TSP. | FRESHLY GROUND PEPPER | 5 ML |
| 4-6 LB. | CHUCK ROAST | 2-3 KG |
| 1/2 CUP | VEGETABLE OIL | 125 ML |
| 3 | CARROTS, PEELED & CUT IN CHUNKS | 3 |
| 3 | YAMS OR SWEET POTATOES, PEELED & CUT INTO 2" (5 CM) PIECES | 3 |
| 1 | MEDIUM ONION, CUT IN QUARTERS | 1 |
| 4 | GARLIC CLOVES, MINCED | 4 |
| 2 CUPS | BEEF STOCK | 500 ML |

TO MAKE JALAPEÑO KETCHUP: PLACE PEPPERS, ONION, GARLIC AND WATER IN A SAUCEPAN. BRING TO A BOIL OVER HIGH HEAT AND SIMMER FOR 15 MINUTES, OR UNTIL PEPPERS HAVE ABSORBED

# COWBOY POT ROAST
## WITH YAMS AND JALAPEÑO KETCHUP

CONTINUED FROM PAGE 226.

SOME LIQUID AND BECOME SOFT. REMOVE PEPPER MIXTURE WITH SLOTTED SPOON TO FOOD PROCESSOR. RESERVE LIQUID. TO FOOD PROCESSOR, ADD BROWN SUGAR, CUMIN, TOMATO PASTE, SALT, PEPPER AND 1/4 CUP (60 ML) RESERVED LIQUID. PURÉE, ADDING MORE PEPPER LIQUID, IF NEEDED, TO REACH DESIRED THICKNESS. ADD SALT AND PEPPER AND MORE BROWN SUGAR IF DESIRED.

MIX TOGETHER FLOUR, SALT AND PEPPER. DREDGE ROAST IN FLOUR MIXTURE.

HEAT OIL IN LARGE OVENPROOF POT. SEAR ROAST FOR 4 MINUTES ON EACH SIDE, OR UNTIL WELL BROWNED.

ADD JALAPEÑO KETCHUP, CARROTS, YAMS, ONION AND GARLIC TO POT. COOK FOR 5 MINUTES. ADD BEEF STOCK; COVER AND BRING TO A BOIL. PLACE POT IN 300°F (150°C) OVEN AND COOK FOR 2½-3 HOURS, OR UNTIL BEEF IS VERY TENDER. SERVES 6-8.

# GINGER'S BEEF STROGANOFF

| | | |
|---|---|---:|
| 2 TBSP. | BUTTER | 30 ML |
| I LB. | BEEF SIRLOIN, CUT AGAINST GRAIN INTO THIN STRIPS | 500 G |
| I CUP | SLICED FRESH MUSHROOMS | 250 ML |
| 1/2 CUP | CHOPPED ONION | 125 ML |
| I | GARLIC CLOVE, MINCED | I |

SAUCE

| | | |
|---|---|---:|
| 3 TBSP. | BUTTER | 45 ML |
| 3 TBSP. | FLOUR | 45 ML |
| 1/2 TSP. | SALT | 2 ML |
| I TBSP. | TOMATO PASTE | 15 ML |
| 10 OZ. | CAN BEEF BROTH | 284 ML |
| I CUP | SOUR CREAM | 250 ML |
| 2 TBSP. | SHERRY | 30 ML |

COOKED BROAD NOODLES FOR 4-6.

IN A FRYING PAN, MELT BUTTER AND BROWN MEAT QUICKLY. REMOVE TO A CASSEROLE. REDUCE PAN HEAT AND ADD MUSHROOMS, ONIONS AND GARLIC (ADD MORE BUTTER IF NECESSARY). COOK 3-4 MINUTES, UNTIL ONION IS TRANSLUCENT. REMOVE AND ADD TO CASSEROLE.

TO MAKE SAUCE: MELT BUTTER IN FRYING PAN; ADD FLOUR, SALT AND TOMATO PASTE. SLOWLY STIR IN BROTH; COOK AND STIR UNTIL THICKENED. ADD SAUCE TO CASSEROLE AND STIR.

WHEN READY TO SERVE, ADD SOUR CREAM AND SHERRY TO CASSEROLE; BAKE AT 275°F (130°C) FOR 1/2 HOUR, OR UNTIL WARMED THROUGH. SERVE OVER BROAD NOODLES. SERVES 4-6 - BUT CAN BE EASILY DOUBLED.

# TEX-MEX FAJITAS

OLÉ YOUSE GRINGOS!!

| | | |
|---|---|---|
| 2 LBS. | FLANK STEAK OR 3 CHICKEN BREASTS, SKINNED, BONED & HALVED | 1 KG |

MARINADE

| | | |
|---|---|---|
| ½ CUP | VEGETABLE OIL | 125 ML |
| ⅓ CUP | LIME JUICE | 75 ML |
| ⅓ CUP | RED WINE VINEGAR (ELIMINATE FOR CHICKEN) | 75 ML |
| ⅓ CUP | CHOPPED ONION | 75 ML |
| 1 TSP. | SUGAR | 5 ML |
| 1 TSP. | OREGANO | 5 ML |
| | SALT & PEPPER TO TASTE | |
| ¼ TSP. | CUMIN | 1 ML |
| 2 | GARLIC CLOVES, MINCED | 2 |
| 6 | LARGE FLOUR TORTILLAS | 6 |

TOPPINGS

ONION SLICES, SAUTÉED
GREEN & RED PEPPER STRIPS, SAUTÉED
SHREDDED LETTUCE
GUACAMOLE, SOUR CREAM & SALSA

TO MAKE MARINADE: COMBINE INGREDIENTS IN A SHALLOW CASSEROLE. SCORE BOTH SIDES OF STEAK; ADD TO MARINADE; COVER AND MARINATE IN REFRIGERATOR FOR SEVERAL HOURS. REMOVE FROM MARINADE AND BARBECUE. SLICE IN THIN STRIPS ACROSS THE GRAIN. WRAP IN WARM TORTILLAS WITH ONIONS, PEPPERS AND ANY OR ALL OF THE TOPPINGS. SERVES 6 GRINGOS.

# THE BEST DARN CHILI AROUND

MAKE A DAY OR SO AHEAD, THE FLAVOR IMPROVES AND SO DO THE REVIEWS.

| | | |
|---|---|---|
| 6 OZ. | HOT ITALIAN CHICKEN SAUSAGE | 170 G |
| 2 CUPS | CHOPPED ONION | 500 ML |
| 1 CUP | CHOPPED GREEN PEPPER | 250 ML |
| 8 | GARLIC CLOVES, MINCED | 8 |
| 1 LB. | GROUND SIRLOIN | 500 G |
| 1 | JALAPEÑO PEPPER, SEEDED & CHOPPED | 1 |
| 2 TBSP. | CHILI POWDER | 30 ML |
| 2 TBSP. | BROWN SUGAR | 30 ML |
| 1 TBSP. | GROUND CUMIN | 15 ML |
| 3 TBSP. | TOMATO PASTE | 45 ML |
| 1 TSP. | DRIED OREGANO | 5 ML |
| | SALT & PEPPER TO TASTE | |
| 2 | BAY LEAVES | 2 |
| 1¼ CUPS | MERLOT OR OTHER RED WINE | 300 ML |
| 2 | 28 OZ. (796 ML) CANS WHOLE TOMATOES WITH JUICE, CHOPPED | 2 |
| 2 | 14 OZ. (398 ML) CANS KIDNEY BEANS, DRAINED | 2 |
| | SOUR CREAM | |
| | CHEDDAR CHEESE, SHREDDED | |
| | GREEN ONIONS, CHOPPED | |

HEAT A LARGE DUTCH OVEN OVER MEDIUM-HIGH HEAT. REMOVE CASINGS FROM SAUSAGE. ADD SAUSAGE, ONION, GREEN PEPPER, GARLIC, BEEF AND JALAPEÑO TO POT; COOK ABOUT 8 MINUTES, OR UNTIL SAUSAGE AND BEEF ARE BROWNED, STIRRING TO CRUMBLE.

# THE BEST DARN CHILI AROUND

CONTINUED FROM PAGE 230.

ADD CHILI POWDER, BROWN SUGAR, CUMIN, TOMATO PASTE, OREGANO, SALT, PEPPER AND BAY LEAVES. COOK FOR 1 MINUTE, STIRRING CONSTANTLY. STIR IN WINE, TOMATOES AND KIDNEY BEANS; BRING TO A BOIL. COVER; REDUCE HEAT AND SIMMER FOR 1 HOUR, STIRRING OCCASIONALLY.

UNCOVER AND COOK FOR 30 MINUTES, STIRRING OCCASIONALLY. DISCARD BAY LEAVES. GARNISH EACH SERVING WITH A DOLLOP OF SOUR CREAM, A SPRINKLING OF CHEDDAR CHEESE AND GREEN ONIONS. SERVES 8-10.

TEACHER: NAME THE FOUR SEASONS.

CHILD: SALT, PEPPER, MUSTARD AND VINEGAR.

# SATURDAY NIGHT SPECIAL

... OR SUNDAY ... OR MONDAY ... OR TUESDAY

| | | |
|---|---|---|
| 1/2 LB. | SPAGHETTI, BROKEN IN PIECES | 250 G |
| 1 LB. | GROUND BEEF | 500 G |
| 1 | SMALL ONION, CHOPPED | 1 |
| 1 | GREEN PEPPER, CHOPPED | 1 |
| 1 CUP | FRESH MUSHROOMS, SLICED | 250 ML |
| 12 OZ. | CAN KERNEL CORN OR 1 CUP (250 ML) FROZEN CORN | 341 ML |
| 1 CUP | GRATED CHEDDAR CHEESE | 250 ML |
| 10 OZ. | CAN TOMATO SOUP | 284 ML |
| 14 OZ. | CAN TOMATOES | 398 ML |
| 3/4 TSP. | SALT | 3 ML |
| 1/2 TSP. | CHILI POWDER | 2 ML |
| 1/2 TSP. | WORCESTERSHIRE SAUCE | 2 ML |

IN A POT, BRING SALTED WATER TO A BOIL AND COOK SPAGHETTI UNTIL TENDER. DRAIN. IN A FRYING PAN, BROWN BEEF AND ONION. ADD GREEN PEPPER AND MUSHROOMS AND COOK UNTIL TENDER. IN A LARGE CASSEROLE, COMBINE BEEF MIXTURE WITH THE OTHER INGREDIENTS AND MIX WELL. BAKE AT 325°F (160°C) FOR 45 MINUTES. SERVE WITH FRENCH BREAD AND A TOSSED SALAD. SERVES 6-8.

THE TROUBLE WITH LIFE IS THERE'S NO BACKGROUND MUSIC.

## PLAYOFF CASSEROLE

A.K.A. CHOP, CHOP CASSEROLE - IT'S IN - IT'S OUT -
IT'S IN - IT'S OUT - SORRY LINDA -
YOU LOSE!

(LINDA HAS BEEN SUBMITTING THIS RECIPE FOR YEARS
- IT JUST DIDN'T MAKE THE CUT.)

BENIGN: WHAT YOU GONNA BE WHEN YOU IS DONE BEING EIGHT.

# BRAISED SHORT RIBS

MAKE THIS A DAY AHEAD. NOT ONLY WILL THE FLAVORS BE MELLOW . . . SO WILL YOU!!!

| | | |
|---|---|---|
| 1/3 CUP | FLOUR | 75 ML |
| | SALT & PEPPER TO TASTE | |
| 1/2 TSP. | PAPRIKA | 2 ML |
| 3-4 LBS. | BEEF SHORT RIBS, BONE-IN | 1.5-2 KG |
| 2 TBSP. | VEGETABLE OIL | 30 ML |
| 2 | MEDIUM ONIONS | 2 |
| 1/2 CUP | TOMATO SAUCE | 125 ML |
| 1/2 CUP | BARBECUE SAUCE | 125 ML |
| 2 TBSP. | MOLASSES | 30 ML |
| 2 TBSP. | CIDER VINEGAR | 30 ML |

COMBINE FLOUR, SALT, PEPPER AND PAPRIKA. TRIM EXCESS FAT FROM RIBS. DREDGE RIBS IN FLOUR MIXTURE AND BROWN IN OIL ON ALL SIDES. REMOVE TO CASSEROLE.

CHOP ONION INTO LARGE CHUNKS AND PLACE ON TOP OF BROWNED RIBS.

WHISK TOMATO SAUCE, BARBECUE SAUCE, MOLASSES AND CIDER VINEGAR TOGETHER IN A SAUCEPAN. BRING TO A BOIL AND POUR OVER RIBS AND ONIONS. COVER AND BAKE AT 275°F (130°C) FOR 3-4 HOURS.

ON A COOL FALL NIGHT YOUR FAMILY WILL DELIGHT IN THE TASTE OF BARBECUE. SERVE WITH MASHED POTATOES AND A GREEN VEGETABLE. SERVES 4.

# COOKIES

Lemon Shortbread Cookies
Aunt Mary's Sugar Cookies
Sensational Pecan Sables
Wafer Puffs
French Button Cookies
Ginger Cookies
Mrs. Smith's Oatcakes
Oatmeal Crispies
Toffee Cranberry Crisps
Skor Bar Cookies
Better-Than-Mom's Oatmeal Cookies
Carrot Hermits
The "Best" Chocolate Chip Cookies

# SQUARES

Brownies
Chewy Chocolate Peanut Bars
Chocolate Raspberry Truffle Squares
Brandied Cranberry Apricot Bars
Dream Slice
Krispie Granola Bars
Salted Peanut Bars

# — LEMON SHORTBREAD COOKIES —

THE CHRISTMAS BAKING LIST JUST INCREASED BY ONE! HIDE THEM BEFORE THE CHILDREN DISCOVER YOUR NEW BEST RECIPE!

| | | |
|---|---|---|
| 3/4 CUP | BUTTER, SOFTENED | 175 ML |
| 1/3 CUP | ICING (CONFECTIONER'S) SUGAR | 75 ML |
| 1 TSP. | GRATED LEMON ZEST | 5 ML |
| 1 TBSP. | FRESH LEMON JUICE | 15 ML |
| 1 1/4 CUPS | FLOUR | 300 ML |
| 1/2 CUP | CORNSTARCH | 125 ML |

### FROSTING

| | | |
|---|---|---|
| 3/4 CUP | ICING SUGAR | 175 ML |
| 1/4 CUP | BUTTER, SOFTENED | 60 ML |
| 1 TSP. | GRATED LEMON ZEST | 5 ML |
| 1 TSP. | FRESH LEMON JUICE | 5 ML |

IN A LARGE BOWL, CREAM BUTTER AND SUGAR. MIX IN LEMON ZEST AND JUICE. ADD FLOUR AND CORNSTARCH; MIX THOROUGHLY. DIVIDE DOUGH IN HALF. SHAPE EACH HALF INTO A 1" (2.5 CM) ROLL. WRAP IN PLASTIC WRAP AND REFRIGERATE FOR AT LEAST 1 HOUR, OR UNTIL READY TO BAKE. PREHEAT OVEN TO 350°F (180°C). USING A SHARP KNIFE, CUT ROLLS INTO 1/4" (6 MM) SLICES. PLACE EACH SLICE 2" (5 CM) APART ON UNGREASED COOKIE SHEETS. BAKE FOR 8-12 MINUTES, OR UNTIL SET. DO NOT BROWN. COOL COMPLETELY.

TO MAKE ICING: IN A SMALL BOWL COMBINE SUGAR, BUTTER, LEMON ZEST AND JUICE. BEAT UNTIL LIGHT AND FLUFFY. FROST COOLED COOKIES. MAKES 4 DOZEN.

# AUNT MARY'S SUGAR COOKIES

THE KIDS CAN DECORATE THESE FOR A SPECIAL OCCASION – HALLOWEEN, CHRISTMAS, VALENTINE'S DAY OR BIRTHDAYS. AUNT MARY WOULD BE PROUD!

| | | |
|---|---|---|
| 2 CUPS | WHITE SUGAR | 500 ML |
| 2 CUPS | BUTTER, ROOM TEMPERATURE | 500 ML |
| 4 | EGGS, BEATEN | 4 |
| 1/2 TSP. | LEMON EXTRACT | 2 ML |
| 5 CUPS | FLOUR | 1.25 L |
| 2 TSP. | CREAM OF TARTAR | 10 ML |
| 1 TSP. | BAKING SODA | 5 ML |
| | SUGAR FOR SPRINKLING | |

IN A LARGE BOWL, CREAM SUGAR AND BUTTER. ADD BEATEN EGGS AND LEMON EXTRACT. SIFT DRY INGREDIENTS; ADD TO EGG MIXTURE. MIX WELL. CHILL FOR 15 MINUTES; ROLL ON GENEROUSLY FLOURED SURFACE TO 1/8-1/4" (3-6 MM) THICK. CUT WITH A 3" (8 CM) COOKIE CUTTER AND SPRINKLE WITH SUGAR. PLACE ON UNGREASED COOKIE SHEETS AND BAKE AT 350°F (180°C) FOR 10-12 MINUTES, UNTIL EDGES ARE LIGHT BROWN. MAKES 9 DOZEN COOKIES.

# SENSATIONAL PECAN SABLES

SABLE IS THE FRENCH WORD FOR SAND, WHICH BEST DESCRIBES THEIR DELICATE CRUMBLY TEXTURE.

| | | |
|---|---|---|
| 3/4 CUP | PECANS, TOASTED | 175 ML |
| 2 TBSP. | ICING (CONFECTIONER'S) SUGAR | 30 ML |
| 1 1/4 CUPS | FLOUR | 300 ML |
| 1/2 TSP. | SALT | 2 ML |
| 1/4 TSP. | BAKING POWDER | 1 ML |
| 1/2 CUP | BUTTER, SOFTENED | 125 ML |
| 2/3 CUP | ICING (CONFECTIONER'S) SUGAR | 150 ML |
| 1/2 TSP. | VANILLA | 2 ML |
| 1 | LARGE EGG, SEPARATED | 1 |
| | | |
| 32 | PECAN HALVES | 32 |

PULSE TOASTED PECANS WITH 2 TBSP. (30 ML) SUGAR IN A FOOD PROCESSOR UNTIL FINELY GROUND. WHISK TOGETHER FLOUR, SALT, AND BAKING POWDER IN A BOWL. IN A LARGE BOWL, BEAT BUTTER, SUGAR AND VANILLA WITH AN ELECTRIC MIXTURE AT HIGH SPEED UNTIL PALE AND FLUFFY. ADD EGG YOLK AND BEAT WELL. ADD FLOUR MIXTURE AND GROUND-PECAN MIXTURE AND BEAT AT LOW SPEED UNTIL JUST COMBINED. (DOUGH WILL BE CRUMBLY BUT WILL HOLD TOGETHER WHEN SQUEEZED.)

PREHEAT OVEN TO 325°F (160°C). HALVE DOUGH. ROLL OUT 1 PIECE, BETWEEN 2 SHEETS OF WAX PAPER, 1/4" (6 MM) THICK, ABOUT A 9" (23 CM) ROUND. CUT OUT AS MANY ROUNDS AS POSSIBLE WITH A 2" (5 CM) COOKIE CUTTER AND ARRANGE ABOUT

# SENSATIONAL PECAN SABLES

CONTINUED FROM PAGE 238.

2" (5 CM) APART ON LARGE UNGREASED COOKIE SHEETS. ROLL OUT AND CUT REMAINING DOUGH IN SAME MANNER.

BEAT EGG WHITE UNTIL FROTHY, THEN LIGHTLY BRUSH TOPS OF EACH ROUND. PUT A PECAN HALF ON TOP OF EACH ROUND AND BRUSH PECAN LIGHTLY WITH EGG WHITE. BAKE COOKIES IN THE MIDDLE OF THE OVEN UNTIL TOPS ARE PALE GOLDEN, 15-20 MINUTES. COOL COOKIES ON COOKIE SHEETS FOR 2 MINUTES, THEN TRANSFER COOKIES TO RACKS TO COOL COMPLETELY.

STORE IN AN AIRTIGHT CONTAINER. MAKES ABOUT $2\frac{1}{2}$ DOZEN.

A CLEAR CONSCIENCE IS USUALLY THE SIGN OF A BAD MEMORY.

# WAFER PUFFS

THESE LITTLE SANDWICH COOKIES MELT IN YOUR MOUTH AND PUFF UP YOUR CHEEKS!

| | | |
|---|---|---|
| 1 CUP | BUTTER | 250 ML |
| 2 CUPS | FLOUR | 500 ML |
| 1/2 CUP | WHIPPING CREAM | 125 ML |
| SOME | WHITE SUGAR | A BIT |

## FILLING

| | | |
|---|---|---|
| 1/4 CUP | BUTTER | 60 ML |
| 1/2 TSP. | VANILLA | 2 ML |
| 1 | EGG YOLK | 1 |
| 1 1/2-2 CUPS | ICING (CONFECTIONER'S) SUGAR | 375-500 ML |

IN A MEDIUM BOWL, CUT BUTTER INTO FLOUR TO FORM A CRUMBLY MIXTURE. ADD CREAM AND MIX LIGHTLY. ROLL OUT DOUGH TO 1/4" (6 MM) AND CUT OUT IN 1" (2.5 CM) CIRCLES. PRICK WITH A FORK AND SUGAR BOTH SIDES. PLACE ON UNGREASED COOKIE SHEETS AND BAKE AT 375°F (190°C) FOR 7-9 MINUTES.

TO MAKE FILLING: BEAT BUTTER, VANILLA AND EGG YOLK TOGETHER. ADD ENOUGH SUGAR TO MAKE A VERY CREAMY BUT FAIRLY STIFF ICING. SPREAD FILLING BETWEEN 2 COOKIES TO MAKE SANDWICHES.

# FRENCH BUTTON COOKIES

YOU <u>MUST</u> MAKE THESE!

| | | |
|---|---|---|
| 1 CUP | BUTTER, ROOM TEMPERATURE | 250 ML |
| 2/3 CUP | PACKED BROWN SUGAR | 150 ML |
| 1 | LARGE EGG | 1 |
| 1 TSP. | VANILLA | 5 ML |
| 2 1/2 CUPS | FLOUR | 625 ML |
| 1 TSP. | SALT | 5 ML |
| 1/2 CUP | TURBINADO * OR REGULAR SUGAR | 125 ML |

COMBINE BUTTER AND BROWN SUGAR IN A BOWL AND BEAT ON HIGH SPEED UNTIL FLUFFY. ADD EGG AND VANILLA AND BEAT TO COMBINE. ADD FLOUR AND SALT AND BEAT ON LOW SPEED UNTIL FLOUR IS INCORPORATED. ROLL DOUGH INTO THREE LOGS 1 1/2" (4 CM) IN DIAMETER. WRAP IN PLASTIC WRAP AND REFRIGERATE UNTIL FIRM, AT LEAST 1 HOUR. PREHEAT OVEN TO 350°F (180°C). LINE A COOKIE SHEET WITH PARCHMENT PAPER. ROLL COOKIE LOGS IN SUGAR, COATING EVENLY, AND SLICE INTO 1/8" (3 MM) ROUNDS. PLACE COOKIES ABOUT 1" (2.5 CM) APART ON COOKIE SHEETS. USING A SKEWER, POKE 4 HOLES (LIKE BUTTON HOLES) IN EACH COOKIE. BAKE FOR 12 MINUTES, UNTIL GOLDEN BROWN. REMOVE FROM OVEN AND LET COOL COMPLETELY ON WIRE RACKS.

*TURBINADO SUGAR IS STEAM-CLEANED RAW SUGAR. THE COARSE CRYSTALS ARE BLOND-COLORED, WITH A DELICATE MOLASSES FLAVOR.

# GINGER COOKIES

SPICY AND CHEWY!

| | | |
|---|---|---:|
| 1 1/2 CUPS | SHORTENING | 375 ML |
| 2 CUPS | SUGAR | 500 ML |
| 2 | EGGS, BEATEN | 2 |
| 1/4 CUP | MOLASSES | 60 ML |
| 4 CUPS | FLOUR | 1 L |
| 4 TSP. | BAKING SODA | 20 ML |
| 1/2 TSP. | SALT | 2 ML |
| 4 TSP. | GROUND GINGER | 20 ML |
| 2 TSP. | GROUND CINNAMON | 10 ML |
| 2 TSP. | GROUND CLOVES | 10 ML |
| 1/4 TSP. | GROUND WHITE PEPPER (OPTIONAL) | 1 ML |
| | SUGAR | |

IN A LARGE BOWL, CREAM SHORTENING AND SUGAR
TOGETHER. BEAT EGGS AND MOLASSES TOGETHER AND
BLEND WITH CREAMED SUGAR MIXTURE. COMBINE FLOUR,
BAKING SODA, SALT, GINGER, CINNAMON, CLOVES AND
WHITE PEPPER. ADD DRY INGREDIENTS TO CREAMED
MIXTURE AND BLEND WELL. CHILL FOR 1 HOUR. SHAPE
DOUGH INTO 1" (2.5 CM) BALLS AND ROLL IN SUGAR.
PREHEAT OVEN TO 350°F (180°C). PLACE BALLS ON
UNGREASED COOKIE SHEETS 2" (5 CM) APART AND
BAKE FOR 8-9 MINUTES. MAKES ABOUT 6 DOZEN
SPICY COOKIES!

THE ONLY THING BETTER THAN A DRY MARTINI IS TWO DRY
MARTINIS.

# MRS. SMITH'S OATCAKES

A TIMELESS SCOTTISH RECIPE. THEY'RE GOOD ON THEIR OWN OR WITH FRUIT AND CHEESE!

| | | |
|---|---|---:|
| 3 CUPS | FLOUR | 750 ML |
| 3 CUPS | ROLLED OATS (NOT INSTANT) | 750 ML |
| I CUP | SUGAR | 250 ML |
| 2 TSP. | SALT | 10 ML |
| I TSP. | BAKING SODA | 5 ML |
| 1½ CUPS | LARD | 375 ML |
| ¾ CUP | WATER | 175 ML |

ROLLED OATS

IN A LARGE BOWL, MIX DRY INGREDIENTS TOGETHER. CUT IN LARD WITH A PASTRY BLENDER. ADD WATER. USING YOUR HANDS, FORM DOUGH INTO A BALL. PLACE DOUGH ON A CLEAN WORKING SURFACE SPREAD WITH MORE ROLLED OATS AND ROLL TO ¼" (6 MM) THICKNESS. CUT INTO 2" (5 CM) SQUARES; PLACE ON LIGHTLY GREASED COOKIE SHEETS. BAKE AT 375°F (190°C) FOR 20-25 MINUTES. COOL AND STORE IN AN AIRTIGHT CONTAINER. MAKES 6 DOZEN.

HE'S SUCH A DIPLOMAT, HIS FAVORITE COLOR IS PLAID.

# OATMEAL CRISPIES

YOU MUST TRY THESE – THEY'RE VERY MORE-ISH!

| 1 CUP | BUTTER, SOFTENED | 250 ML |
| ½ CUP | SUGAR | 125 ML |
| 1 CUP | FLOUR | 250 ML |
| 1½ CUPS | ROLLED OATS | 375 ML |

ICING (CONFECTIONER'S) SUGAR

PREHEAT OVEN TO 350°F (180°C). IN A LARGE BOWL, BEAT BUTTER AND SUGAR TOGETHER UNTIL CREAMY. COMBINE FLOUR AND ROLLED OATS. MIX INTO CREAMED MIXTURE. SHAPE DOUGH INTO MEDIUM-SIZED BALLS AND PLACE ABOUT 3" (8 CM) APART ON UNGREASED COOKIE SHEETS. FLATTEN WITH A FORK DIPPED IN WATER. BAKE FOR 10 MINUTES. COOL BEFORE REMOVING FROM COOKIE SHEETS.

WHEN COMPLETELY COOL, GENEROUSLY DUST WITH ICING SUGAR. MAKES 3 DOZEN COOKIES.

IT MAY BE THAT YOUR SOLE PURPOSE IN LIFE IS SIMPLY TO SERVE AS A WARNING TO OTHERS.

# TOFFEE CRANBERRY CRISPS

IF YOU'RE A CHEWY COOKIE FAN, FIRE UP THE OVEN – YOU'RE GOING TO ENJOY THESE!

| | | |
|---|---|---|
| I CUP | BUTTER | 250 ML |
| 3/4 CUP | SUGAR | 175 ML |
| 3/4 CUP | PACKED BROWN SUGAR | 175 ML |
| I | EGG | I |
| I TSP. | VANILLA | 5 ML |
| 2 CUPS | FLOUR | 500 ML |
| 1 1/2 CUPS | ROLLED OATS | 375 ML |
| I TSP. | BAKING SODA | 5 ML |
| 1/4 TSP. | SALT | I ML |
| 1 1/2 CUPS | DRIED CRANBERRIES | 375 ML |
| I CUP | TOFFEE BITS (CHECK THE BAKING SECTION OF YOUR SUPERMARKET) | 250 ML |

CREAM TOGETHER BUTTER AND SUGARS. BEAT IN EGG AND VANILLA. COMBINE FLOUR, OATS, BAKING SODA AND SALT; GRADUALLY ADD TO CREAMED MIXTURE. MIX IN CRANBERRIES AND TOFFEE BITS. PLACE TEASPOONFULS OF DOUGH 2" (5 CM) APART ON GREASED COOKIE SHEETS. DON'T MAKE THEM TOO LARGE – THEY SPREAD! BAKE AT 350°F (180°C) FOR 10 MINUTES, UNTIL GOLDEN BROWN. COOL ON A WIRE RACK. MAKES 5 DOZEN.

EAT A LIVE TOAD IN THE MORNING AND NOTHING WORSE WILL HAPPEN TO YOU FOR THE REST OF THE DAY.

# SKOR BAR COOKIES

CHEWY TREATS FOR YOUR FAVORITE PEOPLE.

| | | |
|---|---|---|
| 1 CUP | BUTTER | 250 ML |
| 3/4 CUP | BROWN SUGAR | 175 ML |
| 1/2 CUP | SUGAR | 125 ML |
| 1 | EGG | 1 |
| 2 TBSP. | MILK | 30 ML |
| 2 TSP. | VANILLA | 10 ML |
| 1 3/4 CUPS | FLOUR | 425 ML |
| 3/4 CUP | ROLLED OATS | 175 ML |
| 1 TSP. | BAKING SODA | 5 ML |
| 1/4 TSP. | SALT | 1 ML |
| 4 | SKOR BARS OR ANY CRUNCHY TOFFEE CHOCOLATE-COATED BARS, BROKEN INTO SMALL PIECES | 4-39 G |
| 1 CUP | SLIVERED ALMONDS, TOASTED | 250 ML |

PREHEAT OVEN TO 350°F (180°C). CREAM BUTTER, SUGARS, EGG, MILK AND VANILLA IN A LARGE BOWL. BEAT UNTIL LIGHT AND CREAMY. COMBINE FLOUR, OATS, BAKING SODA AND SALT. ADD TO CREAMED MIXTURE AND BLEND WELL. STIR IN SKOR BAR PIECES AND ALMONDS. DROP DOUGH BY TEASPOONFULS ON GREASED COOKIE SHEETS. (LEAVE ROOM FOR SPREADING – THE COOKIES, NOT YOU!) BAKE FOR 8-10 MINUTES, OR UNTIL GOLDEN. COOL SLIGHTLY, THEN REMOVE TO A COOLING RACK.

NEVER PUT BOTH FEET IN YOUR MOUTH AT THE SAME TIME. YOU WON'T HAVE A LEG TO STAND ON.

# BETTER-THAN-MOM'S
## OATMEAL COOKIES

TALK ABOUT RAVES!

| | | |
|---|---|---|
| 1 CUP | BUTTER | 250 ML |
| 1 CUP | SUGAR | 250 ML |
| 1 CUP | BROWN SUGAR | 250 ML |
| 2 | LARGE EGGS | 2 |
| 2 TSP. | VANILLA | 10 ML |
| 1 1/2 CUPS | FLOUR | 375 ML |
| 1 1/8 TSP. | BAKING SODA | 5.5 ML |
| 1 TSP. | SALT | 5 ML |
| 1 TSP. | CINNAMON | 5 ML |
| 1/2 TSP. | MACE | 2 ML |
| 1/2 TSP. | NUTMEG | 2 ML |
| 1/2 TSP. | GROUND CLOVES | 2 ML |
| 3 CUPS | ROLLED OATS | 750 ML |
| 1 CUP | CHOPPED WALNUTS OR PECANS | 250 ML |
| 1 CUP | GOLDEN RAISINS | 250 ML |

IN A LARGE BOWL, CREAM BUTTER AND SUGARS UNTIL LIGHT AND FLUFFY. BEAT IN EGGS AND VANILLA. IN A MEDIUM-SIZED BOWL, COMBINE FLOUR, SODA, SALT, CINNAMON, MACE, NUTMEG AND CLOVES. GRADUALLY ADD DRY INGREDIENTS TO CREAMED MIXTURE, MIXING UNTIL COMPLETELY BLENDED. MIX IN OATS, NUTS AND RAISINS. PREHEAT OVEN TO 350°F (180°C). LIGHTLY GREASE COOKIE SHEETS AND DROP TEASPOONFULS OF DOUGH ABOUT 2" (5 CM) APART. FLATTEN SLIGHTLY. BAKE FOR 8-10 MINUTES FOR A SOFT COOKIE, 12 MINUTES FOR A CRUNCHY COOKIE. COOL ON WIRE RACK. MAKES ABOUT 4 DOZEN COOKIES.

# CARROT HERMITS

AS HEALTHY AS A COOKIE CAN BE.

| | | |
|---|---|---|
| 1/2 CUP | BUTTER, SOFTENED | 125 ML |
| 1/2 CUP | BROWN SUGAR | 125 ML |
| 1 | EGG | 1 |
| 1 TSP. | VANILLA | 5 ML |
| 3/4 CUP | COARSELY GRATED CARROT | 175 ML |
| 1/2 CUP | SHREDDED COCONUT | 125 ML |
| 1 1/4 CUPS | FLOUR | 300 ML |
| 1/2 TSP. | BAKING POWDER | 2 ML |
| 1/2 TSP. | SALT | 2 ML |
| 1/2 TSP. | CINNAMON | 2 ML |
| 1/4 TSP. | NUTMEG | 1 ML |
| PINCH | CLOVES | PINCH |
| 3/4 CUP | RAISINS | 175 ML |
| 3/4 CUP | CHOPPED PECANS | 175 ML |

PREHEAT OVEN TO 350°F (180°C). CREAM BUTTER WITH BROWN SUGAR UNTIL FLUFFY. BEAT IN EGG. STIR IN VANILLA, CARROT AND COCONUT. COMBINE FLOUR, BAKING POWDER, SALT, CINNAMON, NUTMEG AND CLOVES. STIR INTO CREAMED MIXTURE. STIR IN RAISINS AND PECANS. LINE BAKING SHEETS WITH PARCHMENT PAPER. DROP LARGE SPOONFULS OF DOUGH ONTO BAKING SHEETS. BAKE FOR 10-12 MINUTES, OR UNTIL BROWNED. MAKES 2 1/2 DOZEN COOKIES.

WHO DO PILGRIMS' PANTS FALL DOWN? BECAUSE THEY WEAR THEIR BUCKLES ON THEIR HATS.

# THE "BEST"
## CHOCOLATE CHIP COOKIE

EVERYONE HAS A FAVORITE . . . THIS IS OURS!

| | | |
|---|---|---|
| 2 1/4 CUPS | FLOUR | 550 ML |
| 1/2 TSP. | BAKING SODA | 2 ML |
| I CUP | BUTTER, ROOM TEMPERATURE | 250 ML |
| 1/2 CUP | SUGAR | 125 ML |
| I CUP | BROWN SUGAR, PACKED | 250 ML |
| I TSP. | SALT | 5 ML |
| 2 TSP. | VANILLA | 10 ML |
| 2 | LARGE EGGS | 2 |
| 2 CUPS | SEMISWEET CHOCOLATE CHIPS | 500 ML |

PREHEAT OVEN TO 350°F (180°C). IN A SMALL BOWL, WHISK TOGETHER FLOUR AND BAKING SODA AND SET ASIDE. IN A LARGE BOWL, BEAT BUTTER AND SUGARS ON MEDIUM SPEED UNTIL LIGHT AND FLUFFY. REDUCE SPEED TO LOW AND ADD SALT, VANILLA AND EGGS. BEAT FOR ABOUT I MINUTE, UNTIL WELL MIXED. ADD FLOUR MIXTURE AND BEAT UNTIL JUST COMBINED. STIR IN CHOCOLATE CHIPS. ON A PARCHMENT-COVERED COOKIE SHEET, DROP HEAPING SPOONFULS OF DOUGH ABOUT 2" (5 CM) APART. BAKE FOR 10-12 MINUTES. REMOVE FROM OVEN AND LET COOL ON BAKING SHEETS ABOUT 2 MINUTES. TRANSFER TO WIRE RACK AND COOL COMPLETELY. MAKES 3-4 DOZEN.

# BROWNIES

OUR "BEST"!

| | | |
|---|---|---:|
| 1 CUP | SUGAR | 250 ML |
| 1/3 CUP | BUTTER | 75 ML |
| | PINCH OF SALT | |
| 2 | EGGS, BEATEN | 2 |
| 1/4 CUP | COCOA POWDER | 60 ML |
| 2/3 CUP | FLOUR | 150 ML |
| 1/3 CUP | MILK OR CREAM | 75 ML |
| 1 TSP. | VANILLA | 5 ML |
| 1/2 CUP | CHOPPED WALNUTS OR PECANS | 125 ML |

## MOCHA ICING

| | | |
|---|---|---:|
| 3 TBSP. | COCOA POWDER | 45 ML |
| 2 TBSP. | BUTTER, SOFTENED | 30 ML |
| 3 TBSP. | COFFEE (LIQUID) | 45 ML |
| 2 TSP. | VANILLA | 10 ML |
| | ICING (CONFECTIONER'S) SUGAR | |

PREHEAT OVEN TO 350°F (180°C). IN A LARGE BOWL, CREAM TOGETHER SUGAR AND BUTTER. STIR IN SALT, EGGS, COCOA, FLOUR, MILK, VANILLA AND WALNUTS. POUR INTO A GREASED 8" (20 CM) SQUARE PAN AND BAKE FOR 20-25 MINUTES, OR UNTIL A KNIFE COMES OUT CLEAN WHEN INSERTED IN THE CENTER. COOL ON A WIRE RACK.

TO MAKE ICING: BEAT COCOA, BUTTER, COFFEE, VANILLA AND ENOUGH ICING SUGAR TO REACH DESIRED CONSISTENCY. SPREAD ON COOLED BROWNIES. THIS RECIPE DOUBLES WELL. USE A 9 X 13" (23 X 33 CM) PAN.

# CHEWY CHOCOLATE PEANUT BARS

TASTES LIKE ALMOND ROCA AND MAKES ENOUGH TO TREAT ABOUT FIVE DOZEN CONNOISSEURS.

| | | |
|---|---|---|
| 2 CUPS | ROLLED OATS | 500 ML |
| I CUP | GRAHAM WAFER CRUMBS | 250 ML |
| 3/4 CUP | BROWN SUGAR | 175 ML |
| 1/4 TSP. | BAKING SODA | I ML |
| 1/2 CUP | SALTED PEANUTS | 125 ML |
| 1/2 CUP | CORN SYRUP | 125 ML |
| 1/2 CUP | BUTTER, MELTED | 125 ML |
| I TSP. | VANILLA | 5 ML |
| 6 OZ. | PKG. SEMISWEET CHOCOLATE CHIPS | 170 G |
| 1/2 CUP | PEANUT BUTTER | 125 ML |

PREHEAT OVEN TO 375°F (190°C). GREASE A 15 X 10" (38 X 25 CM) EDGED COOKIE SHEET. IN A LARGE BOWL, COMBINE OATS, CRUMBS, SUGAR, BAKING SODA AND PEANUTS. MIX WELL. COMBINE CORN SYRUP WITH MELTED BUTTER AND VANILLA. STIR INTO OAT MIXTURE AND MIX WELL. PRESS INTO PAN AND BAKE FOR 15 MINUTES. MELT CHOCOLATE CHIPS AND PEANUT BUTTER TOGETHER IN A DOUBLE BOILER. SPREAD OVER WARM, BAKED BARS. COOL 10 MINUTES IN PAN AND CUT INTO 2 X 1" (5 X 2.5 CM) BARS. REFRIGERATE TO SET CHOCOLATE. MAKES 5 DOZEN BARS.

# CHOCOLATE RASPBERRY TRUFFLE SQUARES

DROP DEAD DELICIOUS!

## BROWNIE BASE

| | | |
|---|---|---:|
| 3-1 OZ. | SQUARES UNSWEETENED CHOCOLATE | 90 G |
| 1/3 CUP | BUTTER | 75 ML |
| 1/4 CUP | RASPBERRY JAM | 60 ML |
| 2 | EGGS | 2 |
| 1 CUP | SUGAR | 250 ML |
| 1 TSP. | VANILLA | 5 ML |
| 1/2 CUP | FLOUR | 125 ML |

## TOPPING

| | | |
|---|---|---:|
| 2 TBSP. | WHIPPING CREAM | 30 ML |
| 2 TBSP. | RASPBERRY JAM | 30 ML |
| 2 TBSP. | BUTTER | 30 ML |
| 4-1 OZ. | SQUARES SEMISWEET CHOCOLATE, CHOPPED | 120 G |
| 1 CUP | FRESH RASPBERRIES | 250 ML |

TO MAKE BASE: PREHEAT OVEN TO 350°F (180°C). LINE AN 8" (20 CM) SQUARE PAN WITH FOIL; GREASE AND SET ASIDE. COMBINE CHOCOLATE, BUTTER AND JAM IN A SAUCEPAN. STIR OVER LOW HEAT UNTIL SMOOTH. REMOVE FROM HEAT. BEAT EGGS IN A LARGE BOWL UNTIL FOAMY. MIX IN SUGAR, VANILLA AND CHOCOLATE MIXTURE. STIR IN FLOUR, JUST UNTIL BLENDED. SPREAD BATTER EVENLY IN PAN AND BAKE FOR 20-35 MINUTES, OR UNTIL SET.

CONTINUED ON PAGE 253.

Diddle Diddle Dumplings, page 278

Plum Upside-Down Cakes with Mascarpone Cream, page 290

## CHOCOLATE RASPBERRY TRUFFLE SQUARES

CONTINUED FROM PAGE 252.

COOL COMPLETELY IN PAN ON A RACK.

TO MAKE TOPPING: COMBINE, CREAM, JAM AND BUTTER IN A SAUCEPAN. HEAT TO A SIMMER, STIRRING CONSTANTLY UNTIL MELTED. REMOVE FROM HEAT AND ADD CHOCOLATE, STIRRING UNTIL SMOOTH. LET STAND UNTIL COOL BUT STILL SOFT, ABOUT 30 MINUTES. SPREAD TOPPING OVER BROWNIE BASE. IMMEDIATELY TOP WITH RASPBERRIES AND CHILL UNTIL COLD. CUT INTO SMALL SQUARES. (PICTURED OPPOSITE PAGE 199).

MOTHER TO TEENAGE DAUGHTER: "TONIGHT WAS YOUR LITTLE BROTHER'S TURN TO CHOOSE THE MEAL. WE'RE HAVING GUM."

# BRANDIED CRANBERRY APRICOT BARS

NOT TOO SWEET - GOOD CHRISTMAS BAKING.

## CRUST

| | | |
|---|---|---|
| I CUP | FLOUR | 250 ML |
| 1/3 CUP | PACKED BROWN SUGAR | 75 ML |
| 1/3 CUP | BUTTER | 75 ML |

## THE FRUIT

| | | |
|---|---|---|
| 1/3 CUP | GOLDEN RAISINS | 75 ML |
| 1/3 CUP | DARK RAISINS | 75 ML |
| 1/3 CUP | DRIED CRANBERRIES | 75 ML |
| 1/3 CUP | CHOPPED DRIED APRICOTS | 75 ML |
| 1/3 CUP | BRANDY OR WATER | 75 ML |

## FILLING

| | | |
|---|---|---|
| 2 | EGGS | 2 |
| I CUP | PACKED BROWN SUGAR | 250 ML |
| 1/3 CUP | FLOUR | 75 ML |
| I TSP. | VANILLA | 5 ML |
| 1/3 CUP | CHOPPED PECANS | 75 ML |

ICING (CONFECTIONER'S) SUGAR

TO MAKE CRUST: COMBINE FLOUR AND SUGAR; CUT IN BUTTER UNTIL MIXTURE IS CRUMBLY. PRESS INTO AN UNGREASED 9" (23 CM) SQUARE PAN AND BAKE AT 350°F (180°C) FOR 15-20 MINUTES, UNTIL GOLDEN.

# BRANDIED CRANBERRY APRICOT BARS

CONTINUED FROM PAGE 254.

TO PREPARE FRUIT: PLACE ALL INGREDIENTS IN A SAUCEPAN, BRING TO A BOIL AND REMOVE FROM HEAT. LET STAND FOR 20 MINUTES. DRAIN.

TO MAKE FILLING: BEAT EGGS, ADD BROWN SUGAR, FLOUR AND VANILLA, MIXING WELL. STIR IN PECANS AND COOLED FRUIT.

TO ASSEMBLE: POUR FILLING OVER CRUST AND BAKE FOR 35-40 MINUTES. COVER WITH FOIL FOR THE LAST 10 MINUTES OF BAKING - THE TOP BECOMES VERY BROWN. WHEN COOL, SIFT ICING SUGAR OVER TOP. CUT INTO BARS.

I'M GIVING UP EXERCISE DUE TO ILLNESS AND FATIGUE; I'M SICK AND TIRED OF IT.

# DREAM SLICE

ALWAYS A HIT - ADD TO YOUR CHRISTMAS BAKING.

## CRUST

| | | |
|---|---|---|
| 1 1/3 CUPS | FLOUR | 325 ML |
| 1 TBSP. | SUGAR | 15 ML |
| 3/4 CUP | BUTTER | 175 ML |

## FILLING

| | | |
|---|---|---|
| 2 | EGGS | 2 |
| 1 CUP | BROWN SUGAR | 250 ML |
| 1 TSP. | VANILLA | 5 ML |
| 3 TBSP. | FLOUR | 45 ML |
| 1 TSP. | BAKING POWDER | 5 ML |
| | PINCH OF SALT | |
| 1 CUP | SHREDDED COCONUT | 250 ML |
| 2/3 CUP | CHOPPED WALNUTS | 150 ML |
| 1/4 CUP | SNIPPED GLACÉ CHERRIES | 60 ML |

## BUTTER ICING

| | | |
|---|---|---|
| 1/4 CUP | BUTTER, ROOM TEMPERATURE | 60 ML |
| 2 1/2 CUPS | ICING (CONFECTIONER'S) SUGAR | 625 ML |
| 3 TBSP. | CREAM | 45 ML |

TO MAKE CRUST: PREHEAT OVEN TO 350°F (180°C). COMBINE FLOUR AND SUGAR. CUT IN BUTTER WITH PASTRY BLENDER UNTIL CRUMBLY. PRESS FIRMLY INTO A LIGHTLY GREASED 8" (20 CM) SQUARE PAN. BAKE FOR 20 MINUTES.

TO MAKE FILLING: BEAT EGGS IN A LARGE BOWL, GRADUALLY ADD SUGAR AND VANILLA. MIX FLOUR, BAKING POWDER AND SALT TOGETHER, THEN ADD TO SUGAR MIXTURE. ADD REMAINING INGREDIENTS. SPREAD OVER CRUST.

# DREAM SLICE

CONTINUED FROM PAGE 256.

RETURN TO OVEN – LOWER TEMPERATURE TO 300°F (150°C). BAKE FOR 25-30 MINUTES, UNTIL TOP IS SET AND LIGHTLY BROWN. COOL.

TO MAKE ICING: BEAT INGREDIENTS TOGETHER AND SPREAD OVER COOLED SQUARE. FREEZES WELL.

# KRISPIE GRANOLA BARS

GREAT FOR GOLFERS, TRAIL RIDERS AND SNACKIN!

| | | |
|---|---|---|
| 2½ CUPS | RICE KRISPIES | 625 ML |
| 1 CUP | DRIED APRICOTS, QUARTERED | 250 ML |
| 1¼ CUPS | OATMEAL | 300 ML |
| 1¼ CUPS | SUNFLOWER SEEDS, TOASTED | 300 ML |
| ½ CUP | BROWN SUGAR | 125 ML |
| ¾ CUP | HONEY | 175 ML |
| ¾ CUP | PEANUT BUTTER, SUPER CHUNKY | 175 ML |

IN A MEDIUM BOWL, MIX RICE KRISPIES, APRICOTS, OATMEAL AND SUNFLOWER SEEDS. LINE A 10 X 15" (25 X 38 CM) PAN WITH PLASTIC WRAP. IN A LARGE POT, OVER LOW HEAT, MELT BROWN SUGAR, HONEY AND PEANUT BUTTER UNTIL BUBBLY. STIR SO IT WON'T BURN. STIR IN RICE KRISPIE MIXTURE. POUR INTO PAN AND PRESS DOWN. COOL. REMOVE PLASTIC WRAP AND CUT INTO SQUARES. KEEP REFRIGERATED.

# SALTED PEANUT BARS

BOY - ARE THESE GOOD!!

## CRUST

| | | |
|---|---|---|
| 1 1/2 CUPS | FLOUR | 375 ML |
| 3/4 CUP | PACKED BROWN SUGAR | 175 ML |
| 1/2 TSP. | SALT | 2 ML |
| 1/2 CUP | BUTTER, ROOM TEMPERATURE | 125 ML |
| 3 CUPS | SALTED PEANUTS | 750 ML |

## TOPPING

| | | |
|---|---|---|
| 1/2 CUP | CORN SYRUP | 125 ML |
| 2 TBSP. | BUTTER | 30 ML |
| 1 TBSP. | WATER | 15 ML |
| 1 CUP | BUTTERSCOTCH CHIPS | 250 ML |

PREHEAT OVEN TO 350°F (180°C). COMBINE CRUST INGREDIENTS AND BLEND WELL. PRESS INTO AN UNGREASED 10 X 15" (25 X 38 CM) PAN. BAKE FOR 12 MINUTES. SPRINKLE PEANUTS OVER CRUST. IN A SMALL SAUCEPAN, COMBINE TOPPING INGREDIENTS, BRING TO BOIL AND COOK FOR 2 MINUTES, STIRRING CONSTANTLY. POUR OVER NUTS AND RETURN TO OVEN FOR 15 MINUTES, UNTIL GOLDEN. COOL COMPLETELY BEFORE CUTTING. MAKES 48 BARS.

RESPONDEZ S'IL VOUS PLAID: HONK IF YOU'RE SCOTTISH.

# DESSERTS

Icebox Pudding
Peanut Butter Rice Krispies Ice-Cream Sandwiches
Toffee Crunch Ice-Cream Cake
Pumpkin Crème Brûlée
Triple Chocolate Cheesecake
Vanilla Panna Cotta
Angel Mocha Torte
Lemon Meringue Pie
French Lemon Pie
Pumpkin Chiffon Pie
Old-Fashioned Butter Tarts
Spiced Pecan Whiskey Tart
Fruit Poof
Diddle Diddle Dumplings
Little Sticky Toffee Puddings
Lemon Pudding
Apple Cobbler with Cheddar-Biscuit Topping
Rhubarb Cobbler
Fruit Crisp with Oat Crumble Crust
Apple Crisp with Toffee Sauce
Cajun Bread Pudding
with Rum Sauce and Soft Cream
Plum Upside-Down Cakes with Mascarpone Cream
Chocolate Volcanoes with Raspberry Coulis
Berry-Topped Chocolate Torte
Black Magic Cake
Armenian Orange Cake
Orange Chiffon Cake
Fresh Apple Cake

# ICEBOX PUDDING

LIGHT AND DELICIOUS. A FAMILY FAVORITE FOR AT LEAST THREE GENERATIONS – WHICH IS PROBABLY WHY IT'S CALLED ICEBOX PUDDING!

| | | |
|---|---|---|
| 1/2 CUP | GRAHAM WAFER CRUMBS | 125 ML |
| 1 CUP | WHIPPING CREAM | 250 ML |
| 3 | EGGS, SEPARATED | |
| 1 CUP | SUGAR, DIVIDED | 250 ML |
| 1 TBSP. | GELATIN (1 PKG) | 15 ML |
| | JUICE OF 1 LEMON | |
| | JUICE OF 1 ORANGE | |
| 1/4 CUP | GRAHAM WAFER CRUMBS | 60 ML |

SPREAD 1/2 CUP (125 ML) GRAHAM WAFER CRUMBS IN BOTTOM OF AN 8 1/2 X 4 1/2 X 2 1/2" (22 X 11 X 6 CM) LOAF PAN. WHIP CREAM UNTIL STIFF. IN ANOTHER BOWL, BEAT EGG WHITES UNTIL STIFF. GRADUALLY ADD 1/2 CUP (125 ML) SUGAR AND CONTINUE BEATING. IN A LARGE BOWL, BEAT EGG YOLKS WITH REMAINING SUGAR UNTIL LEMON COLORED. SOFTEN GELATIN IN LEMON AND ORANGE JUICES AND ADD TO YOLK MIXTURE. GENTLY FOLD IN EGG WHITES. FOLD IN WHIPPED CREAM AND POUR INTO LOAF PAN. SPRINKLE WITH REMAINING GRAHAM WAFER CRUMBS. FREEZE AT LEAST 4 HOURS OR OVERNIGHT.

AT LEAST 1 HOUR BEFORE SERVING, LOOSEN EDGES AND INVERT ONTO SERVING PLATE. LEAVE IN REFRIGERATOR.

# PEANUT BUTTER RICE KRISPIE ICE-CREAM SANDWICHES

KEEP THESE IN YOUR FREEZER FOR A SUMMER TREAT!

| | | |
|---|---|---|
| 1 CUP | LIGHT CORN SYRUP | 250 ML |
| 1 CUP | SMOOTH PEANUT BUTTER | 250 ML |
| 6 CUPS | RICE KRISPIES | 1.5 L |
| 1 QT. | VANILLA ICE CREAM, SLIGHTLY SOFTENED | 1 L |

LINE BOTTOM AND SIDES OF A 9 X 13" (23 X 33 CM) BAKING DISH WITH FOIL, LEAVING SOME OVERLAP. IN A LARGE BOWL, MIX CORN SYRUP AND PEANUT BUTTER UNTIL WELL BLENDED. ADD CEREAL AND STIR UNTIL WELL COATED. SPREAD HALF OF MIXTURE IN BAKING DISH. SPREAD ICE CREAM OVER TOP AND FREEZE UNTIL FIRM, ABOUT 30 MINUTES. SPREAD REMAINING CEREAL MIXTURE OVER TOP, WRAP WELL WITH PLASTIC WRAP AND FREEZE AGAIN UNTIL FIRM, AT LEAST 30 MINUTES. USE FOIL OVERLAP TO TRANSFER TO A CUTTING BOARD, DISCARD FOIL AND CUT INTO BARS. MAKES 32 BARS.

I'M NOT CHEAP, BUT I AM ON SPECIAL THIS MONTH.

# TOFFEE CRUNCH
# ICE-CREAM CAKE

A GOOD SUMMERTIME BIRTHDAY CAKE!

## CAKE

| | | |
|---|---|---|
| 1½ CUPS | CRUSHED CHOCOLATE WAFERS | 375 ML |
| ⅓ CUP | BUTTER, MELTED | 75 ML |
| 2 QTS. | VANILLA (OR COFFEE) ICE CREAM, SOFTENED | 2 L |
| 8 | 1½ OZ. (39 G) SKOR CHOCOLATE BARS, CRUSHED | 8 |
| 1¼ CUPS | UNSALTED PEANUTS, COARSELY CHOPPED | 300 ML |

## TOFFEE SAUCE

| | | |
|---|---|---|
| ½ CUP | BUTTER | 125 ML |
| 1 CUP | PACKED BROWN SUGAR | 250 ML |
| ½ CUP | HALF & HALF CREAM | 125 ML |
| 1 TSP. | VANILLA | 5 ML |

TO MAKE CAKE: GREASE A 9 X 13" (23 X 33 CM) PAN OR A 9" (23 CM) SPRINGFORM PAN. COMBINE WAFER CRUMBS AND BUTTER AND PRESS INTO BOTTOM OF PAN. PLACE IN FREEZER FOR 15 MINUTES. SPREAD HALF OF THE ICE CREAM OVER CRUST. SPRINKLE WITH CRUSHED SKOR BARS AND PRESS INTO ICE CREAM LAYER. CAREFULLY SPREAD REMAINING ICE CREAM OVER CRUMBS. SPRINKLE WITH PEANUTS AND FREEZE FOR 2-3 HOURS.

# TOFFEE CRUNCH
# ICE-CREAM CAKE

CONTINUED FROM PAGE 262.

TO MAKE SAUCE: IN A SMALL SAUCEPAN, MELT BUTTER OVER LOW HEAT. STIR IN BROWN SUGAR AND CREAM. COOK AND STIR CONSTANTLY OVER LOW HEAT UNTIL SUGAR HAS DISSOLVED. REMOVE FROM HEAT AND ADD VANILLA.

TO SERVE: REMOVE CAKE FROM PAN AND CUT INTO SLICES. POUR WARM OR COLD TOFFEE SAUCE OVER EACH SERVING.

WHAT DO YOU CALL CHEESE THAT ISN'T YOURS?
NACHO CHEESE!

# PUMPKIN CRÈME BRÛLÉE

ANOTHER THANKSGIVING FINALE FAVORITE! COOL AND STYLISH - IT NEVER FEELS LIKE TOO MUCH. AND - IN THE TRUE SPIRIT OF THE HOLIDAY SEASON - YOU CAN MAKE IT 2 DAYS AHEAD!

| | | |
|---|---|---:|
| 3 CUPS | WHIPPING CREAM | 750 ML |
| 8 | EGG YOLKS | 8 |
| 3/4 CUP | CANNED PUMPKIN | 175 ML |
| 1/3 CUP | SUGAR | 75 ML |
| 1/2 TSP. | CINNAMON | 2 ML |
| 1/4 TSP. | GROUND CLOVES | I ML |
| 1/4 TSP. | GINGER | I ML |
| 1/4 TSP. | NUTMEG | I ML |
| 1 1/2 TSP. | VANILLA | 7 ML |
| | | |
| 1/2 CUP | PACKED BROWN SUGAR | 125 ML |

IN A SAUCEPAN, HEAT CREAM OVER MEDIUM-HIGH HEAT UNTIL STEAMING. IN A BOWL, WHISK TOGETHER EGG YOLKS, PUMPKIN, SUGAR, CINNAMON, CLOVES, GINGER AND NUTMEG. GRADUALLY WHISK IN CREAM. WHISK IN VANILLA. SKIM OFF FOAM. DIVIDE AMONG 8, 6-OZ. (170 ML) RAMEKINS OR CUSTARD CUPS. PLACE IN 2 LARGE SHALLOW PANS AND POUR IN ENOUGH BOILING WATER TO COME HALFWAY UP SIDES OF RAMEKINS.

BAKE AT 350°F (180°C) FOR 30-35 MINUTES, OR UNTIL EDGES ARE SET AND CENTER IS STILL JIGGLY. A KNIFE INSERTED IN THE CENTER SHOULD COME OUT CREAMY.

# PUMPKIN CRÈME BRULÊE

CONTINUED FROM PAGE 264.

REMOVE RAMEKIN FROM WATER AND LET COOL ON RACKS. COVER AND REFRIGERATE UNTIL SET (ABOUT 2 HOURS).

PLACE RAMEKINS ON A RIMMED BAKING SHEET AND PAT TOPS DRY WITH A PAPER TOWEL. SPRINKLE BROWN SUGAR EVENLY OVER TOPS AND BROIL 6" (15 CM) FROM HEAT UNTIL SUGAR BUBBLES AND DARKENS. WATCH CAREFULLY AS THEY CAN BURN. REFRIGERATE AGAIN, UNCOVERED, FOR AT LEAST 30 MINUTES, OR UNTIL READY TO SERVE.

I DON'T KNOW HOW I GOT OVER THE HILL WITHOUT GETTING TO THE TOP.

# TRIPLE CHOCOLATE CHEESECAKE

YOU MIGHT BE FULL TO THE BRIM AND VERY WELL FED, BUT YOU'LL FIND ROOM FOR THIS TREAT AND "WADDLE" OFF TO BED!

## CHOCOLATE CRUST

| | | |
|---|---|---|
| 1½ CUPS | CHOCOLATE WAFER CRUMBS | 375 ML |
| ¼ CUP | BUTTER, MELTED | 60 ML |
| 3 TBSP. | SUGAR | 45 ML |
| ¼ TSP. | CINNAMON | I ML |

## CHOCOLATE FILLING

| | | |
|---|---|---|
| ½ CUP | SOUR CREAM | 125 ML |
| 2 TSP. | VANILLA | 10 ML |
| I TSP. | ESPRESSO POWDER OR INSTANT COFFEE GRANULES | 5 ML |
| 8 | I OZ. (28 G) BITTERSWEET CHOCOLATE SQUARES | 8 |
| 3 | 8 OZ. (250 G) PKGS. CREAM CHEESE, ROOM TEMPERATURE | 3 |
| 3 TBSP. | COCOA POWDER | 45 ML |
| ¼ TSP. | SALT | I ML |
| I CUP | SUGAR | 250 ML |
| 3 | LARGE EGGS | 3 |

TO MAKE CRUST: PREHEAT OVEN TO 400°F (200°C). PLACE WAFER CRUMBS IN A MEDIUM BOWL. ADD BUTTER, SUGAR AND CINNAMON. BLEND WELL. PAT MIXTURE INTO A 9" (23 CM) SPRINGFORM PAN AND PUSH CRUMBS UP SIDES ABOUT I" (2.5 CM). BAKE FOR 10 MINUTES. SET ON A RACK TO COOL. TURN OVEN DOWN TO 300°F (150°C).

# TRIPLE CHOCOLATE CHEESECAKE

CONTINUED FROM PAGE 266.

TO MAKE FILLING: IN SMALL BOWL MIX SOUR CREAM, VANILLA AND ESPRESSO. STIR UNTIL COFFEE IS DISSOLVED. IN A DOUBLE BOILER, MELT CHOCOLATE, STIRRING UNTIL SMOOTH. LET COOL.

IN LARGE BOWL, BEAT CREAM CHEESE, COCOA AND SALT UNTIL SMOOTH AND FLUFFY. ADD SUGAR AND BEAT UNTIL WELL BLENDED. POUR IN MELTED CHOCOLATE AND BEAT AGAIN. ADD SOUR CREAM MIXTURE AND MIX THOROUGHLY. ADD EGGS 1 AT A TIME, BEATING AFTER EACH ADDITION. (DON'T MIX TOO MUCH OR CAKE WILL BE TOO PUFFY.) POUR BATTER OVER COOLED CRUST AND SMOOTH TOP WITH A SPATULA.

*PLACE IN MIDDLE OF OVEN AND BAKE FOR 60-70 MINUTES. THE CENTER SHOULD BARELY JIGGLE WHEN NUDGED. SET ON RACK AND COOL TO ROOM TEMPERATURE. REFRIGERATE TO CHILL THOROUGHLY. CAKE CAN ALSO BE FROZEN. PLACE IN FREEZER, UNCOVERED, UNTIL TOP IS COLD AND FIRM. THEN WRAP IN 2 LAYERS OF PLASTIC WRAP AND 1 LAYER OF FOIL.

TO SERVE: RUN METAL SPATULA UNDER BOTTOM CRUST AND SLIDE CAKE ONTO SERVING PLATE. USE A WARM KNIFE TO MAKE CLEAN CUTS.

*TO AVOID CRACKING: BEFORE BAKING, WRAP OUTSIDE AND BOTTOM OF PAN WITH FOIL AND PLACE A PAN OF WATER ON RACK DIRECTLY BELOW CAKE. SERVES 12 GRATEFUL GUESTS.

# VANILLA PANNA COTTA

YOU'LL NEVER MAKE ANYTHING ELSE THAT'S THIS GOOD AND THIS EASY! THE TEXTURE IS LIKE VELVET!

| | | |
|---|---|---|
| 1 TBSP. | GELATIN (1 PKG.) | 15 ML |
| 1/2 CUP | MILK | 125 ML |
| 3 CUPS | WHIPPING CREAM | 750 ML |
| 1/2 CUP | MILK | 125 ML |
| 1/2 CUP | SUGAR | 125 ML |
| 1 TSP. | VANILLA | 5 ML |

## GARNISH

MANGO, PINEAPPLE, RASPBERRIES, KIWI FRUIT, PEACHES

IN A LARGE BOWL, ADD GELATIN TO COLD MILK AND LET SOFTEN. IN A SAUCEPAN, COMBINE CREAM, MILK, SUGAR AND VANILLA AND BRING TO A BOIL. POUR OVER GELATIN MIXTURE; STIR UNTIL COMPLETELY DISSOLVED. SET BOWL OVER VERY COLD WATER AND CHILL 1/2 HOUR, STIRRING OCCASIONALLY, UNTIL ALMOST SET. POUR INTO 8, 1/2 CUP (125 ML) RAMEKINS AND REFRIGERATE. COVER WITH PLASTIC WRAP IF MAKING THE NIGHT BEFORE. TO SERVE, QUICKLY DIP RAMEKINS IN WARM WATER TO LOOSEN SIDES. INVERT ONTO INDIVIDUAL SERVING PLATES AND SHAKE TO RELEASE. CUT FRUIT INTO SMALL PIECES AND ARRANGE ON EACH PLATE AROUND PANNA COTTA. SERVES 8.

# ANGEL MOCHA TORTE

A CLASSIC ENTERTAINING DESSERT.

## MERINGUES

| | | |
|---|---|---|
| I CUP | SLICED ALMONDS | 250 ML |
| 4 | EGG WHITES | 4 |
| | PINCH OF SALT | |
| I CUP | BROWN SUGAR | 250 ML |

## MOCHA FILLING

| | | |
|---|---|---|
| I CUP | WHIPPING CREAM | 250 ML |
| 1/2 CUP | BROWN SUGAR | 125 ML |
| I TBSP. | INSTANT COFFEE GRANULES | 10 ML |
| | | |
| 4 | 9" (23 CM) CIRCLES OF PARCHMENT PAPER | 4 |

TO MAKE MERINGUES: TOAST ALMONDS; RESERVING SOME FOR DECORATION; CRUSH THE REMAINDER. BEAT EGG WHITES AND SALT UNTIL ALMOST STIFF. GRADUALLY ADD SUGAR; BEAT UNTIL GLOSSY PEAKS FORM. FOLD IN CRUSHED ALMONDS. SPREAD 1/4 OF MERINGUE ON EACH PAPER CIRCLE. DECORATE I CIRCLE WITH RESERVED ALMONDS. PLACE ON 2 COOKIE SHEETS; BAKE AT 250°F (120°C) FOR I HOUR. TURN OFF OVEN AND LEAVE OVERNIGHT. DON'T PEEK!! NEXT DAY, REMOVE MERINGUES AND TAKE OFF PARCHMENT PAPER.

TO MAKE FILLING: WHIP CREAM. FOLD IN SUGAR AND COFFEE GRANULES. PLACE A MERINGUE ON A SERVING PLATE. SPREAD WITH 1/3 OF FILLING. CONTINUE WITH REMAINING MERINGUES, FINISHING WITH DECORATED MERINGUE. REFRIGERATE AT LEAST 2 HOURS BEFORE SERVING. SERVES 8-10.

# LEMON MERINGUE PIE

IN CASE MOM DIDN'T TEACH YOU HOW.

## LEMON FILLING

| | | |
|---|---|---:|
| 1 CUP | SUGAR | 250 ML |
| 1/4 CUP | CORNSTARCH | 60 ML |
| 1 1/2 CUPS | COLD WATER | 375 ML |
| 3 | EGG YOLKS, SLIGHTLY BEATEN | 3 |
| | GRATED ZEST OF 1 LEMON | |
| 1/4 CUP | FRESH LEMON JUICE | 60 ML |
| 1 TBSP. | BUTTER | 15 ML |
| 1 | BAKED 9" (23 CM) PIE CRUST | 1 |

## MERINGUE

| | | |
|---|---|---:|
| 3 | EGG WHITES | 3 |
| 1/3 CUP | SUGAR | 75 ML |

TO MAKE FILLING: IN A MEDIUM SAUCEPAN, COMBINE SUGAR AND CORNSTARCH. GRADUALLY STIR IN WATER UNTIL SMOOTH. STIR IN EGG YOLKS. STIRRING CONSTANTLY, BRING TO A BOIL OVER MEDIUM HEAT AND BOIL FOR 1 MINUTE. REMOVE FROM HEAT. STIR IN LEMON ZEST, LEMON JUICE AND BUTTER. SPOON HOT FILLING INTO CRUST.

PREHEAT OVEN TO 350°F (180°C).

TO MAKE MERINGUE: BEAT EGG WHITES IN A BOWL AT HIGH SPEED UNTIL FOAMY. GRADUALLY BEAT IN REMAINING SUGAR UNTIL STIFF PEAKS FORM. MOUND MERINGUE EVENLY OVER HOT FILLING TO EDGE OF CRUST, SEALING WELL. BAKE PIE FOR 15-20 MINUTES OR UNTIL GOLDEN. COOL ON RACK; REFRIGERATE.

Chocolate Volcanoes with Raspberry Coulis, page 292

Orange Chiffon Cake, page 298

# FRENCH LEMON PIE

LEMON FILLING

| | | |
|---|---|---|
| 4 | EGGS | 4 |
| 1 CUP | LIGHT CORN SYRUP | 250 ML |
| 1 TSP. | GRATED LEMON ZEST | 5 ML |
| 1/3 CUP | LEMON JUICE | 75 ML |
| 2 TBSP. | MELTED BUTTER | 30 ML |
| 1/2 CUP | SUGAR | 125 ML |
| 2 TBSP. | FLOUR | 30 ML |
| | | |
| 1 | UNBAKED 9" (23 CM) PIE SHELL | 1 |
| 1/2 CUP | WHIPPING CREAM | 125 ML |

IN A MEDIUM BOWL, BEAT EGGS; ADD CORN SYRUP, LEMON ZEST, LEMON JUICE AND MELTED BUTTER. MIX SUGAR AND FLOUR TOGETHER, THEN STIR INTO EGG MIXTURE. POUR INTO UNBAKED PIE SHELL AND BAKE AT 350°F (180°C) FOR 50 MINUTES. CHILL.

JUST BEFORE SERVING, WHIP CREAM AND MOUND IT ON TOP OF THE PIE.

WHY ISN'T THE NUMBER 11 PRONOUNCED ONETY ONE?

# PUMPKIN CHIFFON PIE

YOU'LL BE "THANKFUL" FOR THIS ONE.

## PUMPKIN FILLING

| | | |
|---|---|---|
| 1 TBSP. | GELATIN (1 PKG.) | 15 ML |
| 1/2 CUP | COLD WATER | 125 ML |
| 4 | EGGS, SEPARATED | 4 |
| 1 CUP | EVAPORATED MILK | 250 ML |
| 1 CUP | CANNED PUMPKIN | 250 ML |
| 1/2 CUP | BROWN SUGAR | 125 ML |
| 1/2 TSP. | SALT | 2 ML |
| 1/2 TSP. | NUTMEG | 2 ML |
| 1/2 TSP. | CINNAMON | 2 ML |
| 1/4 TSP. | GINGER | 1 ML |
| 1/4 CUP | BROWN SUGAR | 60 ML |
| | | |
| 9" | BAKED PIE SHELL | 23 CM |
| 1 CUP | WHIPPING CREAM, WHIPPED | 250 ML |

TO MAKE FILLING: SOFTEN GELATIN IN COLD WATER. SET ASIDE. IN A DOUBLE BOILER, HEAT EGG YOLKS, MILK, PUMPKIN, BROWN SUGAR AND SPICES. COOK AND STIR FOR 10 MINUTES. REMOVE FROM HEAT; ADD GELATIN, STIRRING UNTIL DISSOLVED. REFRIGERATE UNTIL THICK. BEAT EGG WHITES AND BROWN SUGAR UNTIL THICK. FOLD INTO PUMPKIN MIXTURE.

TURN FILLING INTO PIE SHELL, TOP WITH WHIPPED CREAM AND REFRIGERATE UNTIL READY TO SERVE.

# OLD-FASHIONED BUTTER TARTS

THESE ARE QUICK AND EASY, ESPECIALLY IF YOU
PURCHASE THE TART SHELLS.

## FILLING

| | | |
|---|---|---|
| 1/3 CUP | BUTTER, MELTED | 75 ML |
| 1 1/2 CUPS | BROWN SUGAR | 375 ML |
| 3 | EGGS | 3 |
| 1 TSP. | GRATED LEMON ZEST | 5 ML |
| 1 CUP | CURRANTS | 250 ML |
| 1 TSP. | VANILLA | 5 ML |
| | | |
| 3 | DOZEN UNBAKED TART SHELLS | 3 |

TO MAKE FILLING: IN A MEDIUM BOWL, CREAM BUTTER
AND SUGAR. ADD EGGS 1 AT A TIME, BEATING WITH AN
ELECTRIC MIXER. STIR IN LEMON ZEST, CURRANTS
AND VANILLA.

PREHEAT OVEN TO 375°F (190°C). FILL TART SHELLS AND
BAKE FOR 12-15 MINUTES, OR UNTIL GOLDEN. MAKES
3 DOZEN TARTS.

A HANGOVER IS THE WRATH OF GRAPES.

# SPICED PECAN WHISKEY TART

IF YOU DON'T HAVE A TART PAN - YOU MUST! THE PRESENTATION IS PERFECT AND YOU DON'T HAVE TO ROLL THE PASTRY!

## PASTRY

| | | |
|---|---|---|
| 1¼ CUPS | FLOUR | 300 ML |
| 2 TBSP. | SUGAR | 30 ML |
| ¼ TSP. | SALT | 1 ML |
| ⅓ CUP | COLD BUTTER | 75 ML |
| 2 TBSP. | COLD WATER | 30 ML |
| 1 TSP. | WHITE VINEGAR | 5 ML |

## PECAN WHISKEY FILLING

| | | |
|---|---|---|
| 3 | EGGS | 3 |
| 1 CUP | PACKED BROWN SUGAR | 250 ML |
| ½ CUP | CORN SYRUP | 125 ML |
| ¼ CUP | RYE WHISKY OR BOURBON | 60 ML |
| 2 TBSP. | BUTTER, MELTED | 30 ML |
| ½ TSP. | CINNAMON | 2 ML |
| ¼ TSP. | NUTMEG | 1 ML |
| ¼ TSP. | GROUND CLOVES | 1 ML |
| ¼ TSP. | ALLSPICE | 1 ML |
| 1¼ CUPS | PECAN HALVES | 300 ML |
| 2 TBSP. | CORN SYRUP, WARMED | 30 ML |

WHIPPED CREAM FOR GARNISH

TO MAKE PASTRY: IN A LARGE BOWL, COMBINE FLOUR, SUGAR AND SALT. CUT IN BUTTER WITH PASTRY CUTTER UNTIL MIXTURE RESEMBLES FINE CRUMBS. ADD WATER AND VINEGAR AND MIX UNTIL BLENDED BUT STILL CRUMBLY.

# SPICED PECAN WHISKEY TART

CONTINUED FROM PAGE 274.

SQUEEZE TOGETHER IN SMALL HANDFULS AND PAT EVENLY OVER BOTTOM AND UP SIDES OF A 9" (23 CM) TART PAN WITH A REMOVABLE BOTTOM. PRESS DOWN FIRMLY AND REFRIGERATE FOR 15 MINUTES. (THIS CAN BE MADE AHEAD, COVERED AND REFRIGERATED FOR 24 HOURS.)

PREHEAT OVEN TO 375°F (190°C). IN A BOWL, WHISK TOGETHER EGGS, SUGAR, CORN SYRUP, RYE, BUTTER, CINNAMON, NUTMEG, CLOVES AND ALLSPICE; STIR IN PECANS. SCRAPE FILLING INTO PREPARED TART SHELL.

BAKE ON BOTTOM RACK OF OVEN UNTIL FILLING IS JUST FIRM TO THE TOUCH, ABOUT 45 MINUTES. COVER EDGE OF CRUST WITH FOIL IF IT BECOMES TOO BROWN. BRUSH FILLING WITH CORN SYRUP AND LET COOL ON A WIRE RACK. THIS MAY BE BAKED, COOLED, COVERED AND LEFT STANDING AT ROOM TEMPERATURE FOR UP TO 1 DAY. GENTLY REMOVE SIDES AND BASE. SERVE WITH A DOLLOP OF WHIPPED CREAM. SERVES 12.

DIJON VU: THE SAME MUSTARD AS BEFORE.

# FRUIT POOF

YOU SHOW-OFF YOU!

## PUFF

| | | |
|---|---|---|
| 2/3 CUP | WATER | 150 ML |
| 1/3 CUP | BUTTER | 75 ML |
| 2/3 CUP | FLOUR | 150 ML |

## CRUST

| | | |
|---|---|---|
| 2/3 CUP | FLOUR | 150 ML |
| 1 TBSP. | SUGAR | 15 ML |
| 1/4 CUP | BUTTER | 60 ML |
| | | |
| 3 | EGGS | 3 |

## FILLING

| | | |
|---|---|---|
| 3 1/2 OZ. | BOX INSTANT VANILLA PUDDING | 102 G |
| 1 1/2 CUPS | MILK | 375 ML |
| 1/2 CUP | WHIPPING CREAM | 125 ML |
| 2 CUPS | FRESH, SLICED PEACHES, KIWI HALVED STRAWBERRIES, HALVED GRAPES, BLUEBERRIES OR RASPBERRIES | 500 ML |
| 1/4 CUP | APPLE JELLY, MELTED | 60 ML |

TO MAKE PUFF: COMBINE WATER AND BUTTER IN A MEDIUM-SIZED SAUCEPAN AND BRING TO A BOIL, STIRRING TO MELT BUTTER. ADD FLOUR ALL AT ONCE. COOK AND STIR UNTIL MIXTURE FORMS A BALL THAT DOESN'T SEPARATE. SET ASIDE TO COOL FOR 15 MINUTES.

# FRUIT POOF

CONTINUED FROM PAGE 276.

TO MAKE CRUST: COMBINE FLOUR WITH SUGAR. CUT IN BUTTER UNTIL CRUMBLY. FIRMLY PRESS CRUMBS INTO AN 8" (20 CM) CIRCLE ON AN UNGREASED BAKING SHEET. SET ASIDE.

PREHEAT OVEN TO 400°F (200°C). ADD EGGS TO DOUGH IN SAUCEPAN, 1 AT A TIME, BEATING WELL AFTER EACH ADDITION. GENTLY SPREAD 1/4 OF THE DOUGH OVER CRUST, FORMING A 5" (13 CM) CIRCLE. DROP SPOONFULS OF DOUGH AROUND EDGE OF SMALLER CIRCLE. BAKE FOR 15 MINUTES THEN REDUCE HEAT TO 350°F (180°C) AND CONTINUE BAKING FOR 35-40 MINUTES. COOL.

TO MAKE FILLING: PREPARE PUDDING, USING MILK. BEAT CREAM AND FOLD INTO PUDDING. SPOON FILLING INTO CENTER OF PUFF. ARRANGE FRUIT ON TOP AND BRUSH FRUIT WITH MELTED JELLY. CHILL FOR 2 HOURS. SERVES 8.

READING WHILST SUNBATHING MAKES YOU . . .
WELL . . . RED!

# DIDDLE DIDDLE DUMPLINGS

YOUR SON JOHN (AND THE REST OF THE FAMILY) WILL
LOVE THIS OLD-FASHIONED APPLE DESSERT WITH A
NEW TWIST.

## SAUCE

| | | |
|---|---|---|
| 1 1/2 CUPS | BROWN SUGAR | 375 ML |
| 1 1/2 CUPS | WATER | 375 ML |
| 1/4 CUP | BUTTER | 60 ML |
| 1/2 TSP. | CINNAMON | 2 ML |
| 1/4 TSP. | NUTMEG | 1 ML |

## DOUGH

| | | |
|---|---|---|
| 2 CUPS | FLOUR | 500 ML |
| 2 TSP. | BAKING POWDER | 10 ML |
| 1/2 TSP. | SALT | 2 ML |
| 3/4 CUP | BUTTER | 175 ML |
| 2/3 CUP | MILK | 150 ML |

## FILLING

| | | |
|---|---|---|
| 4 | GRANNY SMITH APPLES | 4 |
| 1/2 TSP. | CINNAMON | 2 ML |

PREHEAT OVEN TO 350°F (180°C).

TO MAKE SAUCE: IN A LARGE SAUCEPAN, COMBINE
INGREDIENTS. BRING TO A BOIL FOR 5 MINUTES. REMOVE
FROM HEAT AND SET ASIDE.

TO MAKE DOUGH: IN A LARGE BOWL, COMBINE FLOUR,
BAKING POWDER AND SALT. USING A PASTRY BLENDER, CUT
IN BUTTER UNTIL PIECES ARE PEA-SIZE. MAKE A WELL IN
CENTER OF FLOUR MIXTURE.

# DIDDLE DIDDLE DUMPLINGS

CONTINUED FROM PAGE 278.

ADD MILK ALL AT ONCE. STIR JUST UNTIL MOISTENED. ON A LIGHTLY FLOURED SURFACE, KNEAD DOUGH GENTLY FOR 10-12 STROKES, OR UNTIL NEARLY SMOOTH. ROLL DOUGH INTO A 10 X 12" (25 X 30 CM) RECTANGLE.

TO MAKE FILLING: PEEL AND GRATE APPLES. SPREAD EVENLY OVER DOUGH. SPRINKLE WITH CINNAMON. STARTING FROM LONG SIDE, ROLL DOUGH INTO A TIGHT ROLL. PINCH SEAM TO SEAL. WITH A SHARP KNIFE, CUT INTO 12, 1" (2.5 CM) THICK SLICES. ARRANGE SLICES FACE UP IN A 9 X 13" (23 X 33 CM) BAKING DISH. POUR SAUCE OVER DUMPLINGS AND BAKE FOR ABOUT 50 MINUTES, OR UNTIL GOLDEN. COOL SLIGHTLY ON A WIRE RACK. SERVE WARM WITH WHIPPED CREAM OR ICE CREAM. (PICTURED OPPOSITE PAGE 252.)

THE QUICKEST WAY TO DOUBLE YOUR MONEY IS TO FOLD IT IN HALF AND PUT IT BACK IN YOUR POCKET.

# LITTLE STICKY TOFFEE PUDDINGS

| 1 CUP | WATER | 250 ML |
|---|---|---|
| 1/2 TSP. | VANILLA | 2 ML |
| 1/2 TSP. | BAKING SODA | 2 ML |
| 1 CUP | DRIED CRANBERRIES | 250 ML |
| 3/4 CUP | BUTTER | 175 ML |
| 2/3 CUP | SUGAR | 150 ML |
| 2 | EGGS | 2 |
| 1 CUP | FLOUR | 250 ML |
| 1/4 TSP. | BAKING POWDER | 1 ML |

## TOFFEE SAUCE

| 1 CUP | BROWN SUGAR | 250 ML |
|---|---|---|
| 1/2 CUP | BUTTER | 125 ML |
| 1/2 CUP | WHIPPING CREAM | 125 ML |

BUTTER 8, 4-OZ. (125 ML) RAMEKINS. BRING WATER TO A BOIL; ADD VANILLA AND BAKING SODA. ADD CRANBERRIES; SET ASIDE TO COOL. CREAM BUTTER AND SUGAR UNTIL LIGHT AND FLUFFY. LIGHTLY BEAT EGGS AND GRADUALLY ADD TO BUTTER MIXTURE IN 3 STAGES. SIFT FLOUR AND BAKING POWDER TOGETHER; GENTLY FOLD INTO BATTER. FOLD CRANBERRY MIXTURE INTO BATTER. PORTION INTO RAMEKINS AND BAKE AT 350°F (180°C) FOR 25 MINUTES.

TO MAKE TOFFEE SAUCE: COMBINE INGREDIENTS IN SAUCEPAN; STIR OVER LOW HEAT UNTIL SUGAR IS DISSOLVED. SIMMER UNTIL THICKENED. TO SERVE, REMOVE PUDDINGS FROM RAMEKINS BY RUNNING A KNIFE AROUND EDGE. INVERT ON PLATE AND DRIZZLE WITH WARM TOFFEE SAUCE. SERVES 8.

# LEMON PUDDING

THE TOP TURNS TO CAKE AND THE BOTTOM TURNS TO SAUCE. SERVE WARM WITH WHIPPED CREAM.

| | | |
|---|---|---:|
| 2 TBSP. | FLOUR | 30 ML |
| 1 CUP | SUGAR | 250 ML |
| 2 TBSP. | BUTTER, ROOM TEMPERATURE | 30 ML |
| 2 | EGGS, SEPARATED | 2 |
| 1 CUP | MILK | 250 ML |
| 1 TBSP. | GRATED LEMON ZEST | 15 ML |
| | JUICE OF 1 LEMON | |

PREHEAT OVEN TO 350°F (180°C). IN A LARGE BOWL, COMBINE FLOUR AND SUGAR. CREAM IN BUTTER. IN A MEDIUM BOWL, BEAT YOLKS AND MILK TOGETHER AND ADD TO CREAMED MIXTURE. BEAT UNTIL SMOOTH. STIR IN LEMON ZEST AND JUICE. BEAT EGG WHITES UNTIL STIFF. FOLD INTO BATTER AND POUR INTO A SHALLOW BAKING DISH. SET DISH IN A PAN OF HOT WATER AND BAKE FOR 35-40 MINUTES, UNTIL TOP IS GOLDEN. SERVES 4-6 (OR 2 DELIGHTED TEENAGERS).

IF JIMMY CRACKS CORN AND NO ONE CARES, WHY IS THERE A SONG ABOUT HIM?

# APPLE COBBLER WITH CHEDDAR-BISCUIT TOPPING

SERVE THIS HOT WITH A SCOOP OF VANILLA ICE CREAM.

## COBBLER

| | | |
|---|---|---|
| ³/₄ CUP | PACKED LIGHT BROWN SUGAR | 175 ML |
| I TSP. | GRATED LEMON ZEST | 5 ML |
| ¹/₂ TSP. | CINNAMON | 2 ML |
| ¹/₄ CUP | BUTTER, DIVIDED | 60 ML |
| IO | GRANNY SMITH APPLES, PEELED, CORED & THINLY SLICED | IO |

## TOPPING

| | | |
|---|---|---|
| 3 CUPS | FLOUR | 750 ML |
| ¹/₄ CUP | SUGAR | 60 ML |
| I TBSP. | BAKING POWDER | 15 ML |
| ³/₄ TSP. | SALT | 3 ML |
| ³/₄ CUP | COLD BUTTER, CUT INTO PIECES | 175 ML |
| I¹/₂ CUPS | COARSELY SHREDDED SHARP CHEDDAR CHEESE | 375 ML |
| I CUP | BUTTERMILK | 250 ML |

TO MAKE COBBLER: PREHEAT OVEN TO 375°F (190°C). IN A LARGE BOWL, MIX BROWN SUGAR, LEMON ZEST AND CINNAMON. IN A 12" (30 CM) FRYING PAN MELT 2 TBSP. (30 ML) BUTTER OVER MEDIUM-HIGH HEAT. ADD HALF THE APPLES; COOK AND STIR UNTIL TENDER, 5 MINUTES. GENTLY STIR INTO SUGAR MIXTURE. REPEAT PROCESS WITH REMAINING BUTTER AND APPLES. TRANSFER FILLING TO A 9 X 13" (23 X 33 CM) BAKING DISH; COVER AND KEEP WARM.

# APPLE COBBLER WITH CHEDDAR-BISCUIT TOPPING

CONTINUED FROM PAGE 282.

TO MAKE TOPPING: IN A LARGE BOWL, COMBINE FLOUR, 1 TBSP. (15 ML) SUGAR, BAKING POWDER AND SALT. WITH A PASTRY BLENDER, OR 2 KNIVES USED SCISSOR-FASHION, CUT IN BUTTER UNTIL MIXTURE RESEMBLES COARSE CRUMBS. STIR IN CHEESE AND BUTTERMILK. TURN DOUGH ONTO A WORK SURFACE (DOUGH WILL BE CRUMBLY). KNEAD UNTIL DOUGH IS SMOOTH AND HOLDS TOGETHER. UNCOVER FILLING. DROP DOUGH IN WALNUT-SIZED PIECES OVER APPLE MIXTURE TO COVER; SPRINKLE WITH REMAINING SUGAR. BAKE UNTIL FILLING IS HOT AND BUBBLING AND BISCUITS ARE GOLDEN, 35-40 MINUTES. LET STAND FOR 15 MINUTES BEFORE SERVING. TOP WITH VANILLA ICE CREAM.

MORE THINGS I LEARNED FROM MY CHILDREN:

IF YOU HOOK A DOG LEASH OVER A CEILING FAN, THE MOTOR IS NOT STRONG ENOUGH TO ROTATE A 42-POUND BOY WEARING BATMAN UNDERWEAR AND A SUPERMAN CAPE.

# RHUBARB COBBLER

THERE MUST BE SOME RHUBARB IN YOUR FREEZER! THIS IS ALWAYS A HIT.

| | | |
|---|---|---|
| 4 CUPS | RHUBARB, CUT IN 1/2" (1.3 CM) PIECES | 1 L |
| 3/4-1 CUP | SUGAR | 175-250 ML |
| 1 1/4 CUPS | FLOUR | 300 ML |
| 3 TBSP. | SUGAR | 45 ML |
| 1 TBSP. | BAKING POWDER | 15 ML |
| 1/4 TSP. | SALT | 1 ML |
| 1/3 CUP | BUTTER | 75 ML |
| 1 | EGG, BEATEN | |
| 1/2 CUP | MILK | 125 ML |

PREHEAT OVEN TO 375°F (190°C). COMBINE RHUBARB AND SUGAR AND PLACE IN A SHALLOW, GREASED 9" (23 CM) BAKING DISH. TO MAKE BATTER, COMBINE FLOUR, SUGAR, BAKING POWDER AND SALT. CUT IN BUTTER TO MAKE A CRUMBLY TEXTURE. COMBINE EGG AND MILK AND ADD TO DRY INGREDIENTS. STIR WITH A FORK TO MAKE A STIFF BATTER. DROP BATTER BY SPOONFULS ON TOP OF RHUBARB AND BAKE FOR 35-40 MINUTES. SERVE WARM WITH ICE CREAM OR WHIPPED CREAM. SERVES 6.

SNOWMEN FALL FROM HEAVEN UNASSEMBLED.

# FRUIT CRISP WITH
## OAT CRUMBLE CRUST

DID YOUR MOTHER ALWAYS PUT OATS IN THE CRUST? THIS IS FOR YOU.

| 6 CUPS | APPLES, PEELED & SLICED OR ANY COMBINATION OF THESE FRUITS: BERRIES, RHUBARB, STRAWBERRIES, RASPBERRIES, BLUEBERRIES, PEARS OR APRICOTS | 1.5 L |
|--------|----------------------------------------------------------------------------------------------------------------------|-------|
| 1/3 CUP | SUGAR | 75 ML |
| 2 TBSP. | FLOUR | 30 ML |
| 1 TBSP. | GRATED LEMON ZEST | 15 ML |
| 1/2 TSP. | CINNAMON | 2 ML |

### OAT CRUST

| 1/2 CUP | BUTTER, SOFTENED | 125 ML |
|---------|------------------|--------|
| 1/2 CUP | BROWN SUGAR | 125 ML |
| 1/2 CUP | FLOUR | 125 ML |
| 2/3 CUP | ROLLED OATS | 150 ML |

TO MAKE CRISP: PLACE PREPARED FRUIT IN A 2-QUART (2 L) BAKING DISH. COMBINE SUGAR, FLOUR, LEMON ZEST AND CINNAMON. ADD TO FRUIT AND TOSS TO COAT.

TO MAKE CRUST: MIX CRUST INGREDIENTS WITH A PASTRY BLENDER UNTIL CRUMBLY. SPRINKLE OVER FRUIT MIXTURE. BAKE AT 350°F (180°C) FOR 45 MINUTES, UNTIL CRISP IS BUBBLING. SERVES 8.

# APPLE CRISP
## WITH TOFFEE SAUCE

SERVE WARM WITH TOFFEE SAUCE. AN EXCELLENT DESSERT FOR LARGE FAMILY GATHERINGS – DOWN HOME AND DELICIOUS!

| | | |
|---|---|---|
| 1/2 CUP | SUGAR | 125 ML |
| 1/4 CUP | FLOUR | 60 ML |
| 1 TBSP. | CINNAMON | 15 ML |
| 1/2 TSP. | SALT | 2 ML |
| 1 CUP | LIGHT CREAM | 250 ML |
| 1 TBSP. | FRESHLY SQUEEZED LEMON JUICE | 15 ML |
| 8 | GRANNY SMITH APPLES, PEELED, CORED & SLICED IN WEDGES | 8 |
| 1 1/2 CUPS | FLOUR | 375 ML |
| 1 CUP | PACKED BROWN SUGAR | 250 ML |
| 2 TSP. | CINNAMON | 10 ML |
| 1/4 TSP. | SALT | 1 ML |
| 3/4 CUP | COLD BUTTER | 175 ML |

### TOFFEE SAUCE

| | | |
|---|---|---|
| 1 CUP | PACKED BROWN SUGAR | 250 ML |
| 1/2 CUP | BUTTER | 125 ML |
| 1/2 CUP | LIGHT CREAM | 125 ML |

PREHEAT OVEN TO 350°F (180°C). BUTTER A 9 X 13" (23 X 33 CM) BAKING DISH. IN A LARGE BOWL, COMBINE SUGAR, FLOUR, CINNAMON AND SALT. GRADUALLY STIR IN CREAM AND LEMON JUICE. TOSS APPLES IN CREAM MIXTURE. SPOON INTO PAN. COMBINE FLOUR, SUGAR, CINNAMON AND SALT. CUT IN BUTTER UNTIL

## APPLE CRISP
## WITH TOFFEE SAUCE

CONTINUED FROM PAGE 286.

MIXTURE IS CRUMBLY. SPREAD OVER APPLES AND PAT DOWN LIGHTLY. BAKE AT 350°F (180°C) FOR 45 MINUTES.

TO MAKE TOFFEE SAUCE: COMBINE INGREDIENTS IN SAUCEPAN; STIR OVER LOW HEAT UNTIL SUGAR IS DISSOLVED. SIMMER UNTIL THICKENED. SERVES 10-12.

IF LAWYERS ARE DISBARRED AND CLERGYMEN ARE DEFROCKED, DOESN'T IT FOLLOW THAT ELECTRICIANS CAN BE DELIGHTED, MUSICIANS DENOTED, COWBOYS DERANGED, MODELS DEPOSED, TREE SURGEONS DEBARKED, AND DRY CLEANERS DEPRESSED?

# CAJUN BREAD PUDDING
## WITH RUM SAUCE AND SOFT CREAM

YOUR GUESTS WILL BE INCLINED TO EXCLAIM, "DON'T Y'ALL JUST LUUVE THIS!!!"

### PUDDING

| | | |
|---|---|---:|
| 1/3 CUP | BUTTER, MELTED | 75 ML |
| 16 CUPS | FRENCH BREAD CUBES, DAY OLD, LIGHTLY PACKED | 4 L |
| 3 | EGGS | 3 |
| 1 1/2 CUPS | SUGAR | 375 ML |
| 2 TBSP. | VANILLA | 30 ML |
| 1 TSP. | NUTMEG | 5 ML |
| 1 1/2 TSP. | CINNAMON | 7 ML |
| 3 CUPS | MILK | 750 ML |
| 3/4 CUP | GOLDEN RAISINS | 175 ML |
| 1 CUP | CHOPPED TOASTED PECANS | 250 ML |

### RUM SAUCE

| | | |
|---|---|---:|
| 1 CUP | BUTTER | 250 ML |
| 1 1/2 CUPS | SUGAR | 375 ML |
| 2 | EGGS, BEATEN UNTIL FROTHY | 2 |
| 1/4-1/2 CUP | DARK RUM | 60-125 ML |

### SOFT CREAM

| | | |
|---|---|---:|
| 2 CUPS | WHIPPING CREAM | 500 ML |
| 1/3 CUP | ICING SUGAR | 75 ML |
| 1 TBSP. | VANILLA | 15 ML |
| 2 TBSP. | BRANDY | 30 ML |
| 2 TBSP. | FRANGELICO LIQUEUR | 30 ML |
| 1/4 CUP | SOUR CREAM | 60 ML |

TO MAKE PUDDING: POUR A SMALL AMOUNT OF MELTED BUTTER IN A 9 X 13" (23 X 33 CM) PAN; SWIRL TO COVER BOTTOM AND SIDES. PLACE BREAD CUBES IN PAN.

# CAJUN BREAD PUDDING

CONTINUED FROM PAGE 288.

IN A LARGE BOWL, BEAT EGGS AND SUGAR UNTIL THICKENED, 3-4 MINUTES. ADD VANILLA, NUTMEG, CINNAMON, MILK AND REMAINING BUTTER. BEAT ON LOW TO COMBINE. STIR IN RAISINS AND PECANS; POUR OVER BREAD. ALLOW BREAD TO ABSORB LIQUID, 30-45 MINUTES. PRESS BREAD DOWN OFTEN TO COVER ALL CUBES. PREHEAT OVEN TO 350°F (180°C). BAKE UNTIL CRUSTY AND GOLDEN BROWN, 45-60 MINUTES. COOL AND SLICE INTO SQUARES.

TO MAKE SAUCE: CREAM BUTTER AND SUGAR UNTIL LIGHT AND FLUFFY. COOK IN DOUBLE BOILER FOR 20 MINUTES, WHISKING OFTEN. IN A BOWL, WHISK 2 TBSP. (30 ML) BUTTER-SUGAR MIXTURE INTO BEATEN EGGS, THEN WHISK IN 2 TBSP. (30 ML) MORE. WHISK EGG MIXTURE INTO BUTTER MIXTURE. COOK AND WHISK OVER SIMMERING WATER FOR 4-5 MINUTES. COOL SLIGHTLY. WHISK IN RUM. (BY NOW YOU'RE PROBABLY ALL WHISKED OUT – TASTE THE SAUCE – YOU'LL KNOW IT WAS WORTH IT!)

TO MAKE CREAM: BEAT INGREDIENTS UNTIL SOFT PEAKS FORM, 3-4 MINUTES. DO NOT OVERBEAT. COVER AND REFRIGERATE UNTIL SERVED.

TO SERVE: ON INDIVIDUAL PLATES, PLACE A SPOONFUL OF WARM RUM SAUCE, A SQUARE OF PUDDING AND A LARGE DOLLOP OF SOFT CREAM. SERVES 12-14.

# PLUM UPSIDE-DOWN CAKES WITH MASCARPONE CREAM

### SUPERBULOUS!

| | | |
|---|---|---:|
| 1/2 CUP | BUTTER, ROOM TEMPERATURE | 125 ML |
| 3/4 CUP | PACKED BROWN SUGAR | 175 ML |
| 6 | MEDIUM-SIZED RIPE, FIRM RED PLUMS, PITTED & THINLY SLICED | 6 |
| 1/2 CUP | MILK | 125 ML |
| 1 TBSP. | FRESH LEMON JUICE | 15 ML |
| 1 1/2 CUPS | FLOUR | 375 ML |
| 1 TSP. | BAKING POWDER | 5 ML |
| 1/4 TSP. | BAKING SODA | 1 ML |
| 1/2 TSP. | CINNAMON | 2 ML |
| 1/4 TSP. | SALT | 1 ML |
| 1/2 CUP | BUTTER | 125 ML |
| 1 CUP | SUGAR | 250 ML |
| | GRATED ZEST OF 1 ORANGE | |
| 2 | LARGE EGGS | 2 |
| 2 TSP. | VANILLA | 10 ML |

### MASCARPONE CREAM

| | | |
|---|---|---:|
| 1 CUP | WHIPPING CREAM | 250 ML |
| 6 TBSP. | MASCARPONE CHEESE (ITALIAN CREAM CHEESE) | 90 ML |
| 2 TSP. | SUGAR | 10 ML |
| 1/4 TSP. | VANILLA | 1 ML |

TO MAKE CAKES: BUTTER 8, 8-OZ. (250 ML) RAMEKINS OR AN 8 X 11" (20 X 28 CM) BAKING DISH. PREHEAT OVEN TO 350°F (180°C). IN A MEDIUM SAUCEPAN OVER MEDIUM HEAT, COMBINE BUTTER WITH BROWN SUGAR, WHISKING UNTIL SMOOTH AND COMBINED. IMMEDIATELY POUR INTO BUTTERED RAMEKINS, DIVIDING EVENLY.

# PLUM UPSIDE-DOWN CAKES WITH MASCARPONE CREAM

CONTINUED FROM PAGE 290.

ARRANGE A LAYER OF PLUM SLICES IN EACH RAMEKIN, OVER-LAPPING SLIGHTLY. IN A SMALL BOWL, COMBINE MILK AND LEMON JUICE (DON'T WORRY – IT CURDLES). IN ANOTHER BOWL, SIFT TOGETHER FLOUR, BAKING POWDER, BAKING SODA, CINNAMON AND SALT. USING A MIXER, CREAM BUTTER WITH SUGAR AND ORANGE ZEST. ADD EGGS AND VANILLA, MIX WELL. ADD DRY INGREDIENTS ALTERNATELY WITH MILK MIXTURE, MIXING JUST TO COMBINE. DIVIDE BATTER AMONG RAMEKINS. PLACE ON A RIMMED BAKING SHEET OR, IF USING BAKING DISH, PLACE DIRECTLY ON OVEN RACK. BAKE UNTIL CAKES ARE FIRM TO THE TOUCH AND JUICES ARE BUBBLING, 35–40 MINUTES. COOL ON A RACK. BEFORE SERVING, HEAT OVEN TO 350°F (180°C). SET RAMEKINS ON A BAKING SHEET AND HEAT UNTIL JUST WARMED, ABOUT 5 MINUTES. RUN A SMALL KNIFE AROUND THE INSIDE EDGE OF EACH RAMEKIN AND INVERT ONTO A PLATE. TOP WITH A DOLLOP OF MASCARPONE CREAM. SERVES 8.

TO MAKE MASCARPONE CREAM: BEAT ALL INGREDIENTS IN A SMALL BOWL UNTIL PEAKS FORM. (PICTURED OPPOSITE PAGE 253.)

# CHOCOLATE VOLCANOES WITH RASPBERRY COULIS

A GUARANTEED HIT – EASY AND ABSOLUTELY DELICIOUS! PREPARE AND FREEZE THESE SERVING-SIZED DESSERTS AHEAD OF TIME, THEN COOK THEM WHILE YOU ENJOY YOUR DINNER.

| | | |
|---|---|---|
| 1½ TBSP. | INSTANT ESPRESSO GRANULES (INSTANT COFFEE GRANULES MAY BE USED) | 22 ML |
| 1 TBSP. | BOILING WATER | 15 ML |
| ½ CUP | FLOUR | 125 ML |
| ¼ CUP | COCOA POWDER | 60 ML |
| ¾ TSP. | BAKING POWDER | 3 ML |
| 6-1 OZ. | SQUARES SEMISWEET CHOCOLATE | 170 G |
| ⅔ CUP | BUTTER, SOFTENED | 150 ML |
| ½ CUP | SUGAR | 125 L |
| 3 | LARGE EGGS | 3 |

## RASPBERRY COULIS

| | | |
|---|---|---|
| 10½ OZ. | PKG. FROZEN RASPBERRIES, THAWED | 300 G |
| ⅓ CUP | SUGAR | 75 ML |
| 1-2 TBSP. | GRAND MARNIER LIQUEUR | 15-30 ML |

TO MAKE VOLCANOES: DISSOLVE COFFEE GRANULES IN BOILING WATER. SET ASIDE TO COOL. GREASE 6, 4-OZ. (125 ML) RAMEKINS. USING A WHISK, COMBINE FLOUR, COCOA AND BAKING POWDER IN A SMALL BOWL. RESERVE. MELT CHOCOLATE IN A DOUBLE BOILER. ADD BUTTER AND SUGAR AND STIR UNTIL SMOOTH. TRANSFER TO A LARGE BOWL. USING AN ELECTRIC MIXER, BEAT IN EGGS 1 AT A TIME ON MEDIUM SPEED.

# CHOCOLATE VOLCANOES WITH RASPBERRY COULIS

CONTINUED FROM PAGE 292.

ADD DISSOLVED COFFEE AND FLOUR MIXTURE AND CONTINUE BEATING UNTIL FULLY MIXED. RAISE MIXER SPEED TO HIGH AND BEAT FOR 6 MORE MINUTES (THERE MUST BE SOMETHING GOOD ON TV!). POUR BATTER INTO RAMEKINS AND TIGHTLY WRAP WITH PLASTIC WRAP. FREEZE OVERNIGHT OR UP TO 2 WEEKS.

TO MAKE RASPBERRY COULIS: COMBINE RASPBERRIES AND SUGAR IN A BLENDER AND PURÉE UNTIL SMOOTH. STRAIN THROUGH A SIEVE (OR A CLEAN J-CLOTH) TO REMOVE SEEDS. ADD LIQUEUR AND STORE IN REFRIGERATOR.

PREHEAT OVEN TO 375°F (190°C). TAKE RAMEKINS OUT OF FREEZER, REMOVE PLASTIC WRAP. BAKE VOLCANOES FOR 18 MINUTES - NO LONGER! COOL ON RACK FOR 5 MINUTES. THE OUTSIDES WILL BE CRUSTY AND THE CENTERS WILL BE GOOEY - SORT OF LIKE YOUR AVERAGE VOLCANO. TO SERVE, DRIZZLE INDIVIDUAL PLATES WITH RASPBERRY COULIS. INVERT EACH RAMEKIN ONTO A PLATE AND ADD A SMALL SCOOP OF ICE CREAM. (PICTURED OPPOSITE PAGE 270.)

# BERRY-TOPPED CHOCOLATE TORTE

EASY AND ELEGANT. CHOCOLATE, CREAM AND BERRIES ARE PERFECT PARTNERS.

| | | |
|---|---|---|
| 2/3 CUP | GROUND ALMONDS | 150 ML |
| 3 TBSP. | FLOUR | 45 ML |
| | PINCH OF SALT | |
| 3/4 CUP | BUTTER | 175 ML |
| 1/3 CUP | COCOA POWDER | 75 ML |
| 1/2 CUP | SUGAR | 125 ML |
| 3 | EGGS, SEPARATED | 3 |
| 1/2 CUP | SUGAR | 125 ML |
| 3 TBSP. | GRAND MARNIER LIQUEUR OR ORANGE JUICE | 45 ML |
| 1 CUP | WHIPPING CREAM | 250 ML |
| 1 TBSP. | GRAND MARNIER LIQUEUR | 15 ML |
| 2 CUPS | RASPBERRIES | 500 ML |
| | CHOCOLATE CURLS | |

GREASE A 9" (23 CM) SPRINGFORM PAN AND LINE WITH PARCHMENT PAPER. IN SMALL BOWL, COMBINE ALMONDS, FLOUR AND SALT. SET ASIDE. MELT BUTTER IN A SAUCEPAN AND STIR IN COCOA AND SUGAR. IN A LARGE BOWL, BEAT EGG YOLKS UNTIL THICK; GRADUALLY BLEND IN COCOA MIXTURE. STIR IN ALMOND MIXTURE. IN A SEPARATE BOWL, BEAT EGG WHITES UNTIL STIFF. GRADUALLY ADD SUGAR. FOLD WHITES INTO CHOCOLATE MIXTURE. POUR BATTER INTO PREPARED PAN AND BAKE AT 375°F (190°C) FOR 25-30 MINUTES, UNTIL A TOOTHPICK INSERTED IN THE CENTER COMES OUT CLEAN.

# BERRY-TOPPED CHOCOLATE TORTE

CONTINUED FROM PAGE 294.

LET COOL IN PAN FOR 10 MINUTES. RUN A KNIFE AROUND EDGE OF TORTE AND REMOVE SIDES OF SPRINGFORM PAN. TORTE WILL FALL IN MIDDLE. (DON'T WORRY, YOU CAN FILL IT WITH WHIPPED CREAM!)

DRIZZLE 3 TBSP. (45 ML) GRAND MARNIER OVER CAKE. COOL COMPLETELY AND WRAP WITH PLASTIC WRAP. THIS CAN BE STORED IN REFRIGERATOR FOR 2 DAYS.

WHIP CREAM AND FOLD IN GRAND MARNIER. SPREAD ON TORTE AND DECORATE WITH BERRIES AND CHOCOLATE CURLS. SERVES 8.

MIDLIFE CRISIS: WHEN THE ONLY THING YOU RETAIN IS WATER.

# BLACK MAGIC CAKE

FOR CHOCOLATE LOVERS – A DENSE CHOCOLATE CAKE THAT SERVES A CROWD.

| | | |
|---|---|---:|
| 1 CUP | BUTTER, CUT-UP | 250 ML |
| 3/4 CUP | CHOCOLATE SYRUP | 175 ML |
| 6 | MALTED MILK OR MILKY WAY BARS, CUT INTO PIECES | 6 |
| 2 CUPS | SUGAR | 500 ML |
| 1 CUP | BUTTERMILK | 250 ML |
| 1 TSP. | VANILLA | 5 ML |
| 4 | LARGE EGGS, LIGHTLY BEATEN | 4 |
| 2 1/2 CUPS | FLOUR | 625 ML |
| 3/4 CUP | COCOA POWDER | 175 ML |
| 3/4 TSP. | SALT | 3 ML |
| 1/2 TSP. | BAKING SODA | 2 ML |

PREHEAT OVEN TO 325°F (160°C). GREASE A 12-CUP (3 L) BUNDT PAN OR AN ANGEL FOOD PAN. IN A LARGE SAUCEPAN, COMBINE BUTTER, SYRUP AND CHOCOLATE BARS. WHISK OVER MEDIUM HEAT UNTIL BARS ARE MELTED AND MIXTURE IS SMOOTH. BE CAREFUL NOT TO BURN CHOCOLATE. WHISK IN SUGAR, THEN BUTTERMILK, VANILLA AND EGGS. IN ANOTHER BOWL, COMBINE FLOUR, COCOA, SALT AND BAKING SODA; STIR INTO CHOCOLATE MIXTURE UNTIL BLENDED. POUR BATTER INTO PAN. BAKE FOR 1 1/2 HOURS, OR UNTIL A TOOTHPICK INSERTED IN THE CENTER COMES OUT CLEAN. COOL IN PAN ON A WIRE RACK FOR 10 MINUTES. LOOSEN CAKE FROM PAN AND INVERT ONTO RACK TO COMPLETELY COOL. SERVE WITH VANILLA ICE CREAM.

# ARMENIAN ORANGE CAKE

FAST, SIMPLE AND ABSOLUTELY DELICIOUS.

## CAKE

| | | |
|---|---|---|
| 2 CUPS | BROWN SUGAR | 500 ML |
| 2 CUPS | FLOUR | 500 ML |
| 1/2 CUP | BUTTER | 125 ML |
| 1/2 TSP. | SALT | 2 ML |
| 2 TSP. | GRATED ORANGE ZEST | 10 ML |
| 1/2 TSP. | ALLSPICE | 2 ML |
| 1 TSP. | BAKING SODA | 5 ML |
| 1 CUP | SOUR CREAM | 250 ML |
| 1 | EGG, SLIGHTLY BEATEN | |
| 1/2 CUP | CHOPPED MIXED NUTS (WALNUTS, CASHEWS, ALMONDS) | 125 ML |

## TOPPING

| | | |
|---|---|---|
| 1 CUP | WHIPPING CREAM | 250 ML |
| 2 TBSP. | ICING (CONFECTIONERS) SUGAR | 30 ML |
| 1 TSP. | GRATED ORANGE ZEST | 5 ML |
| 2 TBSP. | ORANGE JUICE OR GRAND MARNIER | 30 ML |

TO MAKE CAKE: PREHEAT OVEN TO 350°F (180°C). GREASE A 9" (23 CM) SPRINGFORM PAN. IN A MEDIUM BOWL, COMBINE SUGAR, FLOUR, BUTTER, SALT, ORANGE ZEST AND ALLSPICE. BLEND WITH A PASTRY BLENDER UNTIL CRUMBLY. SPOON HALF INTO PAN. STIR SODA, SOUR CREAM AND EGG INTO REMAINING CRUMBS. POUR INTO PAN; SPRINKLE WITH NUTS. BAKE FOR 40-45 MINUTES; COOL. REMOVE SPRINGFORM AND SLIDE ONTO SERVING PLATE. SERVE WITH TOPPING.

TO MAKE TOPPING: WHIP CREAM UNTIL STIFF. STIR IN REMAINING INGREDIENTS. LET STAND FOR 1 HOUR TO LET FLAVORS BLEND.

# ORANGE CHIFFON CAKE

PARTY TIME!

| | | |
|---|---|---|
| 2 CUPS | FLOUR | 500 ML |
| 1½ CUPS | SUGAR | 375 ML |
| 1 TBSP. | BAKING POWDER | 15 ML |
| 1 TSP. | SALT | 5 ML |
| ½ CUP | VEGETABLE OIL | 125 ML |
| 7 | UNBEATEN EGG YOLKS | 7 |
| ½ CUP | ORANGE JUICE | 125 ML |
| ¼ CUP | WATER | 60 ML |
| 2 TBSP. | GRATED ORANGE ZEST | 30 ML |
| 1 TSP. | VANILLA | 5 ML |
| 7 | EGG WHITES | 7 |
| ½ TSP. | CREAM OF TARTAR | 2 ML |

## ORANGE GLAZE

| | | |
|---|---|---|
| 2 TBSP. | BUTTER, ROOM TEMPERATURE | 30 ML |
| | PINCH OF SALT | |
| | GRATED ZEST OF 1 ORANGE | |
| ¼ CUP | ORANGE JUICE | 60 ML |
| 3 CUPS | ICING (CONFECTIONER'S) SUGAR | 750 ML |

PREHEAT OVEN TO 325°F (160°C). IN A LARGE BOWL, BLEND FLOUR, SUGAR, BAKING POWDER AND SALT. MAKE A WELL IN CENTER OF THE DRY INGREDIENTS. ADD OIL, EGG YOLKS, ORANGE JUICE, WATER, ORANGE ZEST AND VANILLA. BEAT BATTER UNTIL SMOOTH. IN A LARGE MIXING BOWL, BEAT EGG WHITES UNTIL FROTHY. ADD CREAM OF TARTAR. CONTINUE BEATING UNTIL VERY STIFF. USING A SPATULA, GENTLY FOLD EGG WHITES INTO FLOUR-SUGAR MIXTURE.

## ORANGE CHIFFON CAKE

CONTINUED FROM PAGE 298.

POUR BATTER INTO AN UNGREASED 10" (25 CM) TUBE PAN. BAKE FOR 45-60 MINUTES. TEST WITH A TOOTHPICK. INVERT PAN AND ALLOW CAKE TO COOL. RUN A KNIFE AROUND INSIDE OF PAN AND INVERT ONTO A SERVING PLATE.

TO MAKE GLAZE: IN A MEDIUM BOWL, BEAT ALL INGREDIENTS UNTIL GLAZE REACHES CONSISTENCY OF A THIN SPREAD. DRIZZLE ON CAKE OR GLAZE ENTIRE SURFACE. (PICTURED OPPOSITE PAGE 271.)

MONEY ISN'T EVERYTHING . . . BUT IT SURE KEEPS THE CHILDREN IN TOUCH.

# FRESH APPLE CAKE

| | | |
|---|---|---|
| 3 | TART APPLES, PEELED & CHOPPED | 3 |
| 3 TBSP. | SUGAR | 45 ML |
| 2 TSP. | CINNAMON | 10 ML |
| 2 CUPS | SUGAR | 500 ML |
| 1 CUP | VEGETABLE OIL | 250 ML |
| 4 | EGGS | 4 |
| 1/4 CUP | ORANGE JUICE | 60 ML |
| 1 TSP. | GRATED ORANGE ZEST | 5 ML |
| 2 TSP. | VANILLA | 10 ML |
| 3 CUPS | FLOUR | 750 ML |
| 1 TBSP. | BAKING POWDER | 15 ML |
| 1/2 TSP. | SALT | 2 ML |

### CITRUS RUM GLAZE

| | | |
|---|---|---|
| 1 CUP | ORANGE JUICE | 250 ML |
| 2 TBSP. | LEMON JUICE | 30 ML |
| 1 CUP | SUGAR | 250 ML |
| 2 TBSP. | RUM | 30 ML |

COMBINE APPLES WITH SUGAR AND CINNAMON. IN A LARGE BOWL, CREAM SUGAR AND OIL. ADD EGGS, 1 AT A TIME; BEAT AFTER EACH ADDITION. ADD JUICE, ZEST AND VANILLA. COMBINE FLOUR, BAKING POWDER AND SALT. BEAT INTO CREAMED MIXTURE UNTIL SMOOTH. GREASE A 10" (25 CM) BUNDT PAN. POUR 1/3 BATTER INTO PAN, THEN 1/2 THE APPLES. REPEAT 1/3 BATTER, 1/2 APPLES AND FINAL 1/3 BATTER. BAKE AT 350°F (180°C) FOR 60-70 MINUTES, OR UNTIL TOOTHPICK COMES OUT CLEAN. COOL SLIGHTLY BEFORE GLAZING.

TO MAKE GLAZE: COMBINE INGREDIENTS IN POT AND BRING TO A BOIL. DRIZZLE OVER WARM CAKE. COOL BEFORE REMOVING FROM PAN.

# INDEX